PERSONAL CHANGE THROUGH
SELF·HYPNOSIS

PERSONAL CHANGE THROUGH
SELF HYPNOSIS

PAMELA YOUNG

Copyright © 1986 Pamela Young

ISBN: 978-1-925341-39-3

Published by Vivid Publishing
P.O. Box 948, Fremantle
Western Australia 6959
www.vividpublishing.com.au

Cataloguing-in-Publication data is available from the National Library of Australia

First published in Australia by Angus & Robertson Publishers in 1986
First published in United Kingdom by Angus & Robertson (UK) Ltd in 1986
First published in New Zealand by Angus & Robertson NZ Ltd in 1989
Reprinted 1986, 1987, 1989

ACKNOWLEDGEMENTS

I wish to thank the people who gave me permission to use their material and who replied to my letters with such kindness and encouragement; and also Barbara Ashford, Lesley Peter, Peter Luck and the editors, who made comments where appropriate on psychological, medical and communication grounds.

I would also like to thank the group at Macquarie University, in particular Professor A. Gordon Hammer, and my patient fellow workers.

CONTENTS

FOREWORD

I graduated in psychology from the University of New South Wales in 1970 and have worked as a counsellor to university students and staff, at an employee assistance company and in private practice since then.

I began writing this book in 1982 after discovering that self-hypnosis is at least twice as effective as hypnosis by another person (hetero-hypnosis) for reduction or cessation of smoking cigarettes. I believe this also to be the case for other complex issues, such as eating disorders, substance abuse, and gambling.

The book was published in seven countries, including Italy and Iceland.

In the book I have tried to replace popular misconceptions of hypnosis with the concept of the acceptance of suggestions to promote positive change. You will also become aware of the significant contribution Australian practitioners and researchers have made to the study of hypnosis.

In addition to theories and known facts about hypnosis, the book contains basic hypnosis scripts and more than 70 specific scripts. Printed individual scripts are available separately, as are CDs developed from the scripts in the book. The CDs were constructed because it became apparent that not everyone was willing to make their own recording. My partner, Bill Peach (1935-2013) recorded five CDs before he became too ill, and I completed the project in 2014.

I have reprinted the book to accompany the CDs. It is helpful to understand many things about hypnosis before you embark on your own project.

While the references in the book are obviously dated I believe that none of the more recent findings negates or casts doubt on any of the material within.

There have been some fresh therapeutic approaches, in particular Acceptance and Commitment Therapy and the concept of Mindfulness. But at the 20th International Congress of Hypnosis held in Paris in August 2015, researchers and practitioners were still attempting to understand and explain the phenomenon of hypnosis. They were in little doubt that hypnosis had established itself as a legitimate treatment method, partly due to advances in brain imaging and neuroscience. There was a large increase in the number of papers presented by doctors and dentists using hypnosis as the sole anaesthetic for complex surgery. However theories presented at the Congress, some involving quantum physics and Chaos Theory, did little to shed light on the subject.

In my experience the expectation of success with either self-hypnosis or hetero-hypnosis ranges from close to 100% for concentration, motivation and exam nerves, slightly less for public speaking, public performance and job interviews, still high for sporting improvement, anxiety symptoms and sleeping disorders.

I presented my smoking cessation research findings at the International Society of Clinical and Experimental Hypnosis and Psychosomatic Medicine Congress at the Hague, Netherlands in 1978. Subjects using self-hypnosis showed a 75% drop in consumption and a 50% complete cessation rate. The group undergoing hetero-hypnosis were between half and a third as successful.

Individuals differ and in my experience no amount of theorising or testing for hypnotiseability will predict what will actually work for a particular person. The worst outcome is that nothing will change. In my 48 years as a qualified psychologist and hypnosis practitioner there have been no untoward incidents.

CDs and printed scripts and copies of the book are available by visiting the website www.selfhypnosis.net.au or emailing pamelayoung@selfhypnosis.net.au

INTRODUCTION

This book is a guide to self-hypnosis. All you need is a tape recorder and some patience and you should be able to solve almost any problem you may have, from smoking to shyness.

Since 1978 I have been experimenting with a method of self-hypnosis which I am satisfied is quite unique and very effective. It all started in 1977, when I began the practice of taping the procedures of hypnotic induction that I used with students and staff at the New South Wales Institute of Technology, where I am a senior student counsellor. This was mostly in the interest of saving time.

On one occasion, while taping a session with the editor of our student newspaper who wanted to give up smoking, a fault in the system occurred and the tape recording failed to work. I offered to make a substitute tape in the student's absence, and did so feeling a little foolish. For the first time I was addressing remarks to the machine without the presence of a recumbent body. To check if the recording was convincing in these circumstances I settled down on my cushions to listen. Instead of evaluating its quality, I allowed myself to drift along with the recording.

After that I lost interest in smoking.

This was quite startling, as I had smoked quite heavily for twenty-six years and all my attempts to stop had been painful and unsuccessful. It was also surprising because I am a very poor hypnotic subject when other people attempt to hypnotise me and I have proved no more successful when I have tried the traditional methods of self-hypnosis. I have found it difficult to concentrate and keep my mind from wandering. So I began to wonder what caused the difference between others' attempts to hypnotise me and my own rather feeble attempts at self-hypnosis, and the quite dramatic outcome of listening to my own tape.

To help find an answer to this question I enrolled in a higher degree at Macquarie University under the supervision of Professor A. Gordon Hammer. It occurred to me that this form of self-hypnosis might work where hypnosis performed by another person (hetero-hypnosis) did not, because some people are not happy about being "under the control" of another person.

I investigated this idea specifically in relation to cigarette

3

smoking, by having volunteers undergo my Smoking Cessation Programme. They either recorded my experimental version of the basic script (see page 55, Alternative Induction I) and the smoking script (page 70) themselves, or else I made a recording as I carried out the induction myself using the same scripts. They also filled in questionnaires designed to ascertain their beliefs and preferences about the degree to which they retained control over their lives and futures. Then they went away and listened to their recordings at least twenty times in the next month, providing me with constant feedback. At three months and six months intervals after the treatment sessions were completed I sent them questionnaires to find out more about their current smoking habits, if any. My research is still not quite complete, as I need more long-term participants to make certain of its scientific validity, but preliminary results based on the fifty-nine people who have completed it so far look extremely promising. You can read more about this in the section on smoking (page 67).

After the experience with my self-made tape, I began to encourage the students to make their own self-hypnosis cassettes and to help them construct their own individual scripts. In many cases only two sessions are needed — one to sort out what appears to be the problem or problems to be dealt with, and another for the recording. In some cases, however, quite a few sessions are needed before a script can be prepared, if the problems are more obscure or complex. I usually recommend the inclusion of a script suggesting that whatever else happens, the unconscious mind will continue working on the problem, solving it in some safe way, perhaps even without the conscious mind becoming aware of it.

Self-hypnosis is becoming increasingly popular in therapy, and with good reason. It creates in clients a sense of mastery and control, rather than passivity and helplessness: they can take responsibility for their own treatment rather than relying heavily upon others, and can also take most of the credit for their own "cure". What we still do not know is with what type of person and in what type of circumstance this form of self-hypnosis is more likely to be effective than hetero-hypnosis.

The difference between my method and most others is that my method involves the use of formal, carefully worded scripts, as far as possible written by the clients themselves, from which they make tape recordings to be played back when the need arises.

I repeat that this method is for normal, day-to-day problems only. If you are sensible and follow my instructions closely, no harm will come to you and you will find that many desirable changes can be achieved. In time, you should be able to throw your tranquillisers and sleeping tablets down the drain!

However, I will not take responsibility for irresponsible experimentation. Hypnosis is a powerful force for positive change, but it is possible that harm can result from a suggestion that has not been very carefully thought out.

The scripts that form the main part of this book are detailed instructions for the treatment of such clinical problems as overeating, smoking, insomnia, high blood pressure (as an adjunct to your medical treatments), nailbiting, stammering, chronic or recurring pain, warts, migraine; for such problems as lack of confidence and self esteem, inability to speak or perform in public; for problems peculiar to students, such as examination anxiety, loss of interest in studies, inability to concentrate, the need to study in the middle of family hubbub; and for improving performances in various sports.

Most of the scripts were written by me, some were borrowed from the literature on the subject and a few were produced by my students or fellow staff members. That means they have meaning and relevance to *me*, or *someone else*, but to make them *yours* you must rewrite or adapt them so that they become personally meaningful and relevant, tailored to your own situation and your needs. I emphasise this last point as it is most important for the effective use of scripts.

Part One

ISSUES IN HYPNOSIS

1
ALL HYPNOSIS IS
SELF-HYPNOSIS

There has been little research carried out specifically on self-hypnosis, but the research done has shown that, in most cases, self- and hetero-hypnosis are approximately equally effective. Also, most, if not all, hypnotic techniques can be used in self-hypnosis.

Many believe that hetero-hypnosis is really self-hypnosis, and that the presence of a hypnotist simply makes it easier for a person to enter into a trance. In 1891 the eminent physician and psychiatrist Sigmund Freud said:

> *We shall be well-advised to keep silent or only to give occasional help with a suggestion. Otherwise we should merely be disturbing the patient who is hypnotising himself and, if the succession of suggestions does not correspond to the actual course of his sensations, we should be provoking contradiction.*[1]

Professor of Psychiatry at Harvard Medical School and head of a clinic for therapeutic hypnosis in the United States, Dr Fred Frankel, said in 1976: "Clinicians learn readily that they exercise control over most patients only to the extent that the patients are prepared to let them, which leads to the often expressed opinion: 'All hypnosis is self hypnosis.'"[2]

Similarly, many other therapists believe that the person's own hypnotic talent is the only important factor in deciding whether hypnosis can be used effectively in treatment. Such therapists see themselves as guides, helping people to use their own talents to help themselves.

2
A BRIEF HISTORY OF HYPNOSIS

What is hypnosis? How does it work? Does it even exist? These are questions that have been asked for many years. They are still not satisfactorily answered. However, a brief overview of the history of hypnosis and some of the theories on the subject may be of interest.

There is evidence of the use of hypnosis or something very like it in many ancient cultures. But the "modern" history of hypnosis began in the eighteenth century with Franz Anton Mesmer, an Austrian physician, and his concept of "animal magnetism". He attached magnets to his patients' stomachs and legs to promote an artificial tide after they had swallowed a fluid containing iron. The patients reported feeling streams of fluid running through their bodies, and their symptoms would then disappear, at least for a time. When the number of Mesmer's patients increased he invented a group treatment — a large tub called a *baquet*, in which metal rods were placed. Patients holding onto the rods would experience a similar loss of symptoms.

In 1784 the King of France appointed two commissions to investigate animal magnetism and to determine whether Mesmer had discovered a new magnetic fluid, and they concluded that no evidence could be found of the physical existence of such a fluid. The therapeutic effects were put down to imagination, suggestion and imitation. Mesmer was effectively discredited, and died a broken man.

In 1819 a Portuguese priest, the Abbe Jose de Faria, concluded that the phenomenon of animal magnetism was mainly due to the psychic impressionability of the person being magnetised, and was not due to magnetic fluid or to the person doing the magnetising. He was the first to use direct suggestions in experiments and therapy, and for his efforts he was appointed Professor of Philosophy at the Academy of Marseilles.

By the mid-1800s mesmerism was in disfavour in Europe and England, but Mesmer societies were flourishing in the United States. One evening in 1842 in the rooms of the Phreno-Magnetic Society of Cincinnati, an experiment was carried out on a nineteen-year-old member of the Society. A magnetic sleep was induced and his arms and legs became rigid; his eyelids opened and remained so until someone shut them. They elicited from him "a convulsed laugh, which was painful to witness". At their request, he demonstrated aggression, with an intense expression, clenched hands and striking fists. "'Adhesiveness' was now touched; he grasped a gentleman by the hand, clasped him in his arms, placed him upon his lap, and held him there until 'Benevolence' being excited, when he released him . . . "[1]

In 1837 British physician and surgeon John Elliotson published a paper describing his use of mesmeric sleep to achieve painless surgery on a number of patients. Although medical knowledge at that time could offer nothing better than alcoholic intoxication to dull the pain of surgery, his colleagues opposed his use of mesmerism. He was subsequently dismissed from his professorial post at the University College Hospital in London. Early in 1840 W. S. Ward, also a British physician and surgeon, amputated the leg of a patient who was in a mesmeric trance, and the operation was a success. The patient signed a declaration, stating that he had experienced no pain, but when Ward presented this to the Royal Medical and Chirurgical Society in England they refused to believe it, saying that the patient must have been lying. They further stated that if it *were* true, then it was immoral, since pain "is a wise provision of nature, and patients ought to suffer pain while their surgeons are operating".[2]

In 1843 the English physician James Braid renamed the process "hypnosis", from the Greek word *hypnos*, meaning "to sleep", and he was responsible for hypnosis becoming more widely accepted in England. He believed, like Abbe Faria, that the patient's qualities, rather than the hypnotist's, determined the success of hypnosis.

By 1852 a Scottish surgeon, James Esdaile, had performed thousands of minor operations and about 300 major operations in India, using only hypnosis as an anaesthetic.[3] However, the recognised journals of the day were hostile towards him.

Following the discovery of chemical anaesthesia, the use of hypnosis lapsed for many years. Interest was revived towards the end of the nineteenth century and the beginning of the twentieth century, when two groups of French investigators argued bitterly over hypnosis. One was led by the French neurologist Jean Charcot, who taught at the Saltpetrière in Paris, and his pupil Pierre Janet, who saw hypnosis as a pathological state closely associated with hysteria; and the other group was the Nancy school, led by Hippolyte Bernheim and Auguste Liebeault, both physicians, who claimed that hypnosis was not an indicator of psychological disturbance, but was the effect of suggestion.

Another major setback to hypnosis occurred, however, when

Sigmund Freud, who had used hypnosis extensively, abandoned it in favour of the techniques of free association. Freud abandoned hypnosis not just because of the dangers of transference (a young female client supposedly flung her arms around him), but because he found that it did not work for everyone, and also because he felt more comfortable with the technique of psychoanalysis — sitting at the end of a couch and listening to the client talk. He felt that hypnosis had limited applications, obscured patient resistance and created problems in patient management.[4] He did not abandon it entirely, or ideas based on it. He even pointed out that if psychotherapy was ever to become as widely available as other forms of medical care, analysts would have to modify their techniques by returning to experiments with hypnosis.[5] However, the fact that he moved on to a new method of treatment put the clinical use of hypnosis back another fifty or sixty years.

It is only recently that hypnosis has finally regained clinical, medical and dental respectability. The scientific investigation of hypnosis properly commenced with the publication in 1933 of a book on hypnosis and suggestibility by American psychologist Clark Hull[6], and has continued steadily ever since. One of the major contributors to research in hypnosis, whose protégés have carried on the good work in many parts of the world, is Professor A. Gordon Hammer, who started his investigations in the early 1950s at the University of Sydney, and who was recently made a member of the Order of Australia for his services to psychology.

3

THE THEORIES OF HYPNOSIS

In the ongoing arguments about what hypnosis actually *is*, some believe that it is like normal sleep, some that it is a special type of learning and many believe that it is a regression to a more primitive form of mental functioning. Some even suggest possible locations in the older part of the brain where the mechanisms of hypnosis may be located.

At the moment the theorists are roughly divided into those who believe that hypnosis is a special state of mind with distinguishing characteristics, and those who believe that hypnotic subjects are faking so as to trick the hypnotist and make him feel useful, or at best are playing a role and have become so involved in the role they have come to believe in it.

Among the major sceptics, the American psychologist Theodore Xenophon Barber is critical of the concept of a hypnotic state and feels there is no real need to employ such a concept. In fact, when he writes about hypnosis he always uses quotation marks. He has consistently claimed that exactly the same behaviour as that of "hypnotised" people can be produced by "task-motivating" instructions to people in the normal waking state. To replace the concept of an altered state, Barber presents the notion of "believed-in efficacy": that is, whether people believe in the effectiveness of the treatment.[1] Barber gives the following example of "believed-in efficacy":

There are few cases of this kind more remarkable than one related by Mr Woodhouse Braine, the well-known chloroformist. Having to administer ether to an hysterical girl who was about to be operated on for removal of two sebaceous tumors from the scalp he found that the ether bottle was empty and that the inhaling bag was free from even the odor of any anesthetic. While a fresh supply was being obtained, he thought to familiarize the patient with the process by putting the inhaling bag over her mouth and nose, and telling her to breath quietly and deeply. After a few inspirations she cried, "Oh, I feel it; I am going off," and a moment after, her eyes turned up, and she became unconscious. As she was found to be perfectly insensible, and the ether had not yet come, Mr Braine proposed that the surgeon should proceed with the

13

*operation. One tumor was removed without in the least
disturbing her, and then, in order to test her condition, a
bystander said that she was coming to. Upon this she began to
show signs of waking, so the bag was once more applied, with
the remark, "She'll soon be off again," when she immediately
lost sensation and the operation was successfully and
painlessly completed.*[2]

The American social psychologist Theodore Sarbin and his
associates believe that hypnosis is a form of role-playing, and just
as an impassioned actor on the stage loses himself in his role and
is unaware of the audience, the hypnotised person becomes
similarly involved in the role he is playing so that he also loses
self-awareness. He accounts for age regression by saying that
those subjects who demonstrate an aptitude for role-taking in
hypnosis could easily take the role of a young child. He wrote:
"Catalepsies, paralyses, anaesthesias, amnesias, posthypnotic
performances, all are a matter of role-taking on the part of the
subject."[3]

Psychoanalysts believe in the idea of an altered state of
awareness during hypnosis. To them hypnosis is a regression of a
special sub-system of the ego, which works in the service of the
ego, a voluntary handing over of one's control over oneself. (In
psychoanalytic theory the "ego" is the part of the psyche which
experiences the outside world and reacts to it, mediating between
the primitive drives of the "id" on the one hand, and the
requirements of the morals and values of society, the
"superego", on the other hand.) In Freud's mind the ability to be
hypnotised was a mark of health, not of pathology (disease). As
only a part of the ego is regressed, most of the ego is able to
operate normally.

Professor Ernest R. Hilgard, who has been investigating
hypnosis for many years at Stanford University, thinks hypnosis
involves dissociation: that is, the use of a separate system of the
brain controlled by its own mechanism, very much like a
computer programmed to carry out subroutines, but integrated
with the central programme. Hypnotic induction, he feels,
prepares the subject for dissociation by disrupting the normal
processes of remembering and attending. He introduced the
concept of "the Hidden Observer". This separate system can be
communicated with through automatic writing and other means
(hypnotists often use signalling with the little finger) and can
report events that occurred in hypnosis that were otherwise not
available to the conscious mind. Hilgard believes that all normal
children are hypnotiseable and that whether we are still hypno-

tiseable as adults depends on our upbringing, whether or not we were encouraged to be creative, adventurous and imaginative.[4]

Martin Orne from the United States, another very important figure in hypnosis research, working with Australians Peter Sheehan and Fred Evans, also believed in the existence of a hypnotic trance state. He suggested that the main features of this state were that the person feels different in comparison to a normal waking state, has difficulty in resisting a hypnotist's suggestions and can experience distortions of perception, memory or feelings.[5] There is also an ability to tolerate logical inconsistencies. Orne called this "trance logic": a hypnotised person may report seeing the same person in two places at the one time, and will often see one of these doubles as transparent.[6]

A reasonable amount of strong feeling has been generated by this argument. Barber has accused those who say the trance state does exist of "vicious circularity" — the idea of a trance state is inferred by people's behaviour, and then is used to explain that behaviour. And the evidence Barber uses, that of "task-motivational" subjects, has been attacked on the grounds that there is considerable pressure on the subject to perform well, and that "task-motivational" instructions are themselves hypnotic-like suggestions; so that these subjects may be, in fact, in a trance.

The experiences of Jim Jupp, a senior lecturer in psychology at Macquarie University, seem to support this. He administered a standard hypnotic-testing scale, with the suggestions of fingers locking together, arm stiffness, imagining a fly and so on, to his "waking control" subjects. He omitted hypnotic induction and also any references to "hypnosis", "sleep", "relaxation" or "heaviness", but still found difficulty in preventing these subjects from lapsing into a trance-like state even when he requested them to keep their eyes open.[7]

In 1979 a team of academics from Macquarie University, Marita McCabe, John Collins and Ailsa Burns, reviewed the theories and evidence from research and concluded that hypnosis could be regarded as an altered state of consciousness, affecting the subject both psychologically and physically. They considered it to be a regression to a more primitive level of consciousness, the same level that produces fantasy and other primary thought processes, and not simply a result of role-playing or over-eagerness to co-operate.[8]

"Does it really matter?" you may ask. Well, I think it does. My work — and this book — is based on the belief that there is such a thing as a hypnotic state which can be utilised in order to achieve desired changes. The whole process of hypnosis appears, on the face of it, to be a little eccentric, but if the sceptics are right, and the effectiveness of hypnosis is only a function of the belief system of the patient or his or her ability to play a role, then the process is downright foolish. This would place hypnosis in the category of a placebo, such as when the doctor gives you coloured water as a tonic and you get better immediately after taking it. Having said that, the idea has been expressed that the placebo should be treated with more respect than it has been, as being a powerful contributor to the success of treatment. However I still believe that there is something *more* happening in hypnotic treatment.

4

CAN YOU BE HYPNOTISED?

While people seem to be either hypnotiseable or not, nobody has yet been able to make a reliable list of the characteristics that make a person a good subject for hypnosis.

At one time it was thought that people of lower intelligence would be more likely to be able to be hypnotised, but that is not the case. Nor has hypnotiseability been found to be related to psychological disturbance, another popular belief.

Personality traits that *have* been found to be connected with hypnotiseability are adventurousness, creativity, a willingness to disclose personal information about oneself, openness to new experiences, the capacity for intense involvement in some activity and a good imagination. Josephine Hilgard, clinical professor of psychiatry at Stanford University School of Medicine, has carried out a lot of research on this subject. Of the highly hypnotiseable subjects, she found their strongest common characteristics were a capacity for absorption or deep involvement in such things as reading, music, religion, nature and adventure. She found the least hypnotiseable people tended to be involved in competitive sports or theoretical sciences, and she decided that this had something to do with whether a person had a dominant right or left side of the brain for mental processing. The right side of the brain is thought to be the side which governs creativity, imagination and so on.[1]

Josephine Hilgard's theory, supported by her husband Ernest, that encouragement in early childhood of creative and imaginative pursuits is important for adult hypnotiseability, is borne out by the fact that age is strongly associated with hypnotiseability. Children between the ages of seven and fourteen are significantly more hypnotiseable than adults. The peak of hypnotiseability occurs between nine and twelve years of age and declines gradually after that. Most clinicians would agree that it is rare to find a child who cannot by hypnotised, and this fortunate fact has helped many a child in the dentist's chair or suffering from cancer or leukaemia. Children will readily benefit from techniques using the imagination to conjure up favourite TV shows, fantasies in crystal balls, magic carpets and Aladdin's cave.

Normal people have been found to be more hypnotiseable than neurotic people, and among the neurotic people those who are hysterical are more hypnotiseable than those who are not.

(Hysteria is defined as chronic ill-health presumed due to repressed emotions resulting from early childhood traumas.)

Another characteristic believed to be associated with hypnotiseability is alpha brainwave activity. These brainwaves are associated with a relaxed, non-attending state of the individual. A high density of alpha rhythm production is believed to be a feature of hypnotised people in general, and highly susceptible subjects in both the relaxed waking state and the hypnotised state. Some recent research has shed doubts on these beliefs; research carried out by my friend and colleague Barbara Ashford, for example, for her doctoral thesis, has shown that there was no increase in alpha waves occurring when a person was hypnotised, over and above that which occurred when they were in a normal relaxed state.[2] However, nearly all researchers have found that highly hypnotiseable subjects, when in the relaxed waking state, do demonstrate a higher level of alpha production.

Attempts have also been made to predict hypnotic sus-ceptibility by measuring eye movement. Some specialisation of function occurs in either of man's two cerebral hemispheres, as has already been mentioned in connection with Josephine Hilgard's work. In most individuals the left hemisphere is dominant in the capacity to perform verbal and analytical mental activities, and the right hemisphere specialises in visual, spatial and intuitive thought. It has been proposed that eye movement to the right in response to a question is an indication of left hemispheric activity while eye movement to the left is an indicator of right hemispheric activity. There is believed to be a relationship between left eye movers and the ability to be hypnotised, which is consistent with the view that hypnosis is a right hemispheric function.

Ernest Hilgard and his associates tested over 19,000 students with the famous standard scale he and his colleague Dr Andre Weitzenhoffer developed at Stanford University in the late 1950s, and estimated that ninety-one per cent of them could be hypnotised to some extent, and twenty-six per cent were highly responsive to hypnosis.[3] The most common belief is that five per cent of people cannot be hypnotised, but there are many clinicians who believe that anyone who walks through the door is capable of being hypnotised — it is just a matter of finding the right approach.

Freud pointed out that it was possible to produce the greatest of changes through the lightest of trances, so I think you can assume that you have an excellent chance of achieving the changes you would like through the use of hypnosis.

5
WHAT CAN YOU EXPECT?

People who are hypnotised for the first time are frequently disappointed to find they are experiencing nothing over-whelming. They feel mildly relaxed but remain in touch with reality and in control of their thoughts, and may discover that the hypnotist's suggestions are quite resistible. Contrary to what most people believe, a person under hypnosis need not fall asleep, lose contact with his surroundings or relinquish his will. He or she is often able to recall everything that has happened during the trance and acts perfectly normally.

On the other hand, many people report extraordinary or unusual happenings, spontaneous regressions, out-of-body experiences and body-image distortions. It is difficult to decide whether these occur naturally, or are caused by the preconceived ideas of the person being hypnotised or the subtle cues and hints of the hypnotist. A lot of interest in the unusual effects of hypnosis has revolved around amnesia. For a long time it was considered a genuine major feature of hypnosis, but recently doubts about this have been expressed. Most therapists today would expect their patients to remain aware of everything that is said and remember it afterwards, and to experience very little naturally occurring amnesia. Fred Evans of the University of Pennsylvania drew attention to the occasional temporary amnesia that can occur after hypnotic induction. The amnesia is rarely total: recall is partial, fragmentary and lacking in clarity and detail. The person usually cannot recall the events in the order in which they occurred.[1]

I find that a surprising number of people using my method of hypnosis have substantial amnesia or else go to sleep. They usually report not hearing part of the tape, or else the specific script has become a blank. They cannot remember whether they have gone to sleep or not, but are usually inclined to think not, and nearly always wake up when the "wake-up" numbers get to around six or seven. Perhaps this method encourages the person to permit a deeper trance state to develop because there is no lingering doubt about control by the hypnotist. They already know what the script is because they recorded the words themselves, so they do not have to let curiosity interfere with "letting whatever happens happen". Another important factor may be that no-one else need hear their personal secrets, if they talk while under hypnosis. This is a fear that plagues many people. The fear of remaining in trance and not being able to wake up is also common. People who choose not to wake up when the "wake-up" instructions are given simply drift into a normal sleep.

Age regression can result in some interesting hypnotic experiences. People who are regressed generally report that they "re-live" the experiences rather than just remember them. During a hypnosis practice session, I hypnotised a fellow psychologist in his thirties who regretted, and was a little disturbed by, the fact that he could not remember anything before the age of nine years. He asked me to use age regression to help him gain access to some earlier memories. He was quite obviously re-living the scene he regressed to as his face took on a wondering, childlike expression and he reported being in a convent on a hill in Adelaide watching nuns digging up a tree trunk. He was six years old. He "saw" the big hole left by the trunk, his old teachers with spades in their hands, the sun shining and a particularly unusual old tree which was nearby. All of this had actually happened, he recalled later, though he had quite forgotten it. He was so entranced it took several countings to bring him back up through the years — he wanted to stay there. He was quite moved by the experience, and somehow reassured about his previous inability to remember, even though it was just part of a routine training session with no therapeutic intention.

This experience reminded me of the work done in the 1930s and 40s by Dr Wilder Penfield, an American neurosurgeon at Princeton University, who, when he electrically stimulated certain parts of patients' exposed brains, reported that the patients re-lived scenes from the past, saying things like, "I am walking across a field . . ."[2] This is also reminiscent of Pavlov's idea that traces of past experiences are indelibly "etched" into the brain, and can be activated by the proper associational reflexes.[3]

I would not expect you to have any startling experiences if you stick to the basic script and fairly straightforward specific suggestions. But if you are more ambitious and would like to use age regression or some of the testing suggestions I include in the Miscellaneous Ideas and Scripts section, such as the floating hand, then you may experience some of these further effects.

6
CAN YOU DO THE IMPOSSIBLE?

One of the arguments that rages about hypnosis is whether a hypnotised person can transcend normal capabilities. I have heard of hypnotised people performing seemingly impossible feats of strength and endurance, levitating, returning to past lives and so on. But a study of the literature on the subject has not convinced me.

There *are* some quite remarkable reports of cures effected, supposedly due to hypnosis and quite outside the realm of normal expectations. This example is from Bandler and Grinder's *Frogs Into Princes*:

> *I worked as a consultant for the Simontons in Fort Worth ...*
> *We had a student who got a complete remission from a cancer patient. And he did something which I think is even more impressive. He got an ovarian cyst the size of an orange to shrink away in two weeks. According to medical science, that wasn't even possible. That client reports that she has the X-rays to prove it.*[1]

Other surprising successes have been the use of hypnosis to extract the tooth of a haemophiliac patient without any sign of bleeding[2], the eradication of nearly all symptoms in a case of psoriasis[3] and, even more remarkably, "fishskin disease". This is a hereditary problem, medically termed ichthyosiform erythroderma, in which the patient is covered in a horny layer of black skin and scale-like lumps which often ooze blood and smell extremely unpleasant.[4] However, these treatments, which usually involve the control of blood flow (see also headaches, dentistry, warts, blushing and cancer), may not be considered quite so remarkable after a study of the literature involving blood flow.

For many years it has been recognised that certain individuals can *voluntarily* shift blood from one area to another, and make that area warmer. A case is reported of an Indian yogi who can voluntarily raise the temperature in his forehead and induce perspiration only ten minutes after beginning meditation.[5] And experiments have shown that we can be trained to exercise control over a lot of processes once thought to be completely beyond our control — skin temperature, blood pressure, heart rate, rate of saliva and urine formation and secretion of stomach acids.[6] These processes are part of what are known as the sympathetic functions of the autonomic nervous system, which governs the actions of the gastrointestinal, cardiovascular and respiratory systems in our bodies. The sympathetic nervous system swings into action when some emergency faces the individual: digestive processes slow down, the blood flow is shunted to the brain and muscles where it will be needed, the heart beats more rapidly, breathing quickens, the liver releases a supply of sugar for energy, body hairs become erect, the iris of the eye expands and the body is ready for fight or flight.

David Cheek, a Fellow of the American College of Gynaecologists, believes that subtle messages communicated to patients determine how their systems react: "Interning in 1942 at Johns Hopkins Hospital I witnessed an exsanguinating haemorrhage at delivery of a red-headed Irish woman who had been prepared for this trouble by our concern over her history of a 'bleeding tendency'." He said that subsequently he learned that bleeding tendencies are created by the alarms of doctors and can be prevented by attendants who believe in the ability of people to conserve blood with delivery or injury.[7]

The same question arises about feats of strength and endurance. There is enough evidence to show that significant increases in endurance performance can be gained with the use of hypnosis, but whether this reaches the level of transcending what is normal is not known. I would therefore be extremely careful about the wording of sporting or endurance scripts: it is just possible you might cause yourself injury.

One of the most controversial issues is whether people can be regressed back to birth, or to former lives. David Cheek, writing about birth experiences and their connection with various physical ailments in later life, says that people do have power to recall these experiences under hypnosis, even though they occurred before the beginnings of conscious memory. He feels that adverse circumstances such as being unwanted, a painful or difficult delivery, being separated from the mother immediately after delivery and the absence of breastfeeding are connected with headaches, peptic ulcers and asthma, and such problems as period pains, frigidity and habitual abortion in women.

Cheek, working with a subject who was a doctor with a chronic striving to overachieve, established that the problem stemmed from the subject's birth experiences. Under hypnosis the subject was able to see vividly the bedroom of his grandmother's house, his mother lying on the bed, the doctor standing beside her and the nurse holding a baby — himself — in towels and rubbing him briskly. While the doctor was wiping his hands and putting some things away he remarked to the nurse: "Don't waste too much time. I don't think he is worth saving." He was a premature baby weighing only three and a half pounds, delivered at home.

Cheek also traced another fellow medico's persistent headaches to awkward forceps delivery and other associated birth trauma, and was able to substantiate this with the doctor's mother.

I find these notions hard to accept because newborn infants lack language skills. However, there is an increasing amount of research being done in America showing that babies know a lot more than Western science used to think; they see more, hear more, understand more and use quite elaborate perceptual processes. They also demonstrate a variety of skills and actions that seem to have no basis in their previous experience.

At the International Congress of Clinical and Experimental Hypnosis in Melbourne in 1979 an American named Elena Fiore reported that she had used hypnosis to regress over 2000 patients to events of previous lifetimes and found this technique effective in treating a wide range of clinical problems. Still, she had not made up her mind whether these events remembered under hypnosis were based on reality.[8]

However, there *is* general agreement that hypnosis can increase memory skills. Dr Vladimir Raikov, a medical researcher in the Soviet Union, says that experiments involving deep hypnosis have demonstrated that the function of memory can improve between 150 and 200 per cent over that of the ordinary waking state. He has also carried out successful experiments with subjects capable of deep hypnosis to discover and develop their creative abilities in activities such as playing musical instruments, playing chess, drawing, solving mathematical problems and learning foreign languages. Raikov has conducted exciting experiments with age regression, obtaining hypnotic reproduction of characteristics usually only observed in the newborn child, such as the sucking reflex, specific brainwave patterns and eye movements and the Babinski reflex (extension of the toes when the soles of the feet are stroked).[9]

So, can you do the impossible? Probably the safest conclusion is that with hypnosis you can come closer to realising the potential within you in your normal state.

7
MISUSE AND DANGERS OF HYPNOSIS

Another controversial issue, and a longstanding one, is what potential for danger and misuse lies in hypnosis. Sigmund Freud said in 1891:

> Everything that has been said and written about the great dangers of hypnosis belongs to the realm of fable. If we leave on one side the misuse of hypnosis for illegitimate purposes — a possibility that exists for every other effective therapy method — the most we have to consider is the tendency of severely neurotic people, after repeated hypnosis, to fall into hypnosis spontaneously.[1]

Dr Milton Kline, from the Institute for Research in Hypnosis in the United States, laid that worry to rest, pointing out that even with patients taught to use self-hypnosis the development of undesired spontaneous states of hypnosis was not dangerous for either patient or therapist.[2]

The question has arisen as to whether hypnosis can trigger off a psychotic illness. Jacob H. Conn, a medical practitioner connected with Johns Hopkins University Medical School in the United States, discussed this with a number of clinicians experienced with psychotic patients. They all agreed that the psychotic process develops slowly over a period of years and that it is not "precipitated" by one or many hypnotic experiences. In his own practice over a period of thirty years, which included the treatment of over 3000 patients, he had not observed hypnosis "precipitating a psychotic illness".[3]

Opinion seems about equally divided on the question of whether we can get people to do something antisocial, immoral, unethical or against their own interests by using hypnosis.

In 1784 one of the Commissions of Inquiry into animal magnetism, headed by Benjamin Franklin, tendered a secret report to the King of France on the potential moral dangers in the practice of animal magnetism. The Commission reported the following exchange between the Chief of the Paris police and a physician who practised magnetism: "M. Lenoir said to him, 'In my capacity as Lieutenant-General of Police I wish to know whether, when a woman is magnetised and passing through the crisis, it would not be easy to outrage her?' M. Deslon replied in the affirmative.'' The policeman pointed out that M. Deslon had assured him that if the entitlement to practise magnetism remained within the medical profession and was governed by their ethics, then this should not cause any worry, but the Commissioners still had their doubts and came to the conclusion that "such practices may have an injurious reaction upon morality".[4]

Charcot described in 1889 the case of a married woman who had been hypnotised "five times within three weeks and who could think of nothing but her hypnotist, until she ran away from her home to live with him". Although her husband welcomed her back, she later had to be hospitalised for "severe hysterical disturbances".

Experiments dating back to 1903 have been carried out in which hypnotised people were persuaded to steal, put what they thought was poison in someone's tea, throw what they were told was acid at others' faces and reach for a live rattlesnake (in reality a harmless snake). Arguments have not yet been settled as to whether this was because of the power of hypnosis, or because the hypnotised people realised that they were being used for experimental purposes and that the experimenter would not allow anything to happen that was really dangerous.

In 1970 Jacob Conn asked many of the best known practitioners of hypnosis for their opinions on this matter, and summéd up their replies by saying, "Most clinicians believe that a 'trusting' person who is an excellent subject could be manipulated into committing a crime under certain conditions."[5]

My fellow student at Macquarie University, Lann Dawes, found in one experiment that hypnotised subjects could be influenced to bet real money on an almost certain loser much more easily than his control subjects. Both groups were chosen from highly hypnotiseable people. Some of his hypnotised subjects reported that they wanted to call out what looked certain to be the winning colour, but felt an irresistible urge to call out the colour of the loser instead, as they had been instructed to do.

This shows that good subjects can be made to act to some extent against their self-interest, and lends support to those who believe antisocial acts can be elicited under hypnosis. It certainly shows that the hypnotist has increased control over and above that which he already has as the experimenter in an experimental situation.[6] Luckily the use of self-hypnosis removes this particular danger.

Another potential misuse of hypnosis is in criminal investigation and questioning of witnesses. The Presidential address at the International Congress of Clinical and Experimental

Hypnosis in Melbourne in 1979 was given by Martin Orne from the University of Pennsylvania. It was titled ''The Use and Abuse of Hypnosis in Criminal Investigation'' and described various ways in which hypnosis has been used in accessing vital information from witnesses or in clarifying defendants' motives. However, he warned of the potential pitfalls, particularly subjects unconsciously creating stories when real memories are not available (confabulating). As the subjects actually believe in their stories, they become convincing false eyewitnesses with pseudo-memories.[7]

There are occasional reports of suggestions made to a hypnotised subject carrying over post-hypnotically and causing various problems. I recall reading of a badly worded treatment session aimed at discouraging a person from smoking cigarettes. The patient was told he would be sick every time he saw a cigarette, and he was! In the meantime the man who had made the suggestion had moved away and someone else had to repair the damage. There are other tales of uncancelled hypnotic suggestions: one of a school teacher who had the number six wiped from his memory in an experiment in amnesia, and had trouble teaching mathematics until the suggestion was neutralised, and another of a blister which appeared on the hands of an experimental subject every day until it was cancelled. He had been told that a coin was red hot and would burn the hand without causing pain, and as there was no blister at the end of the experiment, the experimenter did not bother to cancel the suggestion.[8]

If you feel at all uncomfortable or ill at ease after playing your tape it would be advisable to re-examine your script carefully and rewrite it, eliminating any possible sources of conflict or disturbance, just to be absolutely sure. However, in my experience the only negative effects have been oversleeping on rare occasions and, sometimes, boredom.

8
THE EFFECTS OF STRESS

Stress is a very fashionable concept at present, and rightly so. While we are living in a sophisticated, complex environment we still have the same simple mechanisms for reacting to real or imagined danger as did our prehistoric ancestors. When a sabre-toothed tiger came rushing out of the forest at them they either froze, ran away or tried to fight. Modern people react to upsets, conflicts and frustrations with much the same repertoire of responses — fight or flight, or stasis (that is, freezing, giving up or putting up with the situation).

This also applies to physiological responses: when our predecessors were afraid, the sympathetic reaction of their autonomic nervous systems galvanised into action: their heart pounded, their blood pressure rose, their pulse rates increased, their mouths and throats became dry, their pupils dilated, they felt dizzy and weak, they trembled, they perspired and hydrochloric acid attacked their stomach walls. They were ready to fight an attacker or to flee.

While there are no sabre-toothed tigers around now, we still have the same physical reactions to stress. Our stressors may be big or small: we lose a loved one, we just miss being run over by a bus, we forget to turn the iron off and remember just as we reach our holiday destination hours away, we worry about things that may never happen, we are bored, unfulfilled, broke, unsuccess-ful. So off go our responses: blood rushes through our veins, en-gorging our arteries, our hearts beat faster and so on. Whereas these reactions helped in our ancestors' survival, today they may be quite inappropriate as a response to a threatening situation.

The effects of stress have been studied extensively by Hans Selye, who graduated in Medicine from the University of Prague in 1925. Ten years later he began work at McGill University in Montreal and from that time onwards he devoted his career to research into "le stress" as he named it, borrowing from engineering terminology. He has written about this research in a book called *The Stress of Life*.[1]

Selye experimented with various animals, exposing them to stressors such as intense light, noxious chemicals, extreme cold and electric shock, which produced all sorts of ailments: kidney diseases, high blood pressure, diseases of the heart and the blood vessels, rheumatism and rheumatoid arthritis, inflammatory diseases of the skin and eyes, infections, allergic and hypersensitivity diseases, nervous and mental diseases, sexual derangements, digestive diseases, metabolic diseases and cancer, and diseases of resistance in general.

He identified what he called the G.A.S. (General Adaptation Syndrome). Having said that "virtually every organ and every chemical constituent in the human body is involved in the general stress reaction", he then went on to draw a broad simplified picture of the G.A.S.

The first stage is the Alarm Reaction. Stress hormones, specific chemical messengers, are released by the endocrine glands into the bloodstream. They produce enlargement of the adrenal cortex (the outer part of the adrenal glands which produces anti-inflammatory hormones) and shrinkage of the thymus, spleen, lymph nodes and lymphatic structures of the body, all of which are made up of innumerable white blood cells and which play an extremely important role in the body's immune-defence systems and allergic responses. As well, deep, bleeding ulcers appear in the lining of the stomach and the large intestine.

The second phase of the G.A.S. is called the Stage of Resistance, in which the body's forces mobilise, adapt and respond in various ways to counteract the damaging effects of the first stage.

The third stage, the Stage of Exhaustion, occurs after prolonged exposure to stressors. Adaptation becomes ineffective, resulting in chronic disorders and, eventually, death.

The Alarm Reaction indicators appeared in a matter of hours in Selye's experimental animals, but it is not so easy to investigate the effects of psychological stress on humans (the section on cancer includes results of some of the research on stress). However, there is general agreement that the same sorts of disorders can be produced in people by conflicts, anxieties and fears, and unpleasant life experiences.

Selye's belief is that "the most important stressors for man are emotional", and he lists the warning signs by which you or your physician can monitor your stress status and take appropriate action (because you can't actually *feel* your adrenal cortex enlarge or your thymus and spleen shrink!). For your physician, the levels of certain substances in the blood, E.E.G. and blood pressure readings, as well as measures of the electrical conductivity of the skin (G.S.R.) are all fairly reliable indicators of whether stress is taking its toll. For yourself, general irritability, depression, pounding or palpitations of the heart, emotional ups and downs, excessive fatigue, inability to concentrate, insomnia, stomach upsets, inexplicable aches and pains, and headaches are among the signs your body uses to warn you that it is undergoing too much stress.

In view of the fact that some problems are more difficult to deal with than others, two investigators in the United States, Thomas H. Holmes and Richard H. Rahe, drew up a social readjustment rating scale, giving each stressor a score, the highest score being 100. The death of a spouse is at the top of the scale, with a score of 100, divorce is next at seventy-three, marriage at fifty, being retrenched at forty-seven, changing jobs at thirty-five, and outstanding personal achievement at twenty-eight, Christmas at twelve, and so on. They believe that if a person's total score is over 150, he or she will become physically or mentally sick.[2] Clearly they consider "good" stressors (for example, marriage, personal achievement, holidays and Christmas) to be as potentially harmful as "bad" stressors.

While not everyone accepts this stress scale or the idea that "good" stressors are as harmful as "bad" stressors, there is general agreement that some form of breakdown will result from an accumulation of stressful situations. Holmes and Rahe tested their stress scale on hospital patients. They asked the patients to rate their lives over the past two years, and concluded that people are more prone to *any* chronic disease if they have been exposed to stress.

While a good deal of stress, especially of the type I see, is caused by "overload" on the mental and physical system, the same effects can be caused by "underload" — boredom, sensory deprivation, repetitive tasks, unchanging or predictable conditions and lack of choice.

People vary in the amount of stress they can withstand before breakdown starts, and they vary in the type of breakdown they have, but it seems that sooner or later something has to give if effective coping skills are not learned.

This book is mainly about combating the effects of stress. You may be able to do so fairly easily with self-hypnosis tapes; you may need to read and analyse yourself for some time before you can solve your problems; you may have friends who can assist you; or you may need professional help. But there is no exaggerating the importance of successfully dealing with stress. Hans Selye says:

What makes me so certain that the natural human life-span is far in excess of the actual one is this: among all my autopsies I have never seen a person who died of old age . . . we invariably die because one vital part has worn out too early in proportion to the rest of the body.[3]

9

COPING WITH STRESS

Hypnosis is not carried out in a vacuum. It is used within the context of some kind of philosophy or theory, translated into a therapy or technique. Neither is it a cure by itself. Hypnosis is a vehicle making the therapy chosen as best suited to the needs of the patient more powerful and more likely to succeed.

Quite often, therapists favouring one kind of approach will reject all other techniques, whereas other therapists will tailor the treatment to the client's needs at the time. Such therapists will use techniques from many different therapies and will treat the client within the context of his or her overall life circumstances.

For the scripts in this book I have used ideas from many different therapies where they were appropriate to the particular problem. However, there are other possible choices apart from the ones I have made, as you will realise once you have read about the therapies and gone through the scripts. You are advised to borrow appropriate ideas and phrases from wherever you can. You may like to explore further by reading books on transactional analysis, Gestalt therapy and other therapies which will provide extra ideas.

Some ways to avoid stress are quite obvious. You *must* have enough sleep; create time for recreation and a social life; and aim for communication and understanding in your relationships. In other words, strive for a well-rounded life. If you place too much importance on one aspect of your life, problems in this sphere will take on much greater emphasis.

If you are bothered by boredom, try to involve yourself in an activity you enjoy; make an effort to change your lifestyle.

Eat a properly balanced diet, making sure that you are taking in the correct amounts of vitamins, minerals and trace elements to keep you healthy. This will reduce the effect of stressful situations.

Aerobic exercise is important, too. Exercises that oxygenate the blood make coping with stress much easier. A person who takes up an exercise such as running, swimming or cycling is less affected by the hormones that produce the "fight or flight" response; the heart becomes accustomed to levelling off at a relatively low rate, and therefore has a built-in protection against the harmful physical effects of psychological stress. These exercises set off the parasympathetic functions of the autonomic nervous system that counter the sympathetic nervous system reactions mentioned earlier. This has the effect of slowing down the breathing and heart rate and aids the flow of blood to the intestines.

Regular aerobic exercise (four to six times a week) causes a decrease in levels of anxiety, feelings of depression, psychosomatic disorders, and an increase in efficiency of sleep, mental alertness, emotional stability, endurance and feelings of relaxation.

A similar effect is produced, and a similar protection from stress obtained, by the various relaxation training procedures — yoga, transcendental meditation, tai chi and, of course, hypnosis.

Relaxation and meditation techniques, preferably practised twice a day, ten to twenty minutes before breakfast and dinner, produce a physical response opposite to that of the "fight or flight" response. There is a marked decrease in the body's own oxygen consumption as body energy resources are taxed less, and an increase in alpha brainwaves, which indicate a relaxed state. Heart rate slows and blood pressure decreases.

It is a good idea to actively seek out activities that help you to relax, such as gardening, listening to music, massage, spas or saunas.

Some handy hints are: drop your shoulders — whenever you tense up your shoulders will rise; and if you are clenching your teeth, relax your jaws. When waiting at traffic lights practise some clenching, relaxing and breathing exercises. If you are hurrying because you are late, tell yourself that you are walking fast or running for the sake of exercise, and you will not feel so distraught. Whenever you are feeling pressured allow yourself a luxury or a treat, or pamper yourself (have a facial or a massage). Have plans for the future (perhaps a short trip) and dwell on them when things are getting you down.

10

THE THERAPIES

There are two main therapeutic approaches — those that try to change a person's behaviour and expect that the person will change along with it (behaviourism), and those that try to get through to the underlying causes of behaviour, and expect that change will occur when these are understood (psychodynamic therapies).

BEHAVIOURISM

Behaviourism is based on theories of human learning stemming from Ivan Pavlov's conditioning of dogs at the beginning of this century. Pavlov was a Russian scientist who taught dogs to associate food with the sound of a buzzer, and subsequently they salivated whenever the buzzer sounded, even when no food was offered. He was also involved in research into hypnosis, with animals as well as humans.[1]

The early behaviourists, in their attempts to gain scientific respectability, were extremely rigid and mechanistic, and refused to allow as evidence anything except behaviour that could be *seen*. Their stimulus-response view of learning threw the baby out with the bathwater, reducing humans to the level of much lower organisms. As someone pointed out, they seemed to suggest that people are essentially ping-pong balls with memories.

Things like emotions, thoughts, wishes, intentions and so on were called "intervening variables" — just a nuisance to be ignored if possible. Later they softened their stance and acknowledged such things as "cognitive" and "affective" behaviours, that is, thoughts and feelings, rather than just actions, and there are now many successful techniques resulting from behaviour modification theories. These are based on the idea that behaviour that goes unrewarded or is punished will generally be eliminated, whereas behaviour that receives a reward of some kind will be retained and strengthened. This leads to the use of what are called aversion techniques, where punishments such as electric shocks, white noise (static) and chemicals that induce nausea and vomiting have been used to treat such problems as alcoholism, sexual deviation and overeating.

Joseph Cautela of Boston College in the United States decided that an idea presented to the imagination would affect behaviour just as if the idea were real, and used decidedly unpleasant imagery as a punishment immediately following undesirable behaviour. For example, the patient imagines in graphic detail the worst kind of hangover resulting from compulsive drinking.[2]

I have a dislike of aversion techniques and prefer to try to find positive reinforcements that will work just as well. Besides, extensive research by the American psychologists N. H. Azrin and W. C. Holz has shown that rewards are more likely than punishments to produce the desired behaviour.[3]

One of the most frequently used behavioural treatments is called systematic desensitisation. This involves training people to relax and then exposing them to a graded series of situations connected with the problem area and letting them experience the anxiety, then relax. For instance, the first item in the hierarchy of the fear of heights might be walking up a few steps, and the last might be standing and looking over a railing on the roof of a tall building. Systematic desensitisation can be carried out either in reality or by imagining the situation. The principle behind this technique, developed by Joseph Wolpe in 1958[4], is that relaxation is antagonistic to the harmful effects of the sympathetic nervous system's responses (anxiety and tension). That is, you cannot be tense and relaxed at the same time. Other techniques are:

• Flooding, which is prolonged and massive exposure to a feared object or situation. For example, a compulsive handwasher who fears dirt is asked to visualise all sorts of scenes involving dirt.

• Massed practice, such as smoking cigarettes rapidly and constantly, or deliberately forcing a facial tic, or stammering repeatedly, for an allotted time.

• A replacement habit, such as fist clenching, which helps to stop habits like nailbiting.

"Time out for worry" is another behaviourist idea that involves setting aside a certain time each day, say an hour, for worrying. As time passes, subjects are advised to make more of this time available for constructive worry or planning, and less time available for useless worry of the "what if" kind.

Behaviourists also favour the use of biofeedback. Electrodes placed on the forehead or the forearm of the subject register an auditory and sometimes visual signal of the level of tension. Biofeedback has been used effectively for insomnia, high blood pressure, tension headaches, ulcers and many other stress-related disorders. It cannot easily be used in conjunction with hypnosis, but I mention it here because much hypnosis research involves comparisons with biofeedback.

ASSERTIVENESS TRAINING

Assertiveness training and rational-emotive therapy are, strictly. speaking, behaviour modification techniques, but they have evolved into major therapeutic approaches in their own right.

In my last year of university I stumbled across a little book in the "stacks", the part of the library you can't borrow from, and even though it was that time of the year when the pressure was really on, I read the whole book.

It was called *Your Perfect Right*[5], and was so interesting I wrote away to California for a copy. Since working as a counsellor I have made three or four bulk orders for the same book, as it is so popular it keeps disappearing. (The book is distributed in Australia by F. S. Symes Pty Ltd, of Brookvale, NSW.)

The following three paragraphs are reprinted from the fourth (1982) edition of *Your Perfect Right*, with permission of the publisher:

> *Has anyone ever cut in front of you in a line? Do you have difficulty saying "no" to persuasive salespeople? Are you able to express warm, positive feelings to someone? Can you comfortably begin a conversation with strangers at a party? Have you ever regretted "stepping on" someone else in trying to gain your own objectives?*
>
> *Many people find situations like these uncomfortable or irritating, and often seem at a loss for just the "right" action. In fact, there is no one "right way" to handle such events, but there are some basic principles which will help you to gain confidence and effectiveness in your relationships with others.*
>
> *Assertive behaviour enables a person to act in his or her own best interests, to stand up for herself or himself without undue anxiety, to express honest feelings comfortably, or to exercise personal rights without denying the rights of others.*

This is a particularly important message for Australians, because we seem to be rarely assertive, but often meek or aggressive. Some of us would never consider complaining about the food or service in a restaurant, and others are eager to make a scene, abuse the waiter and make everyone feel uncomfortable. Assertive behaviour in that situation would be to call the waiter politely, quietly state your case and ask firmly but pleasantly, for what you want. That is your perfect right. The authors define assertiveness as "the right to choose to express your emotions honestly". This does not only involve complaining, but also paying compliments, telling people how you really feel, refusing to do a favour if you don't want to, and so on.

Body disturbances such as headaches, general fatigue, stomach problems, depression, rashes and asthma are often the result of the failure to develop assertive behaviour, and assertiveness training has claimed some quite remarkable "cures" for such problems as sleepwalking, irritable bowel and severe depression, just to name a few. Treatment sometimes has an unexpected by-product — divorce. Naturally, training a previously meek person to speak out can cause quite a few shock-waves in personal relationships. That is why the emphasis is on "choosing" to express emotions honestly. The person may consider the consequences and choose not to be assertive if, for example, there is a risk of breaking up the family.

So it is quite all right to choose not to be assertive, but we have a real problem if we are incapable of it when the occasion really demands it.

RATIONAL-EMOTIVE THERAPY

Rational-emotive therapy is fully explained in a paperback by Albert Ellis and Robert Harper called *A New Guide to Rational Living*.[6]

Many people blow up what are merely difficult situations and experiences into major disasters. Fear of slights or rejections, fear of failure and fear of making a fool of oneself prevent people from making friendly overtures to others. They think, "If I ask so-and-so to go out and they refuse that will prove that I'm worthless, and it will be a calamity."

The American psychotherapist and marriage counsellor Albert Ellis, who developed rational-emotive therapy, would examine this reaction with his "ABC theory of personality and emotional disturbance". He would say that it is not the event at point A (the refusal) that causes the reaction at point C (this is a calamity), but rather the thoughts at point B about what occurs at A (this means I'm worthless). Or, as the Stoic philosopher Epictetus wrote almost 2000 years ago: "Men are disturbed not by things, but by the views which they take of them." So it is not what happens or what people do that is necessarily upsetting, it is one's attitude to it.

Everybody has had experiences which when recalled make them wince. They may, indeed, have acted foolishly, have unwittingly hurt someone's feelings, have drawn unwelcome attention to themselves, have been rejected or have failed at something important. But these should preferably be regarded as incidents to be coped with and forgotten, not as proof that all the negative things we may think about ourselves are true.

Life's genuine tragedies, of course, call for special coping skills, but for those minor setbacks that we tend to exaggerate Ellis details specific ways of countering irrational thoughts, and explains how the therapist can help the patient ferret out and rephrase all those self-defeating sentences he is repeating to himself, with a view to helping the patient learn how to do this by himself.

The therapies so far described are attempts to change a person's *behaviour*, whether it is behaviour that can be seen, or unobservable thoughts and feelings. Many of my scripts contain suggestions from these therapeutic approaches, which will be fairly specific and direct instructions on what changes will be made, and how they will occur. If you favour the behaviourist approach it is a good idea first to analyse how you behave, and then to decide which behaviour needs changing. Try to determine which factors are maintaining the behaviour and how the behaviour was acquired, and decide on the means of producing the change. How much of this behaviour do you really have to keep? What are you achieving by clinging on to this behaviour?

Ask yourself: "Am I taking on too much? Do I have an overly high expectation of myself and others? What are the bad habits I would like to overcome? What would I like to achieve? What are my weaknesses that can be worked on? How can I organise my time, plan my priorities, clarify my value systems?"

Try to analyse your problems logically. What do you want out of life? How do you see yourself in five, ten or forty years time? What would you like to do that you are not doing now? What is stopping you?

It may be helpful to use a Life History Questionnaire. There is an excellent one in Arnold A. Lazarus's book *Behaviour Therapy and Beyond*.[7] Many of my students have found working through such a questionnaire an enlightening experience in itself.

PSYCHODYNAMIC THERAPIES

The psychodynamic approach stems from the work of Sigmund Freud. It stresses the importance of the dynamic forces of unconscious motives, which spring mainly from early childhood experiences.

I will not go into great detail about psychoanalytic procedures because while hypnosis can be an adjunct to psychoanalysis, the process of listening to patients talking freely about themselves for one to three hours a week over long periods has no real relevance to my method of self-hypnosis. However, the importance the psychoanalysts place on unconscious motives and the various defence mechanisms we use is implicit in many of the scripts. A modern psychodynamic approach is dealt with in the works of Milton Erickson[8] and Bandler and Grinder[9], and this can be applied to self-hypnosis.

TECHNIQUES OF MILTON ERICKSON

Arguably the greatest practitioner of hypnotic techniques of this century, the American psychiatrist Milton Erickson was confined to his wheelchair for many years by two attacks of poliomyelitis, one when he was seventeen and another when he was fifty-two. This left him with a lot of pain from muscle and joint difficulties, and he practised self-hypnosis to deal with this. When he turned seventy-five he told an interviewer that it took him an hour after he woke up in the morning to get all the pain out, whereas it used to be easier when he was younger.

He was a very skilled clinician, and many of his followers have devoted much time and effort trying to analyse his procedures, which were unique and varied. He would say things like: "How will you feel, next week, when your behaviour has completely changed?" and severe phobias and antisocial behaviour just seemed to melt away.

Erickson spoke to two levels of the person at the same time, the conscious and the unconscious levels, so that often the actual words did not make all that much sense.

He used many therapeutic tricks, sometimes several at once in what he called his "buckshot approach". An example of his approach is the "double bind", which forces choices out of people. Erickson claimed he got the idea from his father, who would say to his young son on their farm: "Do you want to feed the chickens first or the hogs, and then do you want to fill the woodbox or pump the water for the cows first?"

He used metaphors and anecdotes to weave stories, again effecting seemingly magical cures in this way, and a technique which projected the person into an imaginary future to experience achievement of a goal. He asked patients to visualise all manner of scenes in crystal balls, and made frequent use of age regression and time distortion (making time seem to expand or contract), and what he called pseudo-orientation in time. This consists of leading a deeply hypnotised subject into a dissociated state in which he believes he has already accomplished something that he previously felt was beyond his ability to achieve.

The hypnotist suggests that the patient is in some future time and that he has already experienced that which has not yet happened in reality. This procedure has been successfully used with depressed patients, who have been projected into the future and asked to remember enjoyable experiences and happy times in the past.

Erickson occasionally used behavioural techniques, too. He treated cases of parental dominance by assuring the patient that it is perfectly acceptable to think for oneself, then assigning more and more difficult tasks contrary to parental demands, starting off with a little task associated with intense guilt. Then he would increase the guilt by goading the patient about how the parent would be upset and angry at what had been done. Sometimes he would step in and criticise the parent in front of the patient, saying the patient was no longer going to tolerate certain things or do what the parent wanted. One patient made a breakthrough when he sent his mother a picture of himself apparently drunk, holding a bottle of whisky![10]

Another technique he used was "symptom prescription", asking the person to voluntarily perform the behaviour in hopes of eliminating or gaining control over it. The following case illustrates this procedure:

> A woman came to me with a stomach ulcer; a pain that had incapacitated her at work and home and in all her social relationships. The major issue concerning her was the fact that she could not stand her in-laws visiting her three or four times a week. They came without notice and stayed as long as they pleased. I pointed out to her that she could not stand her in-laws, but she could stand church, and card games with neighbors, and her work. Focusing down on the in-laws, I said, "You really don't like your relatives. They're a pain in the belly every time they come. It ought to be usefully developed; they certainly can't expect you to mop up the floor if you vomit when they come."
>
> Whenever the in-laws dropped in she would rush to drink a glass of milk and subsequently vomit. She would apologize while they mopped up. As a result, the in-laws dropped in less frequently. When they did come uninvited, they received the same treatment until these unwelcome visits ceased. She gave up the stomach ulcer and took pride in her stomach. It was an awfully good stomach that could throw the relatives out.[11]

TECHNIQUES OF RICHARD BANDLER AND JOHN GRINDER

The most recently developed therapy of all, as far as I am aware, is called Neurolinguistic Programming (N.L.P.) and is the result of the authors actually sitting in for many months on the practices of three famous clinicians, Milton Erickson, Fritz Perls and Virginia Satir. Virginia Satir is an extremely effective family therapist in the United States. Fritz Perls, who was born in Germany but left for the United States before World War II, is best known as the founder of Gestalt therapy which, although a valuable tool for therapists, is not easily adapted for use in self-hypnosis.

Richard Bandler and John Grinder analysed what took place in the therapy sessions, both in terms of the use of language and the nonverbal messages that were exchanged. They point out that people have a tendency to respond in predominantly one of the sensory modes — that is, sound, vision, touch or occasionally smell or taste — and that you can find out which mode a person uses most frequently by listening to the kinds of verbs, adverbs and adjectives they use.

Some simple examples are:

• *Vision*: "I can see most of what you are saying clearly, but there are still a few grey areas."

• *Sound*: "Most of what you say sounds OK, but something doesn't quite click."

• *Touch*: "I like the general feel of all that, but it's still a bit rough in places."

• *Taste*: "The general flavour is all right, but some of it is still a bit hard to swallow."

• *Smell*: "I'm on to the scent of most of what you mean, but some parts I find a bit on the nose."

They also noticed that people's predominant sensory mode can be determined by the way their eyes move when they are asked certain questions. If a person is asked, "What was it like when you were ten years old?" his or her eyes will move in a certain direction. Most right-handed people, they believe, will look upwards left for visual accessing of remembered material, upwards right for visual accessing of imagined material, sideways or downwards left for auditory accessing of remembered material, sideways right for auditory accessing of imagined material and downwards right for accessing touch, smells or tastes.

The importance of these findings lies in improving communication with other people. They say if you wish to communicate well with a person, use the same sensory modes, and if you want to alienate the person, deliberately mismatch their mode. They suggest pacing or mirroring, that is, matching another person's verbal or non-verbal behaviour with the idea of eventually leading the other person into new behaviour by changing what you are doing. Another example of pacing is tuning into another person's breathing.

I found Bandler and Grinder's book *Frogs Into Princes* quite fascinating. They believe that the conscious mind is less than the tip of the iceberg, and in therapy they aim at communication with the unconscious processes. They make the assumption that there is part of us that makes us do something we do not want to do, or prevents us from doing what we want, and that this part is, in fact, acting on our behalf, and benefits us in some way. So they do not try to eliminate any behaviour, just to integrate it and help the person find alternative ways of accomplishing the same purpose.

About one case of catatonia, which is a form of schizophrenia in which people remain often in one position, sometimes for years, without communicating, they had this to say:

> *Once you have paced well, you can lead the other person into a new behaviour by changing what you are doing . . . if it is done gracefully and smoothly it will work with anyone, including catatonics. Once I was in Napa State Mental Hospital in California, and a guy had been sitting there for several years on a couch in the day room. The only communication he was offering me were his body position and his breathing rate. His eyes were open, pupils dilated. So I sat facing away from him at about a forty-five degree angle in a chair nearby, and I put myself in exactly the same body position . . . and I sat there for forty minutes breathing with him . . . I tried little variations in my breathing, and he would follow, so I knew I had rapport at that point. I could have changed my breathing slowly over a period of time and brought him out that way. Instead I interrupted and it shocked him. I shouted, "Hey! Do you have a cigarette?" He jumped up off the couch and said, "God! Don't do that!"*[12]

Milton Erickson used formal hypnotic induction in less than twenty per cent of his clinical work, and Bandler and Grinder have gone one step further and do not use formal hypnosis at all, claiming that they achieve the same end without the need for formal hypnosis. They make special use of words, as did Erickson, and the fact that most of the attributes of trance are present in people much of the time — for example, driving from A to B without being consciously aware of the journey, or staring straight at something but not seeing it.

Bandler and Grinder say that being in a trance doesn't mean that you have to be dead: "A lot of people tell me 'Well, I don't think I was in trance because I could still hear things and feel things.' If you can't see and hear things, that's death; that's a different state."[13]

Later in this book I will suggest scripts based on Bandler and Grinder's techniques of changing or rewriting personal histories.

I have by no means exhausted all the available therapies, but most of the suggestions incorporated in my scripts come from the techniques I have covered. Most of the other therapeutic approaches (primal therapies, body therapies, etc.) really require a therapist, and sometimes group work.

11
UNCONSCIOUS MOTIVATION

When I was at university in the 1960s behaviourism was *in* and conscious and unconscious processes were *out*. Since then I have had to acknowledge the vital part unconscious motives play in governing behaviour. However, there are differing views of the unconscious processes. To Freud they were a seething mass of id instincts, that is, sexual and aggressive tendencies, incestuous impulses and castration complexes, within which strong forces demanding life on the one hand and death on the other struggled for supremacy. These id instincts were deeply repressed (pushed out of consciousness) because they conflicted with accepted standards of conduct, but they remained active, indirectly affecting feelings and behaviour. The only evidence for them was via symbolic manifestations such as dreams, slips of the tongue, or pathological symptoms such as hallucinations, delusions, "word salads" (meaningless outpourings of words) and so on.

Milton Erickson's view of the unconscious mind is similar to the 1909 definition of "subconscious" or "co-conscious" given by Morton Prince, an American psychoanalyst practising early this century, as any process "of which the personality is unaware" but "which is a factor in the determination of conscious and bodily phenomena".[1] Erickson regarded the unconscious as a very powerful constructive force for life and growth that should be fully used. He believed that the conscious mind could tell the unconscious mind what it wanted done, but not how or when or where to do it. After many years of practising self-hypnosis for removal of pain, he was able to simply say, "Unconscious, do your stuff." He believed the aim of therapy was not uncovering or releasing repressed emotions, but gaining co-ordination between unconscious and conscious functioning. Like Bandler and Grinder, he believed the conscious mind to be only the tip of the iceberg. He maintained that the patient doesn't consciously know what the problems are, no matter how good a story he might tell, because it is a conscious story.

Most theorists would agree with British scientist Daniel Dunnett, who said after a series of experiments: "Quite outside our consciousness our brain is carrying out elaborate and sophisticated activities."[2] The brain stores all experiences; nothing is ever forgotten — neither sights, smells, feelings, sounds nor tastes. It has recorded everything that has ever happened to you.

Well, almost. Bandler and Grinder tell of a woman who was trying to find out why her unconscious was maintaining her phobia (obsessive fear) of freeways, and after a while the unconscious part that was responsible for this behaviour admitted that it had quite forgotten. Bandler and Grinder felt that this made sense: that if you get caught up in resisting some behaviour for a long time the part of you responsible for this behaviour gets so involved in the fight that it forgets why it organised that behaviour in the first place! They define "conscious" as whatever you are aware of in a moment of time, and "unconscious" as everything else.[3]

Bandler and Grinder believe that there is not just one unconscious, but there are many facets of the unconscious mind. Others speak of layers or levels of unconscious behaviour, and some, such as Ernest R. Hilgard, make several distinctions between various levels and forms of both conscious and unconscious processes, as follows[4]:

• Nonconscious processes are those that lie outside of consciousness altogether, such as the physiological controls of body heat and cold.

• Conscious processes are those familiar in the normal waking condition, with appropriate attention to the information coming from the body and from the environment.

• Preconscious processes are quite readily available memories, not at present in consciousness.

• Dissociated processes are memories and control and monitoring systems that can be brought into consciousness spontaneously (as with multiple personalities) or by techniques such as hypnosis.

• Unconscious processes are those processes that are deeply repressed so that, even though they have some of the characteristics of conscious and dissociated processes, they are available to consciousness only indirectly. They are inferred by behaviour or by such indications as dreams or slips of the tongue.

Hilgard believes that some precision is lost if everything not available to consciousness is called unconscious. I agree with that position but will continue to refer to "the unconscious" or "the subconscious", on occasions somewhat interchangeably. Most people have some concept of what is meant by these, whereas the term "dissociated processes" is relatively unfamiliar.

However, both Albert Ellis and Morton Korenberg, a Canadian psychotherapist, completely rejected the concept of "the unconscious". Korenberg states:

People do things quite consciously ... you hypothesize an unconscious which is driving him to do the wrong thing. Whereas the fact of the matter is that it just gives this particular person less anxiety to do what he always does and which he knows is wrong, than to change and do the right thing; which will make him very anxious. [5]

According to Ellis:

The rational-emotive school holds that there is no such entity as the unconscious or the id ... practically all the important attitudes that exist in this respect are not deeply hidden or deliberately kept out of consciousness because the patient is too ashamed to acknowledge them. They are, rather, just below the level of consciousness ... [6]

I feel that when hypnosis fails to achieve the desired result it is because for some reason the suggestion has not been received, accepted and acted upon at the unconscious level. This could be because whatever you want to change has a lot more psychological importance than you gave it credit for, or perhaps the line of approach or the wording are not appropriate.

You could try using more imaginative wording, or a more oblique approach. For example, you might attack the symptom fairly directly at first, then try approaching the underlying dynamics, perhaps using hypnotic dream scripts or Bandler and Grinder types of scripts. If these attempts do not work, try a thoroughly indirect Ericksonian approach.

Some people think the latter approach might succeed where others fail as it does not arouse resistance in either the conscious or the unconscious mind. That is, it is harder to resist a suggestion that bears hardly any relationship to the required response. This calls for a lot of ingenuity in script-writing, which of course depends on how much time and effort you are prepared to spend on achieving the hoped-for change.

Erickson believed it is important that we give our unconscious as much freedom as possible to work things out; when we do make suggestions, they should be as broad as possible. [7] His reason for believing it is necessary to be indirect rather than direct in approach is that "a patient himself is a person who is afraid to be direct". A healthy person is direct — defines a problem, thinks of alternatives, chooses the one that is most likely to achieve the desired outcome and does it, facing whatever obstacles there may be. However, a person with a disturbance is afraid to do this. [8]

Part Two

THE BASIC SCRIPT

12
TAPE CONSTRUCTION

You need a tape recorder, a microphone and a reasonably good quality blank C90 cassette tape. Leave a short time at the beginning of the tape before commencing the recording; the first bit of the tape does not record.

Speak fairly slowly and deliberately, and at a lower pitch than usual. Leave plenty of time for your instructions or imagery to sink in, and for responses to be made. For example, the relaxation instructions in the basic script include: "Take some time now to become aware of tense areas in your body and either clench or stretch the muscles involved, then relax them" — this process can take quite a while. With instructions you consider particulary important, give them more emphasis or repeat them; and again, leave a sufficient pause for the words to sink in and take effect.

Keep in mind that hypnosis is supposed to involve monotony and repetition, so try not to do anything startling — suddenly raising your voice or coughing, for example. It is better to try to make the recording without stops and starts, as these can be distracting when listening later. Nowadays most recorders have a pause button, which is preferable to using the stop button, as this produces a clicking sound on the tape.

Do not expect to make a perfect recording the first time; you will get better with practice. The important thing is how it sounds to you. If there are distracting parts, or it is too soft or too fast, which is by far the most common problem, then the recording should be made again.

You may think you will be self-conscious about, or critical of, the sound of your own voice. But you will get used to it, and probably find yourself enjoying the sound of your own trusted voice telling you things that are good for you!

Play the tape whenever you want, as often as seems necessary. I think it best to play it three or four times in the first week, then, say, once a week after that, but it is entirely up to you.

Also, the time you choose to play it is up to you. I prefer to put my tape on when I go to bed. That way I usually drift off to sleep near the very beginning, or else into a trance (it is sometimes hard to tell the difference), which continues as a sleep when the recording is finished. Then I usually sleep until morning. People often do not hear very much of the tape at all, at least not consciously. But it seems to work perfectly well that way, perhaps even better than when listened to consciously. If you play the tape in the morning you may fall asleep and be late for work, even though the scripts finish with an inducement to wake up.

Whenever you are listening to your tape, make sure you are quite comfortable. Go to the toilet before turning the tape on, loosen tight clothing, take off watches and rings, and either lie down in a darkened room where you can be sure of not being disturbed, or, as I do, go to bed. It is most important that you are not disturbed, if the tape is to be effective.

The basic script that follows is a relatively standard hypnosis induction aimed at reducing the general effects of day-to-day frustration, conflict and stress.

The "eye roll" induction technique was originally developed by the famous psychiatrist Herbert Spiegel, from Columbia University, as a method of evaluating trance levels.[1] Later it was discovered that in the course of evaluating trance levels by means of the technique, most patients would immediately go into trance. It then became a popular rapid induction technique.

Breathing slowly, relaxing and putting pleasant thoughts into your mind are accepted methods of slowing down physical and mental processes and helping to reduce sensations.

The escalator image used to deepen your trance is also quite commonly used, as are the ego-strengthening techniques. Both are aimed at developing peace of mind.

You may use the basic script as it is, or you may make whatever changes you think necessary. Following the basic script are a number of alternatives for you to consider: a short version and two alternative full-length scripts, and a few other ideas you may wish to experiment with. There is also a basic script specially written for children.

The specific scripts form the main part of this book. Choose from these according to the problem you wish to deal with, insert it in the basic script at the time indicated, either as it is or with the changes you feel are necessary. You may choose to use only the basic script, with no specific script, just for relaxation and ego-strengthening.

You can, of course, write your own complete basic and specific scripts, perhaps just using the following as guidelines.

13
THE BASIC SCRIPT

Lie down and make sure you are quite comfortable.

I'm going to get you into a state where you are more receptive than usual to ideas and suggestions.

I'll do this by narrowing and focusing your attention, by using repetition and monotony. You will be very relaxed during this session and afterwards you'll feel fine, free of tension, calm and refreshed.

Begin by looking up toward your eyebrows. Try to look up still more, and as you continue to look up close your eyelids slowly. Keep your eyes rolled upward, and take a deep breath. Hold. Now exhale and let your eyes relax. Keep your eyes closed, and concentrate on a feeling of floating — a pleasant and welcome feeling of floating . . .

Concentrate now on your breathing . . . slow down your breathing . . . right down . . . breathe in deeply through your nose, and breathe out slowly, very slowly, through your nose . . . every so often take a deep breath down as far as you can, hold it for a while, and then slowly exhale . . .

Now concentrate on relaxing. Breathe slowly and deeply, saying the word "relax" to yourself in your mind as you breathe out . . . letting all tension flow out, drain out of your body. If there are any external noises around, let them flow over and away from you, and recede right into the distance. Pay no attention to them . . .

Make your right fist into as tight a ball as possible, then relax it . . . this will show the contrast between tense and relaxed muscles.

Take some time now to become aware of tense areas in your body, and either clench or stretch the muscles involved, then relax them (*long pause*) . . .

Relax the muscles in your feet, in your knees and your thighs. Feel the tension flow out, down through your legs, out through your feet and toes. Tighten up your stomach muscles, tighten your abdomen, then relax . . .

Let tension drain away from chest and back muscles . . . let your forehead go smooth, jaws go slack . . . let the little muscles around your eyes loosen, eyelids heavy . . . let any tension go out of your scalp, let your scalp loosen . . .

49

Clench the muscles in your neck, push your head forward
on to your chest, then push it on to your back ... feel the
tension in the back of your neck ... and then release it ...
let all the tension flow out, out of your neck, down through
your shoulders and arms, out through your hands and fingers
... just let it all drain away ...

Now ... let your mind take you to your favourite relaxing
image or memory, a time when you felt really good ...

By slowing your breathing down, relaxing and filling your
mind with pleasant images, you can be in control of tension
at all times and be generally more calm and tranquil and
much less easily upset ...

The suggestions I make later will be accepted by your
unconscious mind and you will make these things an
automatic part of your way of life ... whenever tense
situations occur you will react by relaxing, slowing down
your breathing and putting pleasant thoughts in your mind.

Let your body relax more and more fully into the kind of
comfort you really want and need. While you do that I am
going to keep on talking ... you may find that you are
aware of everything I say and remember it clearly, or you
may remember very little. Even if you do not listen
consciously, your unconscious mind will take careful note of
what I say ... whatever you do with your conscious
attention will be all right, just let me have your unconscious
attention.

You're relaxed now, and you'll become even more relaxed.

You are in a building several storeys high, a department
store, and between the different floors there are escalators. I
want you to go down two of these floors using the
escalators to do so. Now, step on the first step, take hold
of the black rubber railing and imagine that you feel yourself
going down, down, down, as I count from ten to zero
(counting slowly) ten ... nine ... eight ... moving down,
seven ... six ... five ... further down, four ... three ...
two ... deeper and deeper, one ... zero ... right down,
deeply, deeply relaxed ...

You are now on the floor below, now walk the short
distance around to the next escalator, step on the first step,
take hold of the black rubber railing, and go down, down,
down, as I count from ten to zero (slowly) ten ... nine ...
eight ... moving down, seven ... six ... five ... further
down, four ... three ... two ... deeper and deeper, one
... zero ... right down, deeply, deeply relaxed ...

You feel really good right at this moment ... in future

you will be able to recapture this feeling whenever you wish
... you can do this by saying the word "relax" to yourself
in your mind, and slowing down your breathing ...

You're so relaxed now that your mind has become
sensitive and receptive to whatever gets put into it ...
whatever is put into your mind will sink deeply into the
unconscious part of it and will cause a deep and lasting
impression.

Whatever gets put into your unconscious mind will
exercise more and more influence over the way you think,
and feel and behave ... you will become more calm and
composed, more placid and tranquil ... you will respond to
situations which used to make you tense by relaxing,
breathing deeply and thinking of pleasant memories ...

From this time forward you will feel more alert and
energetic ... you won't think nearly so much about yourself
and your difficulties ... you will become more and more
interested in whatever you're doing, in whatever is going on
around you ... you will be able to think more clearly,
concentrate better, give your undivided attention to
whatever you are doing ... you will work more effectively
and with more interest ...

You will be more and more confident, confidence will
grow daily ... you will be confident that you are able to do
what you want to do, what you have to do and what you
ought to be able to do ... you will be more and more
independent, more able to stick up for yourself and stand on
your own two feet ... you'll find you won't get nearly so
upset about things that used to upset you, things you have
no control over or anything that is not very important ...
you will feel calm, remote and detached, you just won't get
upset. Any time you have been miserable belongs already in
the past and does not trouble you any more; if you
remember it, it does not distress you ...

(At this point the specific script is inserted.)
Now it really doesn't matter what your conscious mind
does, because it is your unconscious mind that will find
new, safe possibilities for solving your problems, solutions
that your conscious mind is unaware of or may have
forgotten. Your unconscious mind knows a lot more about
you than you do — it has stored away many memories and
experiences and dreams and it will start to develop trains of
.thought, perhaps without your conscious mind becoming
aware of even the conclusions ... so you don't know
whether they will be communicated to your conscious mind

or whether this is even necessary . . . and you can benefit
from these trains of thought. Even if you aren't totally in
touch with these things you will be adequately in touch, and
your unconscious will continue thinking, reconstructing,
learning, rearranging . . . perhaps in pleasant dreams that
you may or may not remember and that are comforting and
satisfying . . . it will leave the unpleasantnesses and
unhappinesses of the past in the past, and you will look
forward to new happinesses, new experiences, good days
coming, and you will look back five years from now at the
happiness of these years . . .

(*Waking up:*)
Now, still relaxed, let your mind wander on to your
favourite relaxing scene for a while, a time when you felt
really good . . .

If you wish to continue sleeping then you will pay no
attention to the instructions I am about to give you to
awaken. You will continue to sleep a restful, deep,
replenishing sleep until you need to awaken; then you will
wake up bright and alert . . . but if you wish to wake up, or
need to wake up, then in a moment I will count from zero up
to ten . . . at seven your eyes will open, and at ten you will
arouse yourself . . . you will feel fine, free of tension, quite
relaxed, calm, contented, alert, wide awake and refreshed
. . . you'll find that next time you will be able to go into an
even deeper state of relaxation much more quickly. Zero . . .
one . . . two . . . three . . . four . . . five . . . six . . . seven
. . . eyes open . . . eight . . . nine . . . ten . . . wide awake.

POSSIBLE CHANGES TO THE BASIC SCRIPT

If you wish to shorten the basic script you could start your script
at the section beginning: "Concentrate now on your breathing . . ."

The eye-roll technique is not essential, although it starts the
process working by making you feel a little dizzy and light-
headed.

You could shorten the relaxation training instructions
similarly by using larger muscle groups than I have done, or
perhaps just by giving the instruction to relax the whole body.

Some people might respond to a more active induction, either
in imagination or in reality. If you play sports, and sporting
people are not regarded as being very amenable to the traditional
hypnotic induction methods, then perhaps you could imagine
yourself on a running machine or a stationary bicycle while
listening to the tape. Or you could imagine that you are running

or swimming long distances, as a replacement for the relaxation instructions.

It is probably a good idea to shorten or vary the script if you have been listening to the full version for some time. In fact, after a while you can make a new ending for your tape: "In future when I say the word Persephone (or Aristotle, or any word that doesn't come up in everyday conversation), you will immediately go into a deep trance."

After you have played this a few times you can then construct another tape beginning: "As you hear me say Persephone, Persephone, Persephone, you will go into a deep, deep trance ... ", and then go straight into ego-strengthening suggestions.

Other rapid inductions include:

• Breathing in rapidly fifteen or twenty times and at the same time concentrating on your hand rising from your knee.

• Holding a pen between your fingers — soon you will not be able to hold it, and as you let the pen drop you will go into a deep trance.

• Lying on the floor on a mat or long cushion, lifting your head from the floor, closing your eyes and very, very slowly lowering your head back to the floor — when your head touches the floor, your entire body will become limp and relaxed.

Where the script says, "Now let your mind take you to your favourite relaxing image or memory", I have not described a scene, because my scene may not be to everyone's taste. I like lying on the beach, or snow skiing, or having a massage, but other people's tastes run to, say, walking in forests or gardens, lying in haystacks on warm autumn afternoons, or taking a warm bath. The following is a beach scene I rather like, to give you some guidelines. You can write something similar for your favourite relaxing scene or memory, if you wish:

> You are walking along the beach at the beginning of a warm summer's day ... the sun is a golden yellow, not yet too hot ... the sky is brilliant blue, the sand pale gold in the sunlight ... you can feel the cool, firm sand beneath your feet, and taste and smell the salt in the air from the ocean spray ... if you lick your lips you really can taste it ...
>
> Listen to the sound of the waves breaking on the shore, the cries of the seagulls whirling about in the sky ...
>
> Now you come to a sandhill ... covered with a few small bushes, with tiny yellow flowers, and longish fine grass ... you sit down and look out to sea ... you feel perfectly tranquil and calm ... nothing can interfere with the secure, happy feeling. Everything is back in perspective as you gaze

> at the blue and silver of the sea ... a gentle breeze blows,
> then dies down, blows again, then dies down ... lulling you
> into stronger feelings of peace and security ... you close
> your eyes to the sun's warmth, dozing and daydreaming.

You may wish to alter the escalator image for deepening trance. If you don't fancy an escalator, perhaps a lift, perhaps walking down stairs into a garden (adding a description of the garden), or if downwards is not appealing, then try the backwards and forwards motion of a pendulum.

One of my favourites is a little white cloud, warm and comfortable and safe, suspended just above the ground ... rocking gently backwards and forwards in time to your breathing ... as you breathe in it draws you backwards and as you breathe out it glides you forward.

It is obvious that the ego-strengthening section has endless possibilities for addition or alteration. It is useless for a captain of industry to say he will "stick up for himself and stand on his own two feet". But he might add, in the interests of lengthening his life: "You will find it easier to make time for recreation and relaxing social gatherings, and not place too high a demand upon yourself in future."

The script about the unconscious mind I constructed from bits and pieces I read and films I saw of Milton Erickson. It is quite a powerful suggestion, so it is probably a good idea to leave it in. You could add to it though. For example, a slightly more elaborate dream suggestion can be slipped in, after "... perhaps in pleasant dreams that you may or may not remember and that are comforting and satisfying ... ", by adding, " ... these dreams will somehow deal with your problems and contribute in some way to resolving them ... they will be comforting dreams, and the good feelings attached to them will pervade your everyday life for several days, or even longer, after your dreams are over ... "

If you wish to continue sleeping, the last part of the script can be altered to the following:

> You will continue to sleep a restful, deep, replenishing sleep
> until you need to awaken; then you will wake up bright and
> alert ... you will feel fine, free of tension, quite relaxed,
> calm, contented, alert, wide awake and refreshed ... you'll
> find that next time you will be able to go into an even
> deeper state of relaxation much more quickly.

Another thing to consider is whether to construct the script in the first or second person; that is, whether to say "I" or "you".

Looking through the literature I have found that opinion is equally divided where people are talking about traditional self-hypnosis. But with my method I personally find it a little unnerving contemplating the prospect of a disembodied voice, albeit my own, saying "I" this and "I" that, so I always use "you". But the choice is yours.

ALTERNATIVE BASIC SCRIPTS

You may have wondered why I have no traditional suggestions in my script such as floating hands or unbendable arms. Well, I feel that they tend to be a distraction and a bit irritating. But if you like the idea then here is the more formal script I used for my smoking research, which includes some of these suggestions.

ALTERNATIVE INDUCTION I

Now lie down, and shut your eyes. Get comfortable, and listen to what I say. There is nothing very mysterious about hypnosis. We're in a different state from our usual one, but so are we when we're daydreaming, or strongly absorbed in anything.

It comes about as a result of narrowing and focusing attention, by using repetition and monotony. You won't do anything you would not normally find acceptable. The important thing is that by concentrating on things like breathing and relaxing and pleasant images you can move yourself into a state where you are more receptive to ideas and suggestions than usual.

I can assure you that you will be very relaxed during this session. Afterwards you'll feel fine, free of tension, calm, contented and refreshed. You will also learn how to get yourself into a state of mental tranquillity and physical relaxation, and the suggestions made while you are in this receptive state will take root in your mind and produce the changes you want.

You will find you will be able to change your position or do anything you consider necessary to make yourself comfortable.

Now, find a spot on the ceiling which makes you look up and back a little, placing some strain on your eyes. Look steadily at the spot, and listen to what I say. Look at the spot as steadily as you can; if your eyes happen to wander away from it, bring them back to it. After a while, you will find that the spot gets blurry, or perhaps moves about or changes colour. That is all right. Should you get sleepy, that will be fine, too. Whatever happens, let it happen and keep staring at the spot. There will come a time, however, when your eyes will be so tired, your lids will feel so heavy, that you'll find it difficult to keep them open any longer, and they will close, perhaps of their own accord.

When this happens, just let it take place . . .

Now, I want you to concentrate on relaxing. Breathe slowly and deeply, say ''Relax'' to yourself in your mind as you breathe out. Relaxing is simply letting go of tension, being prepared and willing to release your tension. Just letting all the tension flow out, drain out of your body. If there are any external noises around, let them flow over and away from you, and recede right into the distance . . .

Make your right fist into as tight a ball as possible, then relax it. This will show you the contrast between tense and relaxed muscles.

Take some time now to become aware of tense areas in your body, and either clench or stretch the muscles involved, then relax them. Relax the muscles in your feet, in your knees and your thighs. Feel the tension flow out, down through your legs, out through your feet and toes . . . tighten up your stomach muscles, tighten your abdomen, then relax.

Let tension drain away from chest and back muscles . . . let your forehead go smooth, jaws go slack . . . let the little muscles around your eyes loosen, eyelids heavy . . . let any tension go out of your scalp, loosen your scalp . . .

Clench the muscles in your neck, push your head forward on to your chest, then push it on to your back . . . feel the tension in the back of your neck . . . and then relax it . . . let all the tension flow out, out of your neck, down through your shoulders and arms, out through your hands and fingers . . . just let it all drain away. Concentrate on your breathing . . . slow down your breathing . . . right down . . . breathe in deeply and breathe out slowly . . . every so often take a deep breath down as far as you can, hold it for a while, and then slowly exhale . . .

Now . . . I want you to let your mind take you to your favourite relaxing scene or image or memory, a time when you felt really good . . .

Those three things . . . concentrating on relaxing, slowing down your breathing and filling up your mind with pleasant images are ways that you can deal with stress in a conscious way. You'll be in control of your tension at all times, and will be generally more calm and tranquil and much less easily upset.

The suggestions I make later will be accepted by your unconscious mind and you will make these things an automatic part of your way of life ... when tense situations occur you will react by relaxing, slowing down your breathing and putting pleasant thoughts in your mind.

Let your body relax more and more fully into the kind of comfort you really want and need. While you do that I am going to keep on talking. You may find that you are aware of everything I say and remember it clearly, or you may remember very little. Even if you do not listen consciously at all your unconscious mind will be taking careful note of what I say ... whatever you do with your conscious attention will be all right, just let me have your unconscious attention.

You're relaxed now, and you'll become even more relaxed ... as I count backwards from ten down to zero, imagine that you're going down an escalator ... you'll move slowly down and when I get to zero you will have arrived at the bottom ... each number will take you deeper and deeper down ...

Ten ... nine ... eight ... moving down ... seven ... six ... five ... further down ... four ... three ... two ... deeper and deeper ... one ... zero ... right down ... deeply, deeply relaxed ...

You feel really good right at this moment ... in future you will be able to recapture this feeling whenever you wish ... you can do this by saying the word "relax" to yourself in your mind, and slowing down your breathing ...

You're so relaxed now, that your mind has become sensitive and receptive to whatever is put into it ... whatever is put into your mind will sink deeply into the unconscious part of it and will cause a deep and lasting impression.

Whatever is put into your unconscious mind will exercise more and more influence over the way you think, and feel, and behave. You will become more calm and composed, more placid and tranquil ... you will respond to situations which used to make you tense by relaxing, breathing deeply and thinking of pleasant images ... from this time forward you will feel more alert and energetic.

You won't think nearly so much about yourself and your difficulties ... you will become more and more interested in

whatever you're doing, in whatever is going on around you
. . . you will be able to think more clearly, concentrate more
easily, give your undivided attention to whatever you are
doing . . . you will work and study more effectively and with
more interest . . . you will be more and more confident . . .
your confidence will grow daily . . . you will be confident
that you are able to do what you want to do, what you have
to do and what you ought to be able to do.

You will be more and more independent, more able to
stick up for yourself and stand on your own two feet . . .
you'll find you won't get nearly so upset about things which
used to upset you, things you have no control over or
anything that is not very important . . . you will feel calm,
remote and detached, you just won't get upset.

Any time you have been miserable belongs already in the
past and does not trouble you any more; if you remember it,
it does not distress you.

Concentrate on a feeling of heaviness coming over your
body . . . there is a feeling of heaviness coming over your
legs and your arms, your feet and your hands . . . your whole
body feels heavy and limp . . . legs, heavy and limp . . .
arms, heavy and limp . . . like lead . . . eyelids especially
heavy . . . heavy and tired . . . so heavy and tired that when
you try to move your left arm it will feel so heavy that you
just won't want to exert the effort, and will prefer for it to
remain just where it is. See how heavy your left arm is when
you try to lift it . . . that's all right . . . now stop trying to
lift it . . .

In the midst of all this heaviness, I want you to imagine
that your right arm is starting to get lighter . . .

As you concentrate on that feeling of lightness you will
become aware of a tingling sensation in your right arm . . .
you will find that your fingers begin to twitch and your right
hand and arm begin to float upwards . . .

Now your body is returning to normal, right back to
normal . . . not heavy any longer . . . your left hand and arm
returning completely to normal, no longer heavy . . . your
right hand and arm returning to normal, no longer light . . .
quite relaxed and normal . . .

Your unconscious mind is capable of redirecting the flow
of blood from one place to another . . . concentrate hard for
a while . . . you will find that you can direct a supply of
blood to your right hand . . .

As I continue to speak you will redirect sufficient blood to
your right hand to make it warmer and quite pink, and it

will stay that way until I ask you to wake up. Then, it will gradually return to normal . . . breathe slowly and deeply . . . warm and comfortable . . . listening to the things that I say . . . no cares, no worries now . . . everything seems remote . . .

Your level of hypnosis varies from time to time . . . sometimes you are in a lighter state, sometimes in a deeper state . . . your unconscious mind knows the deepest level you've reached so far . . .

Imagine a ruler standing on its end right in front of you, with the zero millimetres at the top and the 300 millimetres at the bottom . . .

Zero to 100 millimetres is a light state of hypnosis; 100 to 200 millimetres is medium and 200 to 300 millimetres is deep. Imagine an arrow as an indicator, pointing at the zero mark. Picture that arrow; now you can see it. In your mind move the arrow down the ruler until it stops at the greatest depth you've reached . . . watch closely now, the arrow slides down the ruler . . . sliding down . . . you can read the mark it stops at . . . it's clear and vivid now . . . that's fine . . . read it now . . . you will remember that number later . . . from now on you will go even deeper than that level . . .

At this point the specific script is introduced, followed by the concluding waking (or continuing to sleep) instructions.

ALTERNATIVE INDUCTION II

I am going to count from twenty down to zero, and as I do you will allow yourself to enter a deep trance . . .

Twenty . . . nineteen . . . eighteen . . . relaxing completely, your legs, arms, body, your mind, your internal organs . . . put pleasant images into your mind . . . relaxing completely, feeling warm and heavy and comfortable . . . letting all tension flow out, drain out of your body . . . let any noises around you flow over and away from you, and recede into the distance . . . pay no attention to them . . . relaxed, and serene, and calm and content . . .

Seventeen . . . sixteen . . . fifteen . . . breathing slowly and deeply . . . take a deep breath, through your nose if you can, and breathe out very, very slowly, still through your nose . . . now, do it again, a few more times . . . a big deep breath through your nose, breathing out very, very slowly through your nose . . .

Fourteen . . . thirteen . . . twelve . . . (insert the beach image here)

Eleven ... ten ... nine ... *(the escalator script, counting down)*

Eight ... seven ... six ... sleepier and sleepier, drowsier and drowsier ... warm and comfortable ... no worries now ... after you are fast asleep you will have pleasant dreams ... in these dreams you will deal with problems so that they become far less trouble ... these dreams will take you back to times when you have felt good, when you have done something you were pleased with, when you felt confident and sure of yourself ... they will be comforting dreams, and the good feelings attached to them will stay with you for several days or even longer, long after your dreams are over and you have woken up ... you will find that these good feelings will make it much easier to cope with problems that arise, both big and small problems ... you'll feel so confident that you'll find constructive ways to deal with things which used to upset you ... anything which used to make you feel hurt will have very little power to hurt you any more ...

Five ... four ... three ... *(insert specific script here)*

Two ... one ... zero ... sleepier and sleepier, soon your pleasant dreams will start and you'll have a deep relaxing sleep, and wake up feeling really good, full of energy and wide awake at the time that you want to wake up ... fast asleep ...

ALTERNATIVE TRANCE-DEEPENING IMAGES

The escalator image can be replaced by the following, if you wish:

Imagine you are floating on a little white cloud, warm and comfortable and safe, suspended just above the ground ... rocking gently backwards and forwards in time to your breathing ... backwards and forwards ... as you breathe in it draws you backwards and as you breathe out it glides you forward ... each time it goes backwards and forwards you will become more and more relaxed, you will go into a deeper and deeper state of relaxation, you will become more sensitive and receptive to ideas and suggestions ... backwards and forwards, deeper and deeper, further and further, more and more relaxed ...

There is no particular reason why escalators or lifts or steps have to be used as images. Perhaps you would prefer to walk into an imaginary garden, describing the sights and smells and feelings.

Associate Professor Wendy-Louise Walker, from the Department of Behavioural Sciences in Medicine at the University of

Sydney, suggests an image of being in the bush, sitting by a small stream. She describes the scenery, then goes on to say:

> Now imagine that you pick up a leaf lying on the grass beside you and lazily drop it into the water. You watch it float downstream, bobbing in the current like a little boat. Let the leaf take your mind further into hypnosis as it floats downstream. Watch it float along until it disappears from view ... Then imagine that you pick up another leaf, drop it into the clear water and watch it float with the current, taking you further into hypnosis as it floats lightly downstream ... And when it disappears, you will pick up yet another leaf, drop it into the clear, running water of the little stream and let it take you further into hypnosis as it floats downstream.[1]

Walker also recommends using music as a deepening technique, particularly the flute music of Bach and Vivaldi. She avoids music to which hypnotised subjects respond with feelings of sadness.[2]

A SHORTENED VERSION OF THE BASIC SCRIPT

One tends to get tired of the same old script heard over and over again, so here is a shortened version of the basic script:

> Lie down, close your eyes and make sure you are quite comfortable. I am going to get you into a state where you are more receptive than usual to ideas and suggestions ...
>
> Concentrate on your breathing ... slow down your breathing ... right down ... breathe in deeply through your nose, and breathe out slowly, very slowly, through your nose ...
>
> Now, concentrate on relaxing ... breathe slowly and deeply, saying the word "relax" to yourself in your mind as you breathe out ... letting all tension flow out, drain out of your body ... if there are any external noises around, let them flow over and away from you and recede right into the distance ... pay no attention to them ...
>
> Make your right fist into as tight a ball as possible, then relax it ... this will show the contrast between tense and relaxed muscles ... take some time now to become aware of tense areas in your body, and either stretch or clench the muscles involved, and then relax them ... by slowing down

your breathing and relaxing, you can be in control of tension
at all times and be generally more calm and tranquil and
much less easily upset . . .

The suggestions I make later will be accepted by your
unconscious mind and you will make these things an
automatic part of your way of life . . . whenever tense
situations occur you will react by relaxing, slowing down
your breathing . . .

Let your body relax more and more fully into the kind of
comfort you really want and need . . . while you do that I
am going to keep on talking . . . you may find that you are
aware of everything I say and remember it clearly, or you
may remember very little. Even if you do not listen
consciously your unconscious mind will be taking careful
note of what I say . . . whatever you do with your conscious
attention will be all right, just let me have your unconscious
attention . . .

You're relaxed now, and you'll become even more relaxed
. . . (continue with the escalator image)

A BASIC SCRIPT FOR CHILDREN

This would be suitable for children aged about ten, who may have
problems at school, lack of confidence or bed-wetting problems.

By the time I count from twenty down to zero you will be
fast asleep, deeply asleep . . .

Twenty . . . nineteen . . . eighteen . . . when I get to zero
you will be asleep, in a deep comfortable sleep, having
pleasant dreams . . .

Seventeen . . . sixteen . . . fifteen . . . start now by taking
a deep breath through your nose, and breathing out very,
very slowly, still through your nose . . . now do it again, a
few more times . . . a deep, deep breath through your nose,
breathing out very, very slowly through your nose . . .

Fourteen . . . thirteen . . . twelve . . . (insert the beach
image here)

Eleven . . . ten . . . nine . . . you are getting sleepier and
sleepier, drowsier and drowsier . . . warm and comfortable
. . . no worries now . . . after you are fast asleep you will
have pleasant dreams . . . in these dreams you will deal with
problems so that they become far less trouble . . . these
dreams will take you back to times when you have felt good,

when you have done something you were pleased with,
when you felt confident and sure of yourself . . . they will be
comforting dreams, and the good feelings attached to them
will stay with you for several days or even longer, long after
your dreams are over and you have woken up . . . and you
will find that these good feelings will make it much easier to
deal with problems in everyday life, big problems and little
problems . . . you feel so good and confident that you'll find
ways to deal with things which used to upset you . . .
anything which used to hurt you will have very little power
to hurt you any more . . . you'll be much stronger and more
confident, things that used to upset you will just not hurt
you any more, or hardly at all, they'll just be like the water
draining off your body onto a towel after a swim . . .

Eight . . . seven . . . six . . . you'll find when you talk in
front of the class, or do tests, your mind will be clear, you
will be confident and relaxed . . . when you do tests you'll
do as well as you possibly can, you'll think quickly, you'll
be far less worried, far less tense about your exams . . . in
lessons you'll pay closer attention to what is happening,
time will pass more and more quickly and enjoyably . . .
you'll concentrate more while you are listening in class or
while you are studying at home . . . and when you talk in
front of the class you will be at ease and natural . . . you
will look at the faces in front of you and be relaxed and calm
. . . day by day your confidence will grow, steadily, your
mind will be clear, you'll be able to speak up and express
your opinions and respond to comments and questions
easily . . .

Five . . . four . . . three . . . from now on you'll be more and
more confident . . . far less easily hurt . . . if anyone makes
fun of you, it simply won't bother you at all, it just won't
hurt you . . . you'll find clever and polite ways of dealing
with people who used to upset you . . . you'll be able to
make friends easily, get on well with others . . . you'll be
more and more strong and confident, more and more each
day . . .

Two . . . one . . . zero . . . sleepier and sleepier, fast
asleep, soon you will dream your pleasant dreams . . . you'll
have a lovely deep sleep, and you'll wake up feeling really
good, full of energy and wide awake at the time you want to
wake up . . . fast asleep.

Part Three

SPECIFIC SCRIPTS

14

APPETITIVE DISORDERS

It does seem that the appetitive disorders — smoking, drinking, drug-taking and eating — are the most difficult problems to deal with. Many clinicians refuse to see people with these problems, on the grounds that they are wasting their time.

However, as we shall see, hypnosis has produced some good results in the treatment of such disorders.

SMOKING

An overview of the research literature on smoking carried out in 1980 shows that success rates of abstinence for a six-month period range between four per cent and eighty-eight per cent following treatment procedures using hypnosis.[1]

The eighty-eight per cent success rate was obtained by Milton Kline in 1970, with sixty patients taking part in an extended group hypnotherapy programme lasting for twelve hours, from ten am until ten pm in the one day. Apart from discussing their feelings of deprivation, the group went through a kind of systematic desensitisation procedure, with techniques designed to intensify deprivation and conjure up all the satisfying things about smoking, followed immediately by relaxation procedures.[2]

Another high level of success was obtained in 1968, when sixty-four per cent of a group of patients gave up smoking, but they were people hospitalised for serious lung complaints, and therefore more highly motivated than usual.[3]

A group from Montreal in Canada, including expatriate Australian Campbell Perry, found that the only factor related to successful therapeutic outcome was motivation — hypnotic susceptibility had nothing to do with it.[4]

Attempts have been made to stop people smoking by using aversive techniques and other behaviour modification methods, but these have not been found to be as useful as hypnosis.

Anyway, the problem is not quite so much that of giving up smoking as of taking it up again. Most people take it up again one to three months after they receive treatment. Research carried out in 1974 surveyed eighty-nine treatment studies and reported that only twenty-five per cent of those treated were long-term abstainers.[5]

My own smoking research is coming along nicely. There is still a lot of analysing to be done, and I will have to put some more people through the programme, so I have to be fairly cautious about reporting my findings.

My research was intended to see whether certain types of people responded better to self-hypnosis or hetero-hypnosis. I had predicted that people who were amenable to control from external sources would respond better to hetero-hypnosis and that people who preferred to be in control themselves would respond better to self-hypnosis. In fact, of the fifty-nine people who have completed the programme, *both* groups responded better to self-hypnosis.

The poorest results, in terms of giving up smoking completely or in terms of percentage drop in cigarette consumption, were obtained from those who *believed* they were controlled by outside forces (chance or powerful others) but *preferred* to be in control themselves and who underwent hetero-hypnosis. The best results by far were obtained from those who believed they had control over their lives and destinies and liked it that way and who hypnotised themselves. But I was very surprised to find that people who believed they were controlled by external forces and were quite amenable to that, still responded much better to self-hypnosis than to hetero-hypnosis!

Another surprising result was that a large number of smokers using self-hypnosis dropped consumption from between sixty and eighty cigarettes a day down to between five and eight per day (which is statistically regarded as non-smoking), and remained quite happy with the situation over a six-month period, in the sense that they did not feel the need for more cigarettes, although they sometimes expressed regret that they could not cut out smoking altogether.

Most people pointed out that undergoing the programme did not take away the desire to smoke altogether, it just made it easier to control. One of the first people to take part in my programme was at that time the medical reporter for the *Sydney Morning Herald*. He was extremely pleased with the ease with which he had given up. He had been only slightly tempted on a few occasions and found he could swiftly combat these urges.

Those taking part in the programme invariably reported feeling more relaxed and calm. Comments from those who have given up range from "surprised" and "pleased" to "thrilled" and "ecstatic"; "that feeling of well-being can always be felt whenever I play the tape"; "still want one every now and then, and then I play the tape". Some gave up quickly and some towards the end of the programme.

Even those who have continued to smoke have had positive things to say:

I may still smoke — less than half of what I did — but I'm delighted I don't smoke at work any more and don't even miss it. I feel I can control my cigarettes, which was my aim to start with: for me to be master and not the smokes. Sometimes I smoke at a dinner party or when I am out, but then I can stop next day and not miss it. Now I listen to the tape for a course in relaxation I'm doing — biofeedback — but my smoking tape is the best relaxation I've heard.

Another person commented:

I have edited the tape and condensed it to the salient points I feel are contributing to motivation and relaxation. There are some days I do not smoke at all, but somehow I still maintain the habit. The possible reason for this is an extremely traumatic work period and the uncertain future, as my employers are experiencing crises due to the economic climate and are into a severe retrenchment programme. However, I recognise the "danger times" and, hopefully, after my work situation is resolved one way or another, I can decrease my intake in these critical periods. All in all, I am extremely happy with the results achieved, and even if I cannot completely lose the habit, if I maintain the average I burn up at present I will be more than $600 per year better off, and that is no small achievement.

I must confess that although I gave up smoking after listening to my self-made tape, I did take it up again twice. Once was four years later, when my father was rushed to hospital with a stroke, and I unhesitatingly turned into a service station on the way to hospital, bought a packet and smoked the lot. A couple of months later, when things had settled down, I played my tape again. This time it took a few repetitions before it worked, which made me anxious that it had somehow ceased to be effective. After a while, however, I lost the desire for a cigarette, with no craving at all, could not even tolerate the smell of other people's cigarettes and again turned into a smug, intolerant non-smoker.

Two years later a problem in my personal life coincided with a spate of broken-hearted students (problems often come in mini-epidemics). It became more and more difficult to deal with my students under the circumstances, and one night I told the crying student opposite me to hold on for a second, dashed out of the office to the bar, bought a packet of cigarettes and two gins and tonic, and returned. We proceeded to demolish them and they cheered us both up, but I was again a smoker (it need only take one). Again, when things had returned to normal, my tapes, along with a bad cold, did the trick.

SMOKING SCRIPT

You will find from now on that you will be more and more strongly aware of the reasons for giving up smoking . . . more and more conscious of the threat to your health, of the increased chance of dying an ugly, painful death from heart disease or cancer . . : of fighting for each breath with bronchitis or emphysema . . . or causing severe damage to the arteries and veins in your limbs . . . you might comfort yourself that those things are a long way off, and that's true, it takes time . . . but you will find you are now more and more aware of interference to the way you would like to be . . . the gradual lowering of fitness that smoking brings about, the shortness of breath when you try to walk, or play sport, or climb stairs . . . the raw throat you get from time to time . . . the bad taste in your mouth . . . the loss of sense of taste and smell.

You will dwell on the cost of smoking per month, per year, and think how you could spend the extra money you would save . . . you will be more and more aware that smoking is becoming less acceptable to others, that it is regarded as anti-social . . . that smoking is dangerous to those around you and you are forcing them to become passive smokers against their will.

You say that smoking relaxes you, but you know deep down that it doesn't do so at all . . . it really makes you more tense.

You will find, if you do continue to smoke, you'll be so disgusted and disappointed with yourself that the cigarettes will taste foul, like dead ashes lying overnight in an ashtray . . . you'll be overwhelmed by unpleasant feelings, you will feel sick and queasy, as if you want to throw up but can't . . . you really want to vomit, but can't . . . the room will spin . . . you'll have a vile metallic taste in your mouth, you will break out in a sweat.

As the unpleasant, dangerous aspects of smoking take over in your mind, you will find you do not want to pick up the cigarette in the first place, or you will put it back without lighting it . . . at the very thought of smoking you will have a mental picture of a lighted cigarette with a big red stroke through it, telling you that cigarettes are strictly forbidden.

We know that a rise in tension level signals the urge to smoke ... from now on you will cut that urge off before it starts by relaxing and slowing down your breathing ... as you keep doing this the urge to smoke will disappear.

As well as all this, your unconscious mind knows all your reasons for giving up smoking ... it will find a safe way to get rid of your smoking habit ... soon you will find that you just can't bring yourself to smoke ... you will have no desire at all to smoke, your craving will have disappeared ... smoking will be repugnant to you, and quite remote from your needs ... more and more remote from your needs.

From that time on you will not smoke, you will not even be aware of the smell of others' cigarettes, smoking will rarely, if ever, enter your consciousness ... from that time on you will suffer no withdrawal effects, the unpleasant effects that usually accompany stopping smoking will be kept to an absolute minimum.

As your mastery over the habit increases you will become more and more proud of your self-control and willpower ... you will be healthier, your lungs will feel clearer, you will have far more energy, you will feel good about yourself and the world, you will enjoy life far more ... you will be more calm and relaxed ... there will simply be no need to smoke.

You will find that even though food will taste better and better you will make every effort not to gain weight ... you will have less and less desire for high-calorie, rich, unhealthy foods and more and more interest in low-calorie, healthy food ... you will find, to your pleasure, that while you enjoy food much more you will be able to maintain your desired weight while protecting your body against the poison of further smoking ... as you cease to smoke and continue to concentrate more on enjoying low-calorie, healthy foods, you will feel stronger and stronger, healthier and healthier ... your resistance to illness and disease will increase steadily, day by day.

Make whatever changes to this script you think are necessary. You may find the following story of some use. One of my subjects found hetero-hypnosis to be ineffective, and analysed the possible reasons. She concluded that most of the script, as well as the fact that it was administered by another person, made her feel rebellious and antagonistic. Her subsequent alteration, as follows, and her self-administration, produced better results:

You will find from now on that you will be more and more
strongly aware of the reasons for giving up smoking . . . you
will become more and more aware of the interference
smoking has on the way you would like to be, you will
resent the effect it has almost certainly had on your singing
voice . . . you will dwell on the possibility that you may be
able to sing almost as well as you did before if you cease to
smoke . . . you are aware that there are far more effective
means of controlling catarrh . . . you will look forward to
getting rid of the bad taste you have had in your mouth from
time to time . . . you know that none of the reasons you had
for smoking are now valid . . . that an apple is now cheaper
than a cigarette . . . you are aware that smoking is becoming
less acceptable to others, that it is regarded as anti-social . . .
and that it has an adverse effect on many people.

You say that smoking relaxes you, but in fact it does not
do so at all . . . it really makes you more tense.

As the unpleasant, dangerous aspects of smoking take over
in your mind, you will find you do not want to pick up the
cigarette in the first place, or you will put it back without
lighting it.

We know that a rise in tension level signals the urge to
smoke . . . from now on you will cut that urge off before it
starts by relaxing and slowing down your breathing . . . as
you keep doing this the urge to smoke will disappear.

This subject found the rest of the script acceptable and added it to
her individual script. She found that the first part of my original
script was irrelevant to her particular reasons for taking up
smoking in the first place: she was very poor when she was
young, and often smoked instead of eating, as it was then a lot
cheaper than most food. Also, somewhat irrationally, she had
taken it up to get rid of her catarrh. She had also found the
aversive suggestions quite objectionable, so she omitted these.

OVEREATING

By convention, obesity is said to be present when the body weight
exceeds by twenty per cent the standard weight listed in the usual
height–weight tables. Obesity can result from an increase in
the number of fat cells (hyperplastic obesity) or an increase in fat-
cell size (hypertrophic obesity).

People whose obesity began in adult life generally suffer from
the latter. People whose obesity began in childhood generally

suffer from hyperplastic obesity or combination hyperplastic-hypertrophic obesity, and may have up to five times as many fat cells as either persons of normal weight or those suffering from pure hypertrophic obesity. The prognosis for weight reduction is generally poor, particularly for those who became obese during childhood.

My own experience of treating overeaters has not been very gratifying. I have conducted several group sessions, together with the Institute's doctor, and found generally that people would lose weight while the sessions continued and put the weight back on when they stopped. Hypnosis was not involved in the group sessions, and I have only seen about half-a-dozen people for individual hypnosis sessions dealing with overeating. Of those who have lost a significant amount of weight, some attributed this to hypnosis, others to willpower. Those who have not lost any weight are not very impressed with my procedure at all.

Overeating is one of the more difficult problems to tackle. There are complex factors causing overeating, both conscious and unconscious. I have read that the urge to overeat probably goes back to prehistoric times. When some catastrophe was about to occur, even if it was only that winter was approaching, prehistoric people would eat to capacity to better withstand the approaching trauma. So eating in response to stress or emotional upheavals probably has an instinctive basis, not just a psychological cause.

Be that as it may, there are both simple and complex reasons for overeating: as an emotional comforter; as a way of warding off sexual attention; to punish parents for real or imagined wrongs; as a celebration when something good happens; because things have gone wrong; because of sensory stimulation, like sights and smells, which cause you to eat when you are not even hungry; because you are fearful, frustrated or in conflict; because you are bored, anxious or depressed; for social reasons, for enjoyment; out of habit; as an attention-getting device — for so many reasons other than simply as a response to hunger.

Research carried out in 1976 listed some unusual ways in which obese people behave differently from normal people. Normal people eat more when they are calm than when they are frightened, and when they are deprived rather than well fed. Fear and satiety have no effect on the amount of food eaten by overweight people. Also, normal people who are deprived buy more food in a supermarket than they would buy if they had just eaten. Overweight people actually buy more food if they have recently eaten.[6]

A team at Macquarie University has been carrying out a large-scale weight-control programme that they intend to run over a period of three years. There are group or individual sessions with counselling that aims to change the bad habits associated with obesity, and there are hypnotic sessions. The hypnotic sessions involve ego-building suggestions as well as suggestions of ''dissatisfaction with one's present physical disposition, wanting to become slender, being satisfied with a small quantity of food, enjoyment in eating foods which give strength and a proper balance of minerals and vitamins, a temporary dislike of fats, sweets and starches, a new pleasure in eating foods the body needs, using up fat deposits and exercising each day (walking at least two kilometres)''.[7] Also built into the script are behaviour-modification suggestions such as eating only at one place in a particular room, serving food on smaller plates, eating slowly, thoroughly chewing food, and so on.

The unique aspect of this treatment is that photographs of the patients are taken with a special camera, showing how they would look if they were the weight they would like to be. Suggestions are made that patients will keep this picture in mind, especially if they are in danger of breaking their diet.

The programme is still underway so results are not yet available.

My personal experience was that after I gave up smoking I put on six kilograms in weight, so I made myself an overeating tape from the script quoted in this section.

The first thing that happened was that I developed a harmless type of diarrhoea, which began after I had eaten too much at one sitting. I say ''harmless'' because there was no accompanying nausea or discomfort, just a sudden attack of diarrhoea, that came on very quickly after the overeating, without any recurrence. As I lost weight quite swiftly, I didn't feel inclined to seek medical attention — I was quite happy with my diarrhoea. During that time I also lost my taste for sweet things almost completely. I gained weight later because although I no longer cared for cakes, chocolates or sweets, I still had a vital interest in hamburgers, chips, pies, and so on.

After I played my tape again a few times I lost interest in all fattening foods and became obsessed by thoughts of lettuce, cucumber, celery and tomato — in winter, too! I ate enormous amounts of these and again my weight settled down.

The following winter I put on a fair amount of weight again. When I listened to my tapes I think my unconscious played a dirty trick on me. The first time I became aware of it I had just cooked roast lamb with sweet potatoes, pumpkin, potatoes, peas and mint sauce — one of my favourite meals. I was surprised at

how tasteless and uninteresting dinner was and blamed a watery
mint sauce or perhaps a flavourless gravy for ruining the meal,
until everyone complimented me on how tasty it was. They
assured me that I was imagining the lack of taste in the gravy and
sauce, as they were delicious and the sauce was very strong. I
realised that my unconscious had come up with a new system
that affected my taste buds at a most inconvenient time. I again
lost weight.

It is now a year later and I am gaining weight again. I have
played my tape twice in the last two days. I wonder what will
happen this time!

Bandler and Grinder, writing in *Frogs Into Princes* (p. 48), have
the following to say:

> *A long time ago we had been trying to find expedient ways of
> helping people to lose weight. Most of the vehicles that were
> available at that time didn't seem to work, and we discovered
> that there were some real differences between the way people
> have weight problems. One of the major things we discovered
> is there were a lot of people who had* always *been fat . . . When
> they got skinny, they freaked out because they didn't know
> how to interact with the world as a skinny person. If you've
> always been fat, you were never chosen first to be on a sports
> team. You were never asked to dance in high school. You never
> ran fast. You have no experience of certain kinds of athletic
> and physical movements.*
>
> *So instead of trying to get people to adjust, we would simply
> go back and create a whole new childhood and have them grow
> up being a skinny person . . .*

In general, the research suggests that hypnosis is the most
successful treatment for overeating. William Kroger, who has
utilised hypnosis research in teaching, writing and clinical
practice for over forty years, both in his psychiatric practice in
Beverley Hills, California, and in his work as Clinical Professor
in the Department of Anaesthesiology, at the University of
California, Los Angeles, researched the various treatments and
concluded: "The selective utilization of hypnotherapy as an
integral part of psychotherapy has probably produced better
results in the treatment of obesity than any other therapeutic
approach up to the present time."[8]

OVEREATING SCRIPT

And now I want you to have a clear image, in your mind, of
yourself standing on the scales and the scales registering the

weight you wish to be. See this very clearly, for this is the weight you will be. See yourself looking the way you would like to look with the weight off those parts of the body you want the weight to be off, as if you are looking at yourself in a mirror the way you wish to be. See this very, very vividly, and summon this image into your mind many times during the day, particularly just after waking in the morning and before going to sleep at night. Also, have it vividly in your mind before eating meals. And this is the way you will look, and this is the weight you will be. As you believe this, so it will happen.

When you have attained this weight, you will be able to maintain it, you will find yourself eating just enough to maintain your weight at the weight you would like to be.

Until you *do* attain this weight you will find you have less and less desire to eat between meals. You simply will not want to. Also, you will find you will be content with smaller meals. There will be no sense of unhappiness or dissatisfaction; smaller meals will be quite satisfactory to you, and you will have no desire to eat large meals.

Also, you will have less and less desire for high-calorie, rich, unhealthy foods. Day by day your desire for such foods will become less and less, until very soon you will have no desire at all for rich, high-calorie foods. Instead, day by day you will desire low-calorie, healthy foods and these will replace the high-calorie foods, the rich foods, you have eaten in the past.

As you lose weight and approach, closer and closer, the weight you wish to be, you will find yourself growing stronger and stronger, healthier and healthier. Your resistance to illness and disease will increase day by day. With less weight you will feel better and better, and your health will become better and better.

From now on, as you lose weight and your health continues to improve, you will be more motivated to do some regular daily exercise. This too will make you feel better and better. Every so often you will replace eating a meal with some type of exercise.

You have set a goal for the weight you wish to become. You will find that you are able to regulate and monitor your food and drink intake so that you achieve and maintain your goal. You will be more and more aware of the undesirable effects of being overweight : . . you don't feel comfortable, your appearance suffers and your health is threatened. To your surprise and pleasure, achieving and maintaining your weight goal will require very little effort; it will be quite easy.

When you have reached your desired daily calorie intake, any extra food you eat will be tasteless and uninteresting, it may even taste quite unpleasant ... and your stomach will feel uncomfortably distended, full and distended.

Your unconscious mind will in some safe way change your body processes to make your weight loss easier ... it will help you become a less efficient user of food; much more of the unhealthy food you eat will be eliminated as waste and more of the valuable food will be assimilated into your body.

Remember, you will be able to achieve and maintain your desired weight surprisingly easily, almost effortlessly ... your increasing calmness and confidence also will make the need for too much food quite remote ... soon you will find that you just won't eat too much, you just won't bother.

POSSIBLE CHANGES TO OVEREATING SCRIPT

If you have problems imagining yourself on the scales, picture yourself fitting into the size of clothing you wish to fit into. Behaviour modification suggestions can be incorporated into the script if you wish, for example:

In future you will take smaller mouthfuls of food each time, and you will chew each mouthful slowly and thoroughly ... you will slow down your eating considerably and in order to get the most satisfaction from each mouthful you will roll the food from the front of the tongue to the back of the tongue and from side to side ... in this way you will more readily satisfy the thousands of taste cells that are located all over your tongue ... less food will be required and your calorie intake will be lessened ... You will use smaller plates and knives and forks ... you will replace utensils after each mouthful and pick them up only after each mouthful has been finished.

Every time the thought of food arises at an inappropriate time you will find pleasant ways of distracting yourself till the thought of food fades ... You may do some exercise, or read a favourite book, watch television, go for a walk.

Try drinking a cup of hot water with a beef stock cube twenty minutes before your meal. Every time you eat a meal leave one mouthful behind on the plate. At the end of six months or a year you will have left many calories uneaten.

You can also use one of the painkilling techniques, perhaps a glove anaesthesia script:

> Your unconscious mind may decide to pull an imaginary
> anaesthetic glove on to your right hand ... it may choose a
> gardening glove or a leather glove for driving a car, or a long
> evening glove ... as the glove works on to your hand the
> areas it covers become numb and insensitive, first the
> fingers, then the hand ... wherever you place this numb
> hand, that part of you will also become numb and
> insensitive.

After rubbing your stomach with your anaesthetised hand the
hunger pangs will disappear.

If you have a picture of yourself when you were slimmer, keep
it with you and look at it regularly. Eat your meals at one place
especially set aside for the purpose, not when watching TV or
reading. Make a special ritual of your meal, concentrating on it
completely. Fill your stomach with low-calorie foods like lettuce,
cucumber, carrot, tomato, pineapple, asparagus, celery, etc.

ANOREXIA NERVOSA

I have not had any students with anorexia come to see me.
Typically people with anorexia do not believe they have a
problem at all, except to feel that they urgently need to lose
weight, even when they are at death's door.

Anorexia is one of the few psychological disorders that can lead
directly to death. It affects at least one per cent of the population
of girls aged between fifteen and twenty-three years, although it
can occur at any age between twelve and thirty.

Dr Stephen Touyz, who is a consultant at an anorexia clinic at
Royal Prince Alfred Hospital, Sydney, told me that research
carried out in England found that while one in 100 of girls aged
between sixteen and eighteen attending private schools in
London suffered from anorexia, only one in 200 of this same age
group in public schools was affected. He also cited a study carried
out in 1984 by Willi and Grossman in Zurich, which compared
the hospital registers of people being treated for anorexia from
1956 to 1958 with the period from 1973 to 1975. They found an
increase from 0.38 to 1.12 per 100,000 people. So anorexia has
steadily increased in incidence, and is presumably still doing so.

In the late seventies the mortality rate was ten to fifteen per
cent, but since then it has dropped to five per cent, probably due
to improvements in treatment techniques. However, Dr Touyz
described the work of a psychiatrist in Sweden who followed up a
group of anorexics he had dealt with in 1958 over a period of

twenty-five years, and found that in that time seventeen to eighteen per cent had died from a variety of causes. This is a much higher mortality rate than in a normal population.

Because anorexics seek help very rarely (they have a strange euphoria about their condition) often they go unaided until they collapse and have to be hospitalised. When this happens they are violently resentful of treatment and will get up to all sorts of tricks to prevent food being ingested. Fifteen per cent of those treated in hospital later have a relapse.

The onset is gradual, marked by loss of interest in food, constipation, a slowing pulse, swelling of the ankles, pains in the stomach, followed by loss of weight to the point of emaciation, vomiting (sometimes blood), cessation of menstruation and shrinking breasts. The anorexics' perceptions of themselves are in some way altered, they see themselves as much fatter than they really are.

The cause of anorexia in a particular person is not always clear. Research at the University of New South Wales has shown that the biggest difference between anorexics and normal people is in self-image. Anorexics have a very poor self concept, and they are generally very shy, reserved and withdrawn. When you consider the effect of anorexia, that is, a loss of sexual functioning and sexual attractiveness, it is tempting to agree with those who see it as a problem relating to the maturing process and sexual situations, that anorexics have a fear of growing up and becoming adults. Some feel it may be hormonal and others that it is mainly the outcome of the increasing trend towards thinness (a recent study in *Playboy Magazine* showed a substantial average decrease in the vital statistics of females over the last ten years).

At the Royal Prince Alfred Hospital and the Northside Clinic in Sydney, a team, comprising a consultant psychiatrist, clinical psychologist, marital and family therapist, social worker, dietitian, occupational therapist and a variety of nursing staff, uses a number of approaches in its treatment of anorexics.

They have family, group and individual therapy, counselling aimed at dealing with the patient's fears and depression, art therapy, and lenient and flexible behaviour modification techniques with rewards for weight gains. Patients are put to bed; only if they gain 1.5 kilos or more in a week are they allowed up. Most of their time is spent on outings, group meetings or sitting in the sun and reading.

ANOREXIA NERVOSA SCRIPT

From this time forward you will have an increasing desire to return to a weight that is regarded as normal by other people

and standard by weight tables . . . you will be amazed and
disturbed that you have let yourself sink to a weight level
that is dangerous, a level at which many people have died or
caused themselves permanent physical damage . . . you will
be puzzled at how you could have risked death for the goal
you hoped to achieve, and you will from now on have
extreme doubts about the value of this goal . . . you will be
appalled at the danger you have risked.

More and more, from now on, you will be attracted, even
obsessed, by the idea of returning to a weight others consider
reasonable for you . . . you will find healthy, nourishing,
wholesome food irresistible until you do attain this weight
. . . you will find all kinds of food delicious and will crave
them, you won't be able to resist them until you return to
the weight you should be . . . no longer will these foods be
forbidden to you, instead you will feel they are essential,
they are going to save your life and return you to full health
. . . you will eat these foods in a way that will be quite safe,
with a type and level of intake that your body can absorb
and process perfectly safely . . . your stomach will feel
comfortable with these foods, it will stretch to accommodate
them, you will not feel full or uncomfortable or distended,
you will feel quite content and comfortable with the extra
food intake.

Your perception of yourself will change — until you reach
a weight that other people feel is suitable for you . . . you
will always see yourself as thinner than you really are . . .
until that time, when you look in a mirror you will appear
painfully thin, so thin you will be worried about how you
appear . . . you will immediately take steps to improve your
condition.

See yourself, picture yourself in your mind, back at the
weight you should be, picture yourself fitting like a glove
into a size 10, 12 or 14 dress . . . standing on the scales with
the scales registering the weight you should be . . . enjoying
life, feeling healthy and contented, pleased at yourself for
returning to normality.

When you do attain the weight you should be, the weight
other people and the standard tables say you should be, you
will maintain this weight . . . you will eat just the right
amount of good, healthy, nutritious foods, to maintain your
weight at the level it should be . . . you will do a normal
amount of exercise and eat properly to maintain your weight
at the weight it should be.

From now on you will become more and more assertive,

more able to stand up for yourself without anxiety, able to express your feelings comfortably and obtain your rights without interfering with the rights of others ... if you are asked a favour or request you do not wish to grant you will simply say, "I'm sorry, but no."

In interpersonal situations, especially, you will feel free to do what *you* want to do, not what others want you to do ... you have a perfect right to refuse unwelcome advances politely but firmly ... you will be more outgoing and friendly with people, you will be able to talk confidently at parties, accept compliments gracefully and pay other people compliments ... you will look directly at the other person when you are speaking, directly into their eyes as much as seems appropriate ... you will stand and walk and sit confidently and straight, and smile frequently.

BULIMIA

Bulimia is a cycle of binge eating and then purging. People with this disorder eat overwhelming amounts and then induce vomiting. Whereas anorexics often shorten their lives because of tissue damage, bulimics are rather more prone than average to commit suicide.

I have seen students with bulimia. One of them came into my office, slumped into a chair and announced that she had a $40-a-day habit. It was her custom to order three meals at once, eat them and then bring them up. Then she would order three more, and so on.

Somewhere between one and four per cent of young females have this problem. Mostly they are attractive, and in their teens or early twenties. About five per cent of bulimics are male.

When they are not bingeing they are often quite health conscious, but when they binge they head for all the things that are high in fats and carbohydrates.

Bulimics seem to share certain qualities. They are usually perfectionists with high expectations of themselves, lacking in self-esteem and having a strong need for approval from other people. The binge is a source of pleasure and comfort at the start, but afterwards a source of shame, and disgust at their loss of control. The purge restores the feeling of self-control and is quite gratifying at the time, but it is also followed by guilt and misery. It is awful to see these young people trying to fight the problem, missing appointments and dates to go on a binge, then avoiding people because they feel so low, depressed and degraded.

Bulimia can cause a lot of tissue damage — damage to teeth and gums from vomiting, sore throats, stretching of the stomach wall, infection of the salivary glands, causing a chipmunk-like appearance, dehydration, loss of menstrual periods, urinary and kidney problems. The first thing subjects are told in treatment is to STOP PURGING.

BULIMIA SCRIPT

From this time forward you will have less and less desire to binge-eat and purge . . . you will be amazed and disturbed that you have let yourself eat these unhealthy, fattening foods in such large amounts . . . that you have risked physical damage and deterioration of your looks and your living habits when you vomit up this food. The feeling of being ugly and fat . . . the spending of enormous amounts of money . . . ceasing to be reliable and punctual . . . all these things that you have allowed to happen will puzzle and disturb you.

More and more, from now on, you will eat just enough healthy, nourishing, wholesome food to become fit and healthy and return to normality.

When you do achieve this, you will continue to eat just the right amount of good, healthy, nutritious foods, to maintain your weight at the level it should be . . . when you do cease to binge-eat your clothes and mouth will feel clean, your skin will feel clear, free of pimples and dullness . . . you will be more clean, orderly and tidy in your living habits, you will feel better about yourself and enjoy life far more.

From this time on, you won't eat when you are by yourself except for sustenance . . . until your habit has disappeared . . . you will eat when you are with others . . . you will eat slowly, and be more fastidious . . . you will not feel guilty about eating normal, healthy, nutritious food, and you will eat only what you need to sustain yourself in a healthy state.

(At this point introduce the anorexia script at "you will do a normal amount of exercise and eat properly . . . " and continue with it to the end.)

PROBLEM DRINKING

Many people drink alcohol regularly and suffer few ill-effects. You can probably manage six standard drinks a day (four if you are a woman) with a low risk of physical, mental and social problems occurring. (These figures come from a pamphlet entitled *Alcohol*, from the Department of Community Medicine at Royal Prince Alfred Hospital.) This is a general guide and does vary with the individual, depending on age, size, general health, tolerance level and drinking pattern.

If you exceed your personal limit you could expect some degree of damage to your brain, heart and liver to occur, although some people can suffer brain damage from a relatively small daily amount of alcohol.

When people come to see me with a drinking problem, I urge them to attend Alcoholics Anonymous.

There are many reports of the use of hypnosis resulting in abstinence, but in a lot of cases it is difficult to be sure whether this was due to hypnosis itself or to other factors.

Treatments range from teaching people to use self-hypnosis to relax as a replacement for drinking, group hypnosis and discussions about problem-solving techniques and strategies, planning substitute activities that could be carried out instead of drinking, as well as direct hypnotic suggestions for becoming indifferent to alcohol and gradually ceasing to bother with it. In 1976 one researcher claimed that ninety-three out of 150 alcoholics were abstinent one year after he suggested under hypnosis that any future drinking would lead to a reliving of the worst hangover they had ever experienced.[9]

J. Christopher Clarke, Senior Lecturer in Psychology at the University of New South Wales, has written about treating alcoholism by aversion therapy. He says that if an electric shock is used to take away the pleasure of drinking alcohol it must be followed by an illness episode, and that encouraging results have been obtained in this way. However, the usual method of inducing illness is by using strong and potentially lethal drugs such as lithium chloride and apomorphine hydrochloride. As these can be quite dangerous he advises hypnotic suggestions that produce nausea, *not* vomiting (as this represents a release from nausea), and that are aimed at a *particular* form of alcohol — red wine, beer, scotch, or whatever is drunk to excess. If all are taken in excess, he suggests that each one be treated in turn.[10]

Some people suggest that as severe personality disorders are often a feature of the alcoholic these need to be dealt with instead of applying direct suggestion.or aversive techniques. In a review of hypnotic treatments used in conjunction with conventional treatments for alcoholism in 1981, the researchers came to the conclusion that hypnosis contributed nothing to the standard therapies, which conflicts with the majority of the reports.[11]

Perhaps you will have to experiment a little with this script. Try putting together a highly descriptive hangover or nausea image, or try the indirect suggestions in the Erickson and Bandler and Grinder scripts.

PROBLEM DRINKING SCRIPT

From this time onward your unconscious mind, working together with your body, will signal when you have had sufficient alcohol . . . in the past this signal has not been given, or it has been ignored . . . from now on, whenever the amount of alcohol you have consumed is sufficient to give you a pleasant glow, a kindly feeling towards those around you, you will remain at that level by sipping slowly, mixing soda with your alcohol, drinking non-alcoholic drinks or drinking no more.

If you have to drive a car, this signal will let you know when the .05 level has been reached, and you will remain at this level, consuming just enough to keep you at about the .05 level . . . when you do receive the signal that you have had sufficient, your need for a higher intake of alcohol will disappear, you simply won't need any more alcohol content in your blood, you will feel satisfied and satiated with the amount that your mind and body have decided is sufficient . . . you will have a complete, contented feeling, no more need, no more craving, the signal does away with all your previous needs for excess alcohol . . . it will simply not bother you any longer, you will know when you have had enough to drink, and it will be well within the reasonable limits of alcoholic intake.

From this time forward you will find yourself with increased self-confidence, hope for the future and an ability to use relaxation and deep breathing rather than alcohol to feel better.

15

FUNCTIONAL PROBLEMS

I could be challenged about this category. I realise that functional disorders are those disorders for which organic defects can't be positively located, and that in this category are some which have quite definite physical as well as psychological links. However, as it is difficult to categorise them precisely, it seems that "functional" is the most apt term to describe them.

STAMMERING

Many behaviour modification techniques have been used to treat stammering:
* Shadowing, in which the stammerer speaks aloud as closely as possible after another speaker or a recorded voice
* Simultaneous reading, with the stammerer and another person reading from the same book at the same time
* Speaking rhythmically in time to a metronome, or syllable-timed speech, in which words are produced with marked separation between them
* The use of white noise (static) to drown out the sound of the stammerer's voice
* Negative or massed practice, where the stammerer is required to stammer deliberately, or repeat the same passage over and over again.

Systematic desensitisation and hypnosis have been used to try to modify or remove the stammer, and an extremely successful behaviour modification intensive programme has been conducted at Prince Henry Hospital. The programme, the brainchild of Dr Gavin Andrews, a Sydney psychiatrist, involves the patient living in for the two weeks of the treatment, undergoing therapeutic training and group sessions, as well as being placed under a system of rewards and punishments for improvement or backsliding. Various privileges, and some meals, are dependent on the patient showing improvement.

It is thought that stammering is caused by a fault in the feedback control mechanism for speech, and that there is also a connection with anxiety. Some believe that there is a great deal of repressed hostility and insecurity in the stammerer. Stammering occurs when the vocal cords tighten up in spasm, panic making them tighten up even more, so they lock temporarily.

Milton Erickson, writing about stuttering, said that it is a form of aggression against society and people in general, and wondered why the patient would aggress in a way that was so uncomfortable for him:

> I had a patient who was a physician, and who had stuttered all of his life. When he came to me as a patient, I told him very frankly that his stuttering was an aggression and that I would be very glad to take care of it, if he were willing. I stated also that it would not be a pleasant sort of thing. He asked me if I thought stammering or stuttering were very pleasant things. I put him in a trance and worked quite a while with him on the subject of how he felt about speech, and how he felt about people in general. I then built up a negative attitude and aggression toward me which serves the purpose of allowing the patient to vent his aggression on me individually.
>
> As a result, the doctor is in a difficult situation. He speaks clearly and lucidly, has no stammer or stutter. He never fails to send me a Christmas card, but he always writes: "I hate your guts and I'm going to keep right on." Nevertheless, he sends me a Christmas card, and he sends Christmas presents to my children; but he always has a nasty crack for me.[1]

I tried all manner of techniques with a stammerer, including a mixture of biofeedback and Gestalt, to no avail. When I stumbled across my self-recording technique, I hauled my long-suffering stammerer in for one more attack on his affliction. It seemed a very promising idea as, like many stammerers, this person did not stammer when he made a tape recording, or acted on the stage. You can imagine my surprise when, after making a tape and listening to it a couple of times, he came to see me completely fluent, but quite snappy. He really seemed most annoyed. I had made the mistake of not suggesting something onto which he could transfer his masked hostility!

STAMMERING SCRIPT

As your nerves become stronger and steadier, your confidence continues to grow and you become less self-conscious, less preoccupied with yourself, you will find yourself more and more at ease and confident and natural when talking in front of a group — any group . . . in a seminar in your course or in a situation at work you will be able to look at the faces in front of you and feel completely at ease.

In all similar or social situations you will be much less self-conscious, much less aware or concerned about other people's opinions of you ... you will have a steadily increasing confidence, you will be relaxed, secure and at ease in all social situations you have previously found difficult ... your mind will be clear, you will think more clearly and respond fluently to comments and questions ... you will tend to slow down your speech ... you will find yourself becoming more and more fluent and your stammer will gradually disappear ... you will look at the face of the person you are speaking to and maintain a normal facial expression ... remain relaxed and confident and in control of the situation.

You will find you can say the first letter in any word easily from now on ... if there are any particular letters you have had trouble with, in future you will say them as a sound, not as a letter ... you will speak the first syllable without any trouble at all ... you will concentrate on the last syllables ... you will direct your attention to the last syllables and slide over the first few letters.

You will find a way to deal constructively with any pent-up anger or hostility, redirect it to something inanimate ... you will find it easier to express your feelings honestly, and stand up for your rights, even when it is necessary to express annoyance or refuse a favour.

It might be that the blocking of the muscles involved in speaking will be transferred to another part of the body by your unconscious mind ... say, as a twitching of one of the fingers of either the right or the left hand ... which finger would you like to twitch? ... perhaps the little finger on the left hand, or the little finger on the right hand, or even the thumb on the left hand? ... each time you feel that you are going to stammer, you can control it by twitching this finger ... and you can, if you wish, do this with your hand closed ... in this way no-one will see it.

Remember, the more confident and secure and relaxed you become, the more you express your feelings honestly, the more fluent you will become and your stammer will disappear, straight away or gradually ... if an occasional hesitation should occur, it won't bother you at all ... it just won't worry you.

BEDWETTING (ENURESIS)

Bedwetting has mostly been treated with a bell or buzzer that rings the moment urination takes place, or by awakening the child at fixed intervals, unrelated to the time of bedwetting, during the night.

Another method is to train children to increase bladder control and capacity by drinking increased amounts of fluid during waking hours and taking longer and longer between times of emptying the bladder, assuming that this will carry over into sleep.

Having been a bedwetter myself as a child and not wishing to have the added injury of it being thought a neurotic symptom, the explanation I found most acceptable was that the bedwetter is an extremely deep sleeper and the signal that the bladder needs emptying is too weak to be perceived.

A technique used by Milton Erickson was to give an enuretic married couple the task of purposely wetting the bed for a fortnight every night before retiring. Then to sleep in a dry bed one night and examine it in the morning. Only if the bed were wet were they to purposely wet it again for another *three* weeks. He said that after a while the sheer ridiculousness of what was occurring was sufficient to eradicate the behaviour.[2] That seems to me to be going too far, but perhaps if someone is quite old, say fourteen and over, and getting desperate, it is worth a try.

Harry Stanton of the University of Tasmania has had two journal articles published on his method of treating bedwetting, one in 1979 [3] and the other in 1981.[4] I found it surprising that he mentions in one of them that he has not found children easier to hypnotise than adults. He had variable success with hypnotic treatments and decided to use a more indirect approach, modelled on Erickson's techniques.

A method of induction he used frequently was to get children to hold a coin between thumb and forefinger and ask them to imagine that the muscles of the arm, hands and fingers had become tired and that soon they would need to drop the coin. After this he employed an adaptation of an ego-enhancement script to suit a child and included suggestions relating to bedwetting — dry bed, bladder control — and images of gain or loss of power or control as indirectly as possible.

For example, he talked about how the patient learned to speak, walk, ride a bike and so on, and how he lost certain fears as he grew older, incorporating the suggestion that he could also lose the power to urinate while lying down, and would therefore have to get up and go to the toilet. A further phase involved distraction with music or getting the patient to count backwards from 300 down while most of the previous ideas were repeated.

Stanton reports a high success rate — seventy per cent — with this method, and in one of the articles recommends the use of a homeopathic remedy, equisetum — five drops in a little water three times a day — to be used in conjunction with hypnosis.

The following script has been used successfully with children by me and by my fellow counsellor, Stephen Young, who had one of them make his own recording with an adaptation of the basic script for children on page 62.

Don't use the words "wet bed" to an enuretic child. Talk only about a dry bed: "Your bed was three-quarters dry last night."

BEDWETTING SCRIPT

From now on there will be no more need to wet the bed . . . you will no longer wake up cold and wet, your mattress, sheets and blankets soaked . . . you will no longer have your bed smelling of urine . . . when you are asleep and your bladder needs emptying, you will wake up enough to get out of bed, go to the toilet, empty your bladder into the toilet, and return to your bed . . . you will then go back to sleep, soundly asleep, having pleasant dreams.

From now on you will be able to sleep for longer and longer before you will need to go to the toilet . . . soon you will sleep right through most nights without the need to wake up and go to the toilet.

You will become more and more confident and calm, the things that used to upset you won't bother you very much any more . . . you will be calm and relaxed.

Remember, from this time on you will receive the signal that your bladder is sending you to get up and you will rise from your bed, go to the toilet, and return to your bed to go into a sound sleep . . . your sheets will be clean and crisp and fresh . . . you will sleep soundly and peacefully . . . and you will be far more confident and calm.

INSOMNIA

Even without incorporating a specific script for insomnia, many of the people I have seen have reported sleeping better as a consequence of using hypnosis. As insomnia is a debilitating and distressing disorder a few simple suggestions incorporated into the script should bring relief.

In my experience insomniacs have something fairly specific

bothering them and their minds are too actively engaged in going over and over their problems to allow them to settle into sleep. So if you have this problem try to analyse just what is disturbing you, and try to sort it out. Grapple with it in a practical way.

Sometimes insomnia is caused by heavy meals, cigarettes, coffee or alcohol in the evening; or it may represent a more deep-seated psychological problem of left-over childhood guilts, fears or aggressions; or it may be an indicator of depression.

It is not a good idea to take sleeping tablets except perhaps on the odd desperate occasion, as the body quickly adapts to them and more and more of them have to be taken to be effective.

Although insomniacs have genuine sleep problems, they also have a distorted perception of time and believe themselves to have been awake on the average three times longer than they actually have been.

A successful method of treating insomnia was reported by researchers using progressive relaxation to induce hypnosis, then telling their clients to imagine themselves at a blackboard with a piece of chalk and a duster. The clients were then told to imagine drawing a circle on the blackboard and writing the number 100 inside it, then taking the duster and erasing the number slowly using an anticlockwise motion, without touching the edge of the circle. After that they were to write the words ''deep sleep'' just to the right of the circle, then go back to the circle, write the number ninety-nine inside it, erase it as previously instructed. Then they were to write over the words they had previously written, making sure there were no double lines. They were told to continue in this manner, subtracting one number each time until they were asleep. The clients were shown how to put themselves into a trance using self-hypnosis. Using the technique themselves at home the clients increased their average hours of sleep from between three and five, to between six and eight, maintaining this improvement over a one-year period.[5]

INSOMNIA SCRIPT

You will find from now on that you will sleep soundly and peacefully for the length of time that you require . . . your dreams will be pleasant. See yourself in a deep state of repose . . . see your chest moving up and down rhythmically . . . picture yourself deeply asleep . . . you will get drowsy and fall asleep almost as soon as you put your head on your pillow.

If you awaken during the night you will very quickly slip back into a deep sleep, with many pleasant constructive dreams . . . on those rare occasions when you do lie awake and find it a little difficult to sleep, the time will seem to pass far more quickly than usual and you will find ways to put this time to constructive use.

When the number of hours available is not quite sufficient the sleep you do have will be more effective ... every hour will seem like two, and in the morning you will wake up refreshed and alert.

Remember, from now on you will sleep soundly and peacefully for the length of time that you need ... your dreams will be pleasant and will work on sorting out your problems in some way ... you will get drowsy and fall asleep as soon as you put your head on your pillow.

SLEEPWALKING (SOMNAMBULISM)

A study carried out in the 1960s described the following as characteristic of sleepwalkers:

• When sleepwalkers rise from bed at night, the EEG (the machine that monitors brainwaves) shows a sleeping brain wave pattern. If the sleepwalker is only walking for a few minutes, the pattern stays the same, but if the time of walking is extended for much longer the brainwave pattern changes to that of a light sleep or relaxed waking state.

• The sleepwalker moves in a rigid or shuffling manner, has very little awareness of his or her surroundings and has a blank stare. Sleepwalkers rarely reply when spoken to, and if they do reply they tend to mumble or speak vaguely.

• When sleepwalkers are told to wake up they do not do so. It may be necessary to shake the person or speak very loudly, repeating his or her name over and over again.

• Sleepwalkers have amnesia for the walking episode.[6]

Deeply hypnotised people are often labelled "somnambulists" because they bear certain resemblances to sleepwalkers.

I was once asked by a doctor friend to suggest a treatment for sleepwalking and was surprised to find that on looking back through more than ten years of *Psychological Abstracts*, which record international psychological data, I could find only two reported cases of treatment of sleepwalking. When you consider that approximately fifteen per cent of all children between five and twelve years of age indulge in some sleepwalking activity, and some carry on the behaviour into adulthood, it is a wonder there is not more material available on this problem.

One of the treatments I found was the use of assertiveness

training and the other was a long-term psychoanalytic therapy. The assertiveness script (on page 197) should be added to the following script, as one of the supposed attributes of the sleepwalker is lack of assertion. The implication is that, somehow, being meek and submissive contributes to the sleepwalking tendency.

Thomas Eliseo, a psychologist from Illinois, reported on the hypnotic treatment of sleepwalking in a nineteen-year-old student. He had been sleepwalking for two years before he saw the therapist, at least once a month, often up to ten times a month. During these episodes he would do odd things, such as growl like a bear or howl like a wolf. Dr Eliseo found that as the patient was a shy, passive person who had difficulty in expressing anger or annoyance, the sleepwalking episodes were expressions of aggression. The treatment therefore had a heavy emphasis on aspects of being in control, and of assertion. As the treatment progressed to a successful outcome, so did the patient's ability to express his irritation.[7]

SLEEPWALKING SCRIPT

From this time forward you will rarely find it necessary to get out of bed during the night, unless you are completely awake and aware of what is happening around you . . . you will from now on sleep peacefully and soundly when you are in your bed, dreaming constructive, pleasant dreams, and it will be difficult to disturb you . . . if you do get out of bed when you are not awake, the moment your feet touch the ground you will wake up and become alert and aware of what is happening.

Remember, from now on you will sleep soundly and peacefully and undisturbed during the night . . . when you do need to get out of bed, you will be alert and aware and completely awake the moment your feet touch the ground.

SEASICKNESS

I have not come across any reports of treating seasickness with hypnosis in the literature on this problem, but quite some time ago, before I began to encourage self-hypnosis, I made a tape for a student who came to me and announced, "I get seasick and I want to crew in the Sydney to Hobart yacht race."

I wondered what that had to do with me, and looked puzzled, so he continued, "Well, they won't select me unless I stop getting seasick, and I want you to hypnotise me out of it.'' I told him I thought that seasickness was purely physiological, and he said quite firmly, ''I believe it has a psychological component, and I believe hypnosis will help.'' I agreed to help.

I got him to lie down on the cushions, and began my usual induction. I noticed him smiling, and when he finally burst into helpless laughter I became a little peeved, and took on a very authoritarian manner. My suggestions to the student can be used as a general seasickness script:

> You are on a yacht, and it is rocking gently to and fro, to and fro . . . you are resting in your bunk, quite enjoying the gentle motion and the lap of the water on the sides . . . the wind starts to get a little stronger and the rocking becomes a little more pronounced and the water becomes a little rougher and more and more choppy.
>
> A storm is on its way . . . as it comes overhead the yacht begins to pitch and roll . . . the seas are wild . . . you are tossing from side to side in your bunk . . . you have to brace yourself to stop falling out . . . you are feeling more and more nauseated, sicker and sicker, but as the nausea rises it transfers into a warm, pink right hand . . . warmer and pinker as the feeling of nausea subsides . . . finally your nausea is gone altogether, and your hand remains warm and pink.
>
> From this time forward, whenever you begin to feel sick at sea, this feeling will straight away be converted into a warm feeling in your right hand, warmer and pinker as the blood flows into it, and the feeling of nausea will disappear completely.

This suggestion took effect during the hypnotic session, as the student had to brace himself just as if he was in a yacht in a storm at sea. When the session was over his right hand was distinctly redder than the left hand, and he reported that it was very warm. Surprisingly, it had a similar effect on his experiences at sea, because after that he suffered very little from nausea.

NOISES IN THE HEAD (TINNITUS)

About 30 million Americans, 10 per cent of Australians and 17 per cent of British adults suffer to some extent from ringing, buzzing or other noises in the head, mainly localised in the ears. At its mildest it does not interfere with day-to-day living, but as it tends to be more severe it causes irritability and insomnia, and may even lead to psychosis or suicide. It is said that in its severest form it is the third worst ailment of mankind, the worst being severe, unrelievable pain, and the second worst being severe, unrelievable dizziness.

The cause of tinnitus is not very well understood, and its treatment is not very satisfactory. It can accompany a variety of medical and dental problems, or it can appear without any apparent reason. Many sufferers have been told they just have to live with it, and some practitioners believe that it has a psychological component.

There may be actual vibrations in the tissues in or about the head, or there may be apparent irritation of the auditory nerve tissues. Tinnitus has been attributed to the fact that the hair cells in the middle ear, which conduct sound, are somehow artificially stimulated to conduct permanent sound.

A possible treatment of tinnitus is destruction of the auditory nerve, causing total deafness, but even this does not always effectively halt tinnitus. Again, hypnosis has been used to effect, either to minimise perception of the sound being carried, or to make the person less perturbed by it.

In 1982 Crisetta MacLeod-Morgan, John Court and Russell Roberts of Flinders University in South Australia used a combination of relaxation and imagery in hypnosis to treat a series of patients with chronic tinnitus, by training sufferers to use the noise in the ears as a cue for relaxation and peace, whereas before it was a cue for annoyance and irritation.[8]

They used the patient's own preferred images: for example, for one woman with depression and vertigo accompanying the tinnitus they used the idea of a safe place where she could be totally in control. In this place there was a console with two knobs, one to control tinnitus, and one to control her balance. She then experimented in turning the tinnitus knob up and down, finally settling for zero on the tinnitus knob and the mid-point for balance, representing perfect balance.

Another woman referred to them had tried various methods to cure her tinnitus, including a brain scan, jaw re-alignment and ear investigations, and was encouraged to be actively aware of her hum as a cue for relaxation, good feelings and a signal to release all mental and physical tensions. Plato's "harmony of the spheres" was used as an analogy for her hum, as was Pooh Bear's "happy hums".

My first experience with someone with tinnitus was long ago, before I became very involved with hypnosis. A miserable-looking student came in to talk about withdrawing from his course. He had been to a rock concert with very loud music several months before, and ever since had suffered from permanent and severe ringing in his ears. It had affected him so badly he had contemplated suicide, and his ability to concentrate on studying had completely disappeared. The only way he could cope with the sound at night was to play his radio all the time, as he found complete silence unbearable. His results confirmed the drastic effect that tinnitus had had upon him, as he had plummeted from averaging credits to failing all his exams. It did not occur to me to try hypnosis at the time, so I simply had to bid him goodbye.

Using the suggestion that the patient concentrate on noise, some patients have entered a deep trance and the noise has gradually diminished. In this way the ringing or buzzing is used as an induction into hypnotic trance, especially useful for getting to sleep at night. You may include this idea in a script, or some of the Flinders University techniques, or you might suggest deafness for the wavelength at which the tinnitus occurs.

TINNITUS SCRIPT

From this time forward you will pay less and less attention to the noises in your ears . . . it will seem as if they become fainter and further away . . . receding into the distance . . . fainter and fainter . . . further and further away . . . they will flow over and away from you, and recede right into the distance . . . you will pay less and less attention to these noises, you will be less and less sensitive to them . . . and soon they will bother you very, very little.

When you settle down to sleep at night, your unconscious mind will fill your brain with your favourite music, it will seem as if you can actually hear your favourite music being played in your head as you drift off to sleep . . .

(At this point you may include the script for insomnia.)

SHAKING HANDS

A surprising number of people have complained to me that their hands shake uncontrollably, so much so that in social situations they cannot hold a glass or a cup without spilling some of the contents, or at least clattering the cup or drawing attention to themselves in some embarrassing way. They have difficulty in writing, and sometimes are bothered by the rat-a-tatting of their knife and fork on a plate. So they end up either avoiding the situations where this might happen, or avoiding behaviour in public that might draw attention to the problem.

It is surprising that I could not find one journal article dealing with this common problem. So the script that follows is one that I wrote for a patient and have made use of several times since.

SHAKING HANDS SCRIPT

If this is not a very important symptom, then from now on you will find that the shaking of your hands will become less and less obvious . . . soon, very soon, your hands will be steadier . . . the shaking will gradually disappear until it is completely under your control . . . you will be able to hold things firmly and steadily.

You will be able to hold a cup of tea in a saucer without any clattering or spilling . . . you will find you can write clearly and firmly without any tremor at all . . . firmly and steadily . . . totally under your control.

Any small amount of left-over shaking will be converted to a very slight itch on one of your ribs . . . and a couple of second's scratching will eliminate this itch.

If this is a much more important symptom than it should be, then your unconscious mind will need to find ways of changing it . . . it may decide to find other ways to behave that will achieve the same purpose . . . it will give you dreams, pleasant dreams, in which solutions will be found and presented . . . soon you will have other choices of behaviour apart from shaking hands that will accomplish the same purpose.

BREAST ENLARGEMENT

In the United States there are thousands of breast enlargement operations carried out every year, and the number is increasing. It can be assumed that the number of these cosmetic operations is also increasing elsewhere. The operation involves the implantation of a bag filled with a silicone solution between the existing breast tissue and the muscle tissue below.

One study describes the many positive effects of increased breast size that have been reported by patients following surgery, including increased interest in sex, increased frequency of intercourse and increased ability to climax. Two patients reported that they obtained orgasm for the first time. They all reported feeling happier in all areas of life, with a more positive body image, decreased self-consciousness and increased self-esteem. Many felt that their interpersonal and marital relationships had improved.[9] Other studies have found positive effects, except for women who expected too much of the surgery: for example if they expected that it would resolve serious marital problems.

But the surgical procedure is expensive and involves a stay of several days in hospital. In addition, it involves the risks that are associated with any major operation, even though advances in surgery and anaesthesia continue to reduce that risk.

The first report I could find of the successful use of hypnosis to increase breast size was dated 1949, when hypnotic techniques were used to induce breast growth in twenty women aged from twenty to thirty-five. The practitioner suggested that the "inner mind" of the subjects was going to start the same process of breast growth that had occurred during puberty and that the process would continue until their breasts reached the desired size. The subjects pictured themselves the size they wished to be, and used the imagery of warmth and tingling sensations. Seventeen out of the twenty women showed some increase in size, from about one to one and a half inches (2.5 to 3.7 centimetres) and five showed growth of about two inches (five centimetres).[10]

Another successful use of hypnosis to stimulate breast growth was carried out in 1974[11], when thirteen women averaged an increase of 2.11 inches (5.3 centimetres). The explanation put forward was that the endocrine gland, which plays an important role in the development of secondary sex characteristics, was acted upon by the emotions and produced the changes.

Two researchers at the University of Houston suggested it may not be endocrine involvement, but that hypnosis had influenced the circulation of blood, and the resulting congestion of the veins of the breasts caused the extra growth. They tested to see whether breast enlargement could be induced, and also to see whether there were changes in the proportions of the body taking place at the same time. As well as the imagery of warmth (warm wet towels and heat lamps) they also suggested going back in time to when puberty first commenced, and experiencing the sensations that accompanied breast development. They not only produced an increase in breast size, but substantial decrease in waist size, even though none of the women had lost weight (although one of them had gained some).[12]

Another American researcher used similar techniques on twenty-two university students and staff with similar results. The average increase was 1.37 inches (3.5 centimetres), and the women reported other fringe benefits as well. Better bowling scores and improved golf scores were noticed (I can only suppose they were due to the general increase in confidence), and women who had been worried about pendulous breasts before the treatment were pleased with the new fullness and firmness. All women who began the programme with one breast smaller than the other found them to be equal in size at the end of the treatment![13]

BREAST ENLARGEMENT SCRIPT

I want you to have a clear image in your mind of the way you would like to be . . . imagine yourself standing in front of a mirror admiring the improvement in your shape . . . your breasts just the size you would like them to be, your waist smaller, just as you have always wanted it to be . . . see this clearly and vividly . . . your breasts full and firm, no longer sagging or uneven . . . exactly the right size and shape . . . feel how firm they have become even though they are still pliable, and feel how much smaller and tighter your waist has become, and how much flatter your stomach . . . from now on you will bring this image to mind frequently, picturing yourself just the way you want to be . . . because this is how you will be, soon.

Now, I want you to concentrate on a feeling of warmth in your breasts . . . concentrate hard and direct on an extra supply of blood to the arteries and veins in your breasts, making them feel warmer . . . visualise a wet, very warm towel lying over your breasts and helping with the extra feeling of warmth, as the blood congests the veins and starts to enlarge your breasts . . . become aware of your heartbeat and let the pulsing of your heartbeat flow into your breasts.

Let yourself drift back through the past, now, back to the time your breasts were just beginning to grow, when your periods had just commenced . . . experience the feelings again, feelings of growth and tenderness and tightness of the skin over the breasts as if you can feel your breasts grow larger right this moment. As you do this your breasts *will* become larger . . . and firmer . . . and fuller . . . and your waist will become smaller . . . and neater . . . and your stomach will become flatter . . . and as these things happen your confidence will grow, by the day, you will feel more and more pleased about life . . . at the same time your interest in sex will grow . . . and your sexual feelings and sensations will be heightened.

Your unconscious mind will find ways to help achieve your

goal, in safe and clever ways that you may or may not become aware of.

GAGGING

The physical need for a gagging reflex is to regurgitate food or other material lodged in the larynx, and thus prevent choking. This reflex is normally far enough down the throat that it does not interfere with dental treatment, but sometimes abnormal and exaggerated gagging occurs.

Physical problems, such as chronic sinusitis, tonsilitis, or upper respiratory infections may be the cause, or psychological problems, such as fear or anxiety or past traumatic episodes may bring about gagging, making it impossible to proceed with sometimes quite urgent dental treatment.

Jack Gerschman, Graham Burrows and Patrick Fitzgerald working at the Melbourne Pain Management Clinic reported that some patients gag before an impression tray is put into the mouth or at the sight of a mirror or a tongue depressor. Others are unable to use a toothbrush without gagging. The reflex may also occur while an injection is being given, or when an attempt is made to take X-rays of the mouth. In addition, many patients are totally incapable of tolerating dentures in their mouths without being severely ill.[14]

In 1971 an American dentist, Kevin Bartlett, reported the case of a thirty-year-old woman who needed most of her teeth extracted and new dentures inserted. He managed most of the work with the use of hypnosis until it came to inserting the dentures. She could tolerate the dentures quite comfortably while in a trance, but as soon as she was awakened from the trance would begin gagging severely, and continue until the dentures were removed. So Bartlett borrowed an idea from Erickson whereby a post-hypnotic cue for trance induction was given in the course of an apparently normal conversation. The cue for re-awakening was given by a marked change in voice and attitude and by picking up the conversation where it had been left off at the time of the trance induction. This resulted in complete amnesia for the entire trance.

So he placed her in a trance, suggested the cue word, produced amnesia for the cue word, and woke her up. Then he started to chat about golf while he pretended to be adjusting the dentures, and in the course of the conversation said her husband's name loudly. This was the cue word. At that she went into a deep trance, and he inserted and adjusted the dentures, then continued talking about her husband and the game of golf he intended to have with him. The patient woke up and entered into the conversation and, after a while, Bartlett pointed out that her dentures were in place and that she was talking with them and tolerating them well. She continued to wear them without further problems, but could not recall how they had appeared in her mouth.[15]

This technique could not very easily be included in a self-hypnosis script, but the team at the Melbourne Pain Management Clinic report that gagging has been controlled by hypnosis using direct suggestions, even in a very light trance, and even with waking suggestions. They report a technique used in the 1950s in which an eighty per cent success rate was achieved by requiring the patient to stare hard into the dentist's eyes, take a deep breath and hold it while the dentist counted to five. The procedure was repeated and the patient was told convincingly that his gag reflex was eliminated and that he could not gag, no matter how much he tried.

GAGGING SCRIPT

Very soon the problems you have with gagging will be restricted to the occasions when food has gone down the wrong way, and you will very naturally gag to prevent choking. From now on you will be able to tolerate objects of increasing size in your mouth for longer and longer periods of time without feeling uncomfortable.

Imagine you are using a toothbrush and as you clean your teeth you are moving closer and closer to your back teeth, and the back part of your mouth . . . imagine this vividly, brushing the teeth and gums towards the back of your mouth . . . now, relax, breathe slowly and deeply, and think of something pleasant . . . relax your jaw and throat muscles, relax completely.

Now I want you to have a clear image of a dentist inspecting your teeth, looking at them reflected in the mirror he has placed over your tongue . . . feel the cold steel getting closer to your throat as he looks at your back teeth . . . feel the prodding and pricking as he checks your teeth for decay . . . now relax, breathe slowly and deeply as he looks around inside your mouth . . . breathing slowly, relaxed, letting your jaw muscles and chin sag slightly, tongue loose and relaxed.

The dentist is about to give you an injection so he can fill a sensitive tooth . . . imagine the needle sliding into your gum near your back teeth . . . a tiny prick and you feel numbness spreading into your gums and face muscles . . . relaxing completely, feeling calm and breathing slowly . . . your face and jaw muscles relaxed . . . your throat relaxed and the constant feeling of numbness.

This feeling of numbness continues as you imagine the dentist trying out your new set of teeth . . . fitting the dentures into your mouth while you sit comfortably in the chair . . . you become used to the dentures as you sit there calm and relaxed, your throat and face and jaws completely relaxed . . . the numbness gradually fades as it becomes no longer necessary and you tolerate your new dentures very comfortably.

From now on you will have this feeling of relaxation and calmness every time an object of this kind is placed in your mouth . . . you will feel numbness spreading . . . your jaws and mouth and throat and face will be completely relaxed, feeling no discomfort . . . the numbness will gradually fade as you become accustomed to the situation and it no longer bothers you.

16

OBSESSIVE-COMPULSIVE DISORDERS

According to psychoanalytic views, an obsession is an intense idea serving as a defence against a strong unacceptable impulse. For example, your obsessive worry about a parent's health can serve as a defence against forbidden violent impulses toward that parent. An obsession is a persistent and unwelcome idea or set of ideas.

A compulsion is the well-nigh uncontrollable urge to perform some act, or acts, or sometimes quite complex sequences of acts. It is usually supposed that the obsessional thought gives rise to the compulsive behaviour.

A variety of behaviour modification techniques as well as insight attained through long-term psychoanalysis have been used for treating obsessions and compulsions.

OVERSENSITIVITY TO NOISE

Stress often makes people oversensitive to things in the environment and within their own bodies that are usually present but would normally go unnoticed. One of these is noise.

As students are continually under stress they are wide open to these kinds of disorders, and I have often seen students obsessed with noise to the point where it interfered badly with their ability to concentrate on their studies.

The script below was written for a student who came in saying that the noise around him was driving him crazy and he could not study. He had started to perform very poorly, and he was in a very perturbed state. The noises which bothered him so much were the normal suburban sounds — a neighbour's lawnmower, the sound of a car door slamming, dogs barking and so on.

Another student used the script below, altered slightly, after appearing wild-eyed, saying, "I can't stand the noise, it's driving me crazy!" He must have been finally wearing out after several years of successful study, because the noise he was objecting to was the noise he had been listening to for years, the normal living sounds of his father and mother, both in their seventies. He made them sound like juvenile delinquents, conjuring up in my mind scenes of wild abandon, but they were only playing the radio and using the washing machine! It was surprising to see all the signs of a person under severe strain — perspiration, eyes protruding slightly, veins standing out in his forehead, jaws clenched, muscles in his throat and neck working — over what seemed a trivial matter to me. I had difficulty in suppressing a smile, but it was no joke to him.

While students suffer from this problem due to overload on their systems, it can also be brought about by underload. For a while I saw a few people outside the study system. They were mainly young mothers and housewives, married to successful men, and many of them suffered from extreme sensitivity to noise. It seemed to me that their stressors mainly stemmed from boredom, loss of confidence and self-esteem, and from feeling unfulfilled. Most of them had held responsible jobs before they married but they had reached the stage where they could not cope with even simple problems. Most also suffered from physical symptoms, flutterings and palpitations in the heart, for example, so they were not only sensitive to noises around them, but also to ordinary sounds within their bodies.

OVERSENSITIVITY TO NOISE SCRIPT

From now on, when you are at home your perception of outside noise will be altered ... any noises that are around will be fainter, and further away ... more and more, the sounds you once heard as being loud and annoying will become fainter and softer ... further and further into the distance, fading further and further away ... from now on, you will be aware of these sounds but they won't bother you, they won't bother you at all ... they will flow over you, over and away and into the distance ... they simply will not bother you at all ... they will be remote, and faint, and quite unimportant ... you will be calm and detached, calm and detached.

From now on, your unconscious mind will return your sensitivity to sound to a level where you will not be bothered by outside noise ... you will not be bothered at all ... the sounds will just flow over you ... you will be calm and detached ... you will perceive sounds, but they simply won't bother you at all.

OVERSENSITIVITY TO LIGHT

This is a similar obsession to that of being oversensitive to noise, but much rarer. One of the students who came to see me about this could not pay attention to lectures or study in our main building because, he said, "The light is driving me crazy." It sounded to me that it was more likely that his course was driving him crazy, and that he had displaced this onto the light, but there is evidence that some types of lighting can have a detrimental effect on people. Mercury lighting, for example, may influence EEG patterns with its barely detectable flicker. However, I chose to regard his problem as psychological in the absence of any real evidence to the contrary and we constructed the following script.

OVERSENSITIVITY TO LIGHT SCRIPT

From now on that part of you that has been paying far too much attention to the overhead lighting, that part of you that has been irritated and upset by the lighting, is going to pay less and less attention to that lighting . . . it will still be aware that the lighting is there, and sometimes that the lights appear to flicker a little and can be quite bright . . . but it will cease to pay very much attention to these lights, just as if that part of you was extremely alert before but has now become dulled, not able to devote much attention at all to the lights.

These lights won't bother you any more then . . . you will be able to attend to what is happening without noticing them very much . . . as if they have become further away . . . as if they are somehow filtered . . . they just won't seem to bother you any more.

COMPULSION TO STARE

A student who came to see me with this problem said his urge to stare at people had started in lectures one day, when he felt he just had to stare at the person next to him. When the person's attention was drawn to this, he finally looked back at my patient who became overwhelmed with confusion and embarrassment. It had reached the stage where he often had to leave the lecture theatre because of the embarrassment his compulsion was causing him, and naturally enough this had started to have a detrimental effect on his studies.

I found his symptom quite mysterious because it was the only sign of neurosis in a person who was about as normal, well-adjusted and likeable as it is possible to be. We were both extremely puzzled by it and spent a lot of our interview time looking perplexedly at each other.

After making the tape and playing it several times, he felt more relaxed about his problem. The urge to stare had lessened a little in intensity and was not so frequent, but, more importantly, it did not bother him as much any more. It no longer overwhelmed him so much that he had to leave the room whenever it occurred.

COMPULSION TO STARE SCRIPT

From this time forward the need to stare at people will dwindle away and soon disappear altogether . . . soon the urge to stare will be quite, quite remote from your needs . . . you will become more and more interested and absorbed in whatever is going on around you . . . so that the urge to stare just will not enter your head . . . you will be too distracted by whatever is going on around you to bother.

You will be at ease and relaxed, quite comfortable with those around you . . . in future on the very rare occasions you feel the need to stare you will not be bothered by it, it will seem natural and normal . . . it will just not bother you . . . it won't worry you at all.

Your unconscious mind will do its best to resolve this problem in some safe and effective way . . . it will give you less troubling alternative methods to achieve the same results . . . it may allow you to understand why you are staring, or it may not bother . . . it may simply solve the problem satisfactorily without letting you become aware of what has happened . . . when it does this, you will know because you will have no further need to stare at other people . . . the need to stare will no longer be present.

HAIRPULLING (TRICHOTILLOMANIA)

Some people have an irresistible urge to pull out their own hair, from the scalp or eyelashes or eyebrows. This formerly rare compulsion is apparently increasing at a rapid rate, and is far more common in children than in adults. Risk of infection is high and those who eat the hair they have plucked out are prone to forming hairballs, which can be dangerous, sometimes even fatal.

Most studies in the area have been done by psychoanalysts who see the problem as an indication of sexual conflict and unsatisfied sexual tension, as well as being a masturbatory equivalent. Behaviour therapists see it as a disturbance of habit patterns.

In eliminating severe hairpulling of eighteen years' duration in a twenty-six-year-old woman, Dr Thomas Galski, Director of

Mental Health at the John F. Kennedy Medical Center in New Jersey, first used variations of ego-strengthening procedures. Then rather ingeniously, he built up an increased awareness of the feelings attached to hairpulling, the texture, softness and silkiness of the hair, and then suggested increasing sensitivity of the scalp to the point where when she touched her hair preparatory to pulling it out her scalp would feel as if it was severely sunburned. It was important to make her scalp appear sensitive because even when she pulled out large amounts of hair she did not usually feel pain or discomfort.[1]

Alaskan medical practitioner Dr Robert Rowen was asked to treat a twenty-one-year-old prison inmate whose hairpulling had resulted in a severe loss of hair from his scalp. He first used a conditioning technique, associating the act of reaching up to pull out a hair with a post-hypnotic suggestion of nausea and vomiting. After a while the patient stopped practising his self-hypnosis exercises and resumed his habit, as he became tired of vomiting each time he began to pull a hair.

Rowen then established under deep trance the original cause of the habit and the fact that the man got a peculiar pleasurable feeling from pulling hair; he then regressed him to the age of seven, which was when the problem had started. He suggested that beginning at age seven he would feel a slight discomfort when he pulled a hair, and this would increase in intensity so that by age twenty-one each pull would be distinctly uncomfortable but not necessarily painful. He was returned to his present age, and when he began to pull a hair he exclaimed, ''Ouch, that hurt!'' There was no more hairpulling and the hair grew back on his scalp.[2]

In one study the client was told to collect all the hair that she pulled out each day, place it in an envelope, note the time of the occurrence and record her feelings and behaviour. She was also told to record any urges she had to pull her hair. She was then told to do fifteen sit-ups whenever she attempted to pull her hair, and when her urges to pull her hair arose she was to brush or groom her hair.

Hypnotic techniques have also been used, combined with video recordings, to make patients more aware of the habit and of the situations which triggered off the hairpulling. Electric shocks to the backs of the hands while the patient was watching the hairplucking on video produced marked reduction of hairpulling over a long period.[3]

There have been other successful treatments where the habit was simply replaced with a state of relaxation, by training the patient to use self-hypnosis to induce a highly relaxed state whenever the desire to pull hair occurred, and also by systematic desensitisation — that is, training the person to relax at each movement in the chain of events that led to pulling the hair, from the first movement of the hand onward.

Earlier treatments mainly involved psychoanalysis, but this usually produced poor results. Psychotropic drugs, such as amitryptiline and trifluoperazine, have brought about improvement, as has the simple expedient of keeping the hair shaved until the patient loses interest.

HAIRPULLING SCRIPT

From this time forward you will gradually lose interest in pulling out your hair . . . your scalp will become more and more sensitive as you pull each hair out, and it will become more and more unpleasant for you to do so . . . there will be no pleasure in it any more, just annoyance and irritation.

Now, go backwards in time to when your hairpulling first started . . . backwards through the years as if you were flipping through the pages of a book . . . now, experience what was happening at that time, the circumstances that led to you pulling out your hair.

Now, go forward in time to when you no longer pull out your hair . . . keep going forward to the time when there is no further need to pull out your hair . . . experience the changes in thoughts and feelings and actions and attitudes that make it unnecessary for you to pull out your hair.

Now, come back to the present time . . . from this time forward you will experience the necessary changes in thoughts and feelings and actions and attitudes that will make pulling out your hair quite remote from your needs.

Your unconscious mind will arrange this somehow, safely, and it may let you know what is going on, or it may decide not to . . . whatever happens, it will become completely unnecessary to pull out your hair.

TICS AND SPASMS

A tic is a convulsive movement, a spasmodic jerking in a coordinated group of muscles. The term covers compulsive eye-blinking, muscle spasms, throat clearing, lip licking and various facial grimaces.

Freud's quaint description of the underlying problem was that a person with tics suffers from "reminiscences". Modern behaviourists differ little from psychoanalysts in believing that a tic is associated with a fear-related memory. Psychoanalysts believe that the only way to deal with the tic is to recall and re-experience the fear-related incident, whereas behaviourists try to eliminate it by various techniques such as massed practice, in which the person repeats the behaviour deliberately and rapidly for some time. One therapist used white noise (static) immediately following the tic or spasm. Relaxation alone can reduce the behaviour as it tends to increase under tension and anxiety.

In the case of a student from Washington State college, the subject was twenty-one years old and had suffered with severe eye-blinking and a facial grimace for fifteen years. He was introverted and highly anxious and avoided social situations, so treatment was aimed at developing more social contacts, and discussing his feelings of rejection and isolation, followed by hypnosis as a regular therapy. During hypnosis the reason for the development of the tic — a humiliating experience at the age of six at a boys' camp — was uncovered, and the tic disappeared, but later reappeared temporarily when he broke off with a girlfriend.[4]

Hypnosis was used successfully in the case of a fifty-seven-year-old man from Oklahoma, USA, who had a condition called spastic torticollis, in which his head and neck kept pulling to the left, particularly under stress. He had had the condition since he was nine and it had been getting worse and interfering with his public relations work.

With the use of age regression the patient was asked to go back to the time the problem started. He went back to when he was about seven or eight years old and in an operating theatre just after having his tonsils removed. He heard a male voice stating that the patient had expired and then asking someone to turn his head towards the right to see if anything could possibly be done for him. He tried to pull away because he knew he was all right, and then he coughed and started to breathe. The remarks had frightened him so much the incident became a recurring nightmare, especially when he was upset or tense. He then developed his head-pulling to the left, which somehow relieved his tension.[5]

TIC OR SPASM SCRIPT

From now on you will transfer the twitching of your face to the little finger of the left hand . . . all the symptoms will become condensed into your little finger . . . you can, if you wish, choose the time of day that this will occur . . . after this has happened you will give yourself permission for the twitching of the little finger to increase or decrease, then you will gradually lose the twitching of your little finger altogether. Perhaps this will happen next week, or next month . . . soon you will be completely free of movements that are outside your control.

That is a script based on Erickson's method of symptom transformation. You could also build in the dream script (on page 231), asking for some illumination as to the cause of your problem, not forgetting to add that only as much as you can comfortably cope with will be revealed to your conscious mind.

NAILBITING

Milton Erickson used an ingenious "double bind" technique with a twenty-six-year-old student who had been biting his fingernails since he was four years of age. The problem began in an attempt to escape four hours of daily piano practice, but although he chewed his fingernails to the quick, his mother ignored the blood on the piano keys and the piano practice continued, as did his nailbiting.

He had not willingly sought treatment, but was sent by his parents. Erickson pointed out that he had been depriving himself since he was four of the privilege of biting off a good-sized piece of fingernail and instead had been frustrating himself by nibbling away at tiny bits of nail. He convinced the student that he could grow one long fingernail while continuing to nibble away at the other nine digits.

Months later the student returned with a normal set of fingernails, and said, "At first I thought the whole thing hilariously funny, even though you were serious in your attitude. Then I felt myself being pulled two ways. I wanted ten long fingernails. You said I could have only one and I had to end up by biting it off and getting a 'real mouthful of fingernail'." The student became more and more frustrated with biting little bits of nail, and more upset about the idea of destroying his one good nail, so he allowed another nail to grow, and then another, and then said, "To hell with it!"[6]

Other people have used more conventional methods. As usual, there are aversive behaviour methods with fairly gruesome covert suggestions connected with vomit, but I will not go into those. An interesting and fairly successful (though still aversive) method was reported in 1942 when the practitioner suggested to twenty boys in a summer camp while they slept that from then on their nails would taste terribly bitter when they chewed them.[7]

A well-conducted experiment at the University of Montana combined hypnosis and behaviour modification techniques. The team used a standard hypnotic induction and deepening technique, followed by motivation enhancement suggestions and ego-strengthening suggestions. They incorporated personally tailored suggestions into the script, based on the subjects' reasons for wanting to stop their nailbiting. A sample script follows:

> You are very confident of overcoming the nailbiting habit and you have made a commitment to stop biting your nails. You are in complete control of your nailbiting urges and have decided to stop in order to make your hands more attractive and eliminate the frequent painfulness of torn nails. Since you have decided to stop nailbiting, you'll feel proud of yourself, pleased that you have control over your body, and victorious over the diminishing urges to nailbite.

The subjects were then projected into the future, when they had long attractive fingernails, aversive suggestions were made about the unpleasant taste of the nails, and positive suggestions were made about how pleased and refreshed they would feel when they resisted the urge to bite their nails. Later they were taught self-hypnosis to continue the process at home. After a number of follow-ups they showed a dramatic increase in nail length.[8]

NAILBITING SCRIPT

> More and more, your growing calmness and confidence will make biting your nails become remote from your needs . . . from now on, as soon as you start to lift your hand to your mouth you will feel annoyed and irritated with yourself . . . really uncomfortable . . . and you will stop and think what a ridiculous and unnecessary habit biting your nails is.
>
> Straight away you will redirect your hands to your sides, or your pockets, or to some other activity . . . as you do this the feeling of irritation and annoyance will disappear and be replaced by a feeling of wellbeing and pride . . . you will feel relaxed, confident and in complete control.
>
> If you occasionally weaken you will bite just one nail on each hand until gradually you stop biting first one of those nails, then the other . . . very soon you won't want or need to bite your nails at all, you just won't feel the need.
>
> If it is necessary, your unconscious mind will select one or more safe, pleasant replacement activities for your hands and your mouth . . . perhaps a silent whistle with your lips

pursing a little until you no longer feel the need to bite your nails . . . perhaps the little finger on your left hand will twitch slightly whenever you need to bite your nails . . . perhaps just relaxing your body and your mind will be all that is needed to help you give up your nailbiting.

17
FEARS AND PHOBIAS

We all have realistic fears of some things. Fear becomes irrational when it is out of proportion to the real danger, is out of the control of the person, and leads to exaggerated avoidance of the feared situation or object. This type of fear is called a phobia.

Some people believe that phobias are linked to a more primitive level of functioning: that a person develops a phobia to something that has at some stage in man's evolutionary process threatened survival. Researchers in the USA surveyed a random sample of 1000 people in Vermont, and compared the list of common fears in the sample with the list of phobias. They found that the sample of 1000 people shared 2052 common fears, with snakes, heights, storms, flying, dentists and injury heading the list. The same sample shared only seventy-four phobias, of which the commonest were illness and injury, storms, animals, agoraphobia, death, crowds and heights.[1]

There are two classic case studies of the development of phobias in children, the behavioural report of eleven-month-old Albert and the white rat, and the psychoanalytic study of little Hans and his fear of horses. Albert developed a fear of white rats in an experiment (which by today's standards is deplorable) conducted by Watson and Rayner in 1920. They made a sudden loud noise whenever Albert reached out to touch the rat. What had at first intrigued the baby now made him scream in terror. The phobia later generalised to other objects — white rabbits, cotton wool, white handkerchiefs, dogs, fur coats and a mask of Santa Claus with a long white beard.[2] Unfortunately, the orphan was removed from the hospital where he had been living before the experimenters could decondition him.

In 1909 a patient of Sigmund Freud, five-year-old Hans, would not go out into the street because of his intense fear that a horse might bite him. According to Freud, this fear of horses had been converted from a fear that his father would cut off his penis (castration anxiety), caused by a combination of factors: feelings of hostility and jealousy towards his father, who the boy wished would die so that he could marry his mother (the Oedipus complex), together with threats made when he was found masturbating, and the sight of a penis-less girl playmate. This fear, and consequently the fear of horses, was later overcome when Hans was encouraged to imagine his father robbing him of his little penis and replacing it with a bigger one.[3] (The Oedipus complex is, in psychoanalytic theory, supposed to be largely unconscious and to exist in one form or another in every family. It is the unresolved desire of a child for sexual gratification through the parent of the opposite sex. The female equivalent is known as the Electra complex.)

Treatment of phobias almost always involves exposure to the situation the person fears, in relatively comforting circumstances. By far the most common treatment is that of systematic desensitisation, in real life or in imagination. Sometimes flooding is used, sometimes cognitive restructuring and sometimes psychoanalytic uncovering techniques, but the most efficient and least challenged method is that of systematic desensitisation, especially when used in conjunction with hypnosis.

School phobia is a relatively common problem with children and according to those who have worked with this problem it is not so much a fear of school as a fear of leaving home, and represents an unhealthy interdependence or conflict between parent and child. It is sometimes difficult to know whether a child has a school phobia in that sense, or is genuinely afraid of some real situation at school. Social imitation, or modelling, works well with children as does systematic desensitisation. In one case a phobic schoolboy was persuaded to imagine himself being accompanied to school by a comic-book hero. That would have been an even more powerful image if it had been used in conjunction with hypnosis.[4] School phobia has also been successfully treated with psychoanalytic uncovering techniques combined with hypnosis. In this instance, all the children suffered from traumatic backgrounds and had many underlying conflicts and fears.[5]

AGORAPHOBIA

Agoraphobia has the hallmarks of a grown-up's school phobia. The accepted meaning of the word is a fear of crowded places and open spaces, derived from the Greek words *agora*, meaning marketplace or place of assembly, and *phobos*, meaning flight or panic. But like school phobia, a more accurate description of agoraphobia is an exaggeratedly fearful reaction to being away from the safety of home.

My first experience with an agoraphobic was when I was getting out of my car to shop in the middle of the city and a woman grabbed my arm and begged, "Please help me!" She was shaking violently, was whitefaced, and had beads of perspiration on her forehead. I opened the door of the car again and sat her down, opening the window next to her. Then I talked calmly to her until her terror had subsided. It was the first attack she had suffered, as she had not ventured into the city for a long time, preferring to potter around the shops in her home territory. Some agoraphobics cannot bring themselves to move outside their homes, and some are even confined to one or two rooms in the home.

British practitioner M. A. Basker treated two women with agoraphobia by the "clenched fist" method. This is similar to the "anchoring" technique from Bandler and Grinder's neurolinguistic programming. In trance the person is invited to concentrate on a thought, memory, name or feeling which comes to mind after a prearranged signal — for example, the person may wish to recall one of the happiest days of their lives. Then they are asked to close the fist of the dominant hand and recall additional facets of the same memory. This procedure is repeated so that clenching the fist becomes a trigger for the good memory and good feelings. If an unpleasant memory is released by the prearranged signal, the person is to dwell on this for a while, then clench the dominant hand. Basker taught patients to count up to five and vividly imagine agoraphobic scenes and feelings while clenching the non-dominant hand, then count down to zero, imagining scenes of happiness, confidence and relaxation while transferring the fist-clenching to the dominant hand.[6]

Dr Claire Weekes has written an excellent book on agoraphobia[7], which can be supplemented by cassettes and records she has produced, as well as other books. I am sure that her methods have an excellent chance of curing or bringing about considerable improvement in those suffering from this problem, as well as helping them understand what is happening to them and why.

She has treated thousands of agoraphobic patients either in person or by remote direction (with books, cassettes, etc.) and I have extracted some of the information conveyed in her book:

• Roughly sixty per cent of phobic patients could be labelled agoraphobic. Ninety-one per cent were females, mostly married (it seems that men's anxiety usually manifests itself in ways other than agoraphobia). The majority became ill in their twenties or thirties. They represent a cross section of the community and aren't especially neurotic.

• Precipitating causes of agoraphobia in order of frequency were: physical illness (for example, following a surgical operation, difficult confinement, tuberculosis, infection, arthritis), domestic stress in adult life, loss of a loved one, difficulty or pressure at work, domineering, unstable, unhappy or alcoholic parents, the sudden occurrence of frightening symptoms when out of the home, and so on.

Dr Weekes writes about the easy arousal of intense emotional and nervous responses of the agoraphobic. She calls such arousal "sensitisation". In other words, reverberated circuits in the nervous system bring about heightened responses so that a spasm of fear can be felt as a flash of panic. Such a flash naturally brings more fear, which then of course creates more panic, and so a cycle of fear-panic-fear is established. This exaggerated response is the basis of an anxiety attack.

Dr Weekes speaks of two fears: the fear felt originally, which brings exaggerated symptoms, and the fear that the sufferer adds when feeling these symptoms. She calls these "first fear" and "second fear", and adds that the second fear keeps the first fear alive and so keeps the nervously ill person sensitised, hence ill.

The book contains a likely explanation of how sensitisation occurs and points out that agoraphobia is usually a further development after an already sensitised person is suffering from anxiety attacks.

The doctor stresses four concepts in treatment:
- face — do not run away;
- accept — do not fight;
- float — do not tense;
- let time pass — do not be impatient with time.

Sufferers need to accept and go through the first fear, and add as little as possible of the second fear. If they can do this, the panic attacks will gradually cease to matter, until eventually they disappear.

She points out that "the realisation that they were being bluffed by no more than physical feelings of no great medical significance has cured some people".

Treatment by Dr Weekes either personally or by remote direction has led to the recovery of many people from nervous illnesses, including agoraphobia. By "recovery", the doctor means that the sufferers are able to cope with occasional setbacks because they have, through their own efforts, finally reached the stage where their symptoms no longer matter.

AGORAPHOBIA SCRIPT

From this time forward, whenever the feelings of panic start to rise, you will face those feelings and stay with them . . . accept them.

You will relax your body, let your body go slack . . . let go
. . . release your tension . . . take a deep breath . . . breathe
slowly and deeply.

You will let your body loosen, float through what is
happening . . . you will be willing to let time pass . . .
perfectly willing to let the time pass . . . detach yourself
from your feelings about what is happening . . . your
unconscious mind will tell your body that there is nothing
at all physically wrong with it . . . it is simply that your
oversensitive nerves are playing tricks on you.

From now on, a little at a time, you will venture out into
the places which once made you nervous . . . you will find
that from now on you will feel comfortable and at ease,
quite relaxed and calm in these places.

You will feel pleasantly excited, and will look forward to
outings and visits . . . you will look people in the eye,
confidently, and will no longer feel you are the focus of
everyone's attention . . . if people appear to be looking at
you it won't bother you, it will seem just as if they are
observing you with some fairly remote, slight interest . . . it
will not bother you at all . . . you will glance at them
without feeling self-conscious and observe them in turn,
with a little interest . . . you will take more and more
pleasure from venturing out, and you will be able to forget
how you once felt . . . you will take pleasure in observing
other people and seeking their company.

There will be fewer and fewer returns of your feelings of
panic, and they will become less intense . . . immediately
you will slow your breathing down, relax and become calmer
and calmer . . . gradually you will take control over these
feelings and they will fade away . . . very soon they will be a
thing of the past . . . occasional setbacks will only be
temporary . . . they will quickly be followed by successes.

Any left-over feelings will be converted into a tiny inner
trembling or vibration . . . they will soon cease to bother
you . . . they will no longer matter.

ANIMAL PHOBIAS

In a recent journal devoted almost entirely to treatment of
phobias, the authors described techniques for treating various
animal phobias including phobias of dead birds and bovine
sounds. Also included in this issue were reports of a successful

treatment of a twenty-one-year-old female with a slug phobia and a group of nine snake phobics.[8]

Animal phobias are fairly common, particularly of dogs, cats, birds and spiders. Such phobias are usually dealt with in individual therapy sessions.

ANIMAL PHOBIA SCRIPT

As desensitisation is the usual approach to animal phobias, I suggest, if the animal is not dangerous:

> Imagine the animal standing behind the bars of a cage (as at the zoo), imagine this vividly ... now say the word "relax" in your mind, breathe slowly and deeply ... relax your mind and your body.
>
> Now, imagine the animal is ten feet away from you looking at something in the distance, not at you, just standing there ... imagine this vividly, clearly ... now, say the word "relax" to yourself, in your mind ... relax completely, breathe slowly and deeply.
>
> Now the animal is closer, a few feet away, looking at you ... you look back at it steadily and calmly, relaxing, breathing more slowly and deeply ... relaxing your mind and your body.
>
> Imagine someone you greatly admire handling the animal, standing quite close to you and touching the animal, quite enjoying the situation ... relax, breathe slowly and deeply, calmly.
>
> You move closer and put your hand out to touch the animal ... relaxed and calm, you have nothing to fear ... relaxing and slowing down your breathing.
>
> Now you are touching it with your hand ... relaxed and calm ... it all seems so easy ... your fear has gone ... breathing slowly and regularly, relaxing your mind and your body ... quite calm.
>
> From now on whenever you see the animal you will be less and less bothered by it ... less and less fearful until finally you feel completely neutral towards this animal ... completely free of emotion ... it has ceased to be of importance in any way.

SNAKE PHOBIA

University researchers probing into the mysteries of phobias seem to favour snake phobics for their experiments, possibly because the student population from which they usually obtain their "guinea pigs" contains snake phobics in sufficient numbers to make their results valid. Also, non-poisonous reptiles are fairly easily obtainable for experiments.

Nine snake phobics were selected from highly hypnotiseable subjects by a team from a university in New York State, and given four systematic desensitisation treatment sessions as well as five sessions in which a pleasant post-hypnotic dream connected with snakes was suggested. For example, one of the dreams suggested was meeting Robert Redford or Farrah Fawcett (depending on the personal preference) and flirting and talking while he/she nurses his/her pet snake.[9]

SNAKE PHOBIA SCRIPT

Here is a snake phobia hierarchy used in an experiment at Queen's University in Ontario, Canada[10]:

Imagine there is a large, harmless snake, a boa constrictor, in a glass cage, and you are standing and looking at it. Now:

1. You are standing sixteen feet from the cage ... relax, breathe deeply.
2. You are standing eleven feet from the cage (ditto)
3. You are standing seven feet from the cage (ditto)
4. You are standing four feet from the cage (ditto)
5. You are standing two feet from the cage (ditto)
6. You are standing one foot from the cage (ditto)
7. You are looking at the snake through the screen on top (ditto)
8. You are placing a hand against the glass of the cage (ditto)
9. You are lifting the top screen a few centimetres (ditto)
10. You are removing the top screen completely (ditto)
11. You are looking down into the cage with the screen removed (ditto)
12. You are putting a pointer into the cage (ditto)
13. You are touching the snake with the pointer (ditto)
14. You are wearing a leather glove and placing a hand into the cage without touching the snake (ditto)
15. You are touching the snake briefly with the gloved hand (ditto)

FLYING PHOBIA

It is possible that a substantial contribution to flying phobia is made by factors associated with flying, other than the flight itself. The machines selling life insurance, the words *terminal, departure lounge, last and final call* and the demonstration of emergency equipment by flight crew could all add to an aura of impending doom.

Two clinicians from Kentucky needed to give only two treatment sessions to a thirty-year-old woman with a history of severe panic during plane trips. They used Erickson's idea of pseudo-orientation in time (see page 227). The client was asked to imagine and describe her future plane flight as it would be following a complete treatment success. After a slight hitch, to deal with the fact that her real fear was of loss of control — of her life being in the hands of a stranger — she was able to visualise a calm and relaxed trip during which she read and talked to her husband. She soon afterwards completed two journeys with only a slight anxiety in the first one when approaching for landing. A six-month follow-up showed the treatment to be still effective.[11]

A team from Stanford and Columbia Universities treated 178 flying phobia patients with hypnosis used in conjunction with the primary treatment method; that is, they instructed each patient to conceive of the aeroplane as an extension of their own body while maintaining a physical sense of floating and relaxation. In addition, patients were taught to focus on the difference between a probability and a possibility. In essence, rather than being instructed not to worry, patients were instructed how to worry from a new point of view and to use this self-hypnosis exercise in preparation for a trip and during it.

Results were not known for some of the patients, as the follow-ups took place from six months to ten and a half years after the treatment, so a quite conservative estimate was that fifty-two per cent showed some improvement or complete mastery of their phobia. They found a much greater success rate among highly hypnotiseable patients.[12]

Here is a flight phobia hierarchy which can be included in the basic script:

FLYING PHOBIA SCRIPT

1. Imagine it is a pleasant, sunny day at the airport, a day on which nothing can bother you . . . you are at the flight counter, checking your ticket and booking your luggage. Now, relax and slow down your breathing and think of a pleasant scene.
2. You are travelling on the escalator up to the flight lounge. Now, relax . . . (*ditto*)
3. You wander about for a while, watching through the

window the planes taking off and landing. You then go and
take a seat in the flight lounge. (*ditto*)
4. The loudspeaker announces that your flight is boarding.
(*ditto*)
5. You walk along the long corridors to the plane entrance.
(*ditto*)
6. You enter the plane, and the flight attendant shows you
to your seat. (*ditto*)
7. The engine starts, the seat belt sign flashes, and the flight
attendant gives you instructions. (*ditto*)
8. The plane takes off and settles into flight . . . you are still
relaxed, breathing slowly. You start to read a magazine, then
doze off for a while.
9. The plane lands, the door opens and you disembark,
feeling refreshed and eager for what lies ahead.

You can incorporate imagery of sounds and sensations into the
script if you wish, the vibration of the plane, the clunk as the
wheels are lowered, the feeling of the cool air from the air-
conditioner on your face.

While the above script is a counter-conditioning script, the
following one is a more standard systematic desensitisation
script. For this it is necessary to construct a hierarchy of fears
from least stressful to most stressful, and work through these in
real life (if possible) or in imagination, relaxing as you do.

FEAR OF WATER

Fear of water is another common phobia. The following hierarchy
can be included in the basic script:

FEAR OF WATER SCRIPT
1. Imagine you are putting on your swimming costume in
the dressing room at the local swimming pool. Relax,
breathe deeply and think of a pleasant scene.
2. You are walking out to the dressing room onto the
concrete and tiles around the pool and stand there for a
while in the sun, watching the other swimmers. Relax . . .
(*ditto*)
3. You sit at the edge of the pool, dangling your feet in the
water. (*ditto*)
4. Now, you walk down the steps at the shallow end of the
pool and into the water, which is up to your thighs. (*ditto*)
5. You take a deep breath again and while slowly releasing

it put your head under the water ... relax, be calm, think
pleasant thoughts.
6. See yourself swimming, totally relaxed and confident ...
safe and calm and confident as you swim through the water.

DENTAL TREATMENT PHOBIA

Extreme reluctance to visit the dentist has resulted in people
ignoring decaying teeth and sore or bleeding gums, conditions
which may be related to illness in other parts of the body. Some
Freudians believed dental phobia to be an instance of castration
anxiety or of penetration anxiety, and behaviourists put it down
to fear learned during unfortunate experiences in the dentist's
chair.

Dental treatment may of course threaten respiration, particularly when the patient is unable to breathe adequately through
the nose. The patient may not realise that he or she is partly or
even wholly mouth-breathing until in the dental chair with a
mouth full of instruments. This often causes a gagging reflex as
well as feelings of intense anxiety.

I know of one woman who had avoided dentists for over ten
years because of a phobia induced when an orthodontist filled her
mouth with a soft plasticine-like substance to obtain an
impression.

DENTAL TREATMENT PHOBIA SCRIPT

From now on you will feel calm and detached about a visit
to the dentist and the anxiety and discomfort you have
previously experienced will grow less and less until it
completely disappears.

Picture yourself now, quite relaxed, entering the dental
surgery for a check-up, picture the dentist locating a filling
that needs attending to, a decayed tooth that requires a
filling ... you will no longer need an injection because you
will feel no pain or discomfort, but if it really comforts you
to have one you will be conscious of just a tiny prick, and
then numbness. Whether you ask for an injection or not
your perception of pain and discomfort in this situation will
be changed from now on ... your body will release its own
natural painkillers and you will feel no discomfort whatever,
even if the procedure is a complicated one ... you will feel
no pain or discomfort, very little blood will be lost from an
extraction, swelling will be reduced to a minimum, and after

the treatment your mouth will settle down very, very quickly . . . back to normal.

Have a mental image of yourself now, in the dentist's chair as he works on your mouth, relaxed, calm, thinking pleasant thoughts of things to look forward to . . . any discomfort you have experienced in the past is now nonexistent.

You could add the time falsification suggestions from the Erickson section (page 229), or you could make up a systematic desensitisation script from the following hierarchy:

1. You make an appointment to see the dentist.
2. You arrive at the surgery and take your seat.
3. You read a magazine while you wait.
4. Your name is called, and you walk in and sit in the dentist's chair.
5. The dentist proceeds with your treatment, drilling and filling your teeth.
6. You get up and leave, making an appointment for the next treatment.

Erickson treated a patient with a dental phobia who had for years avoided the extensive dental work he needed because of an obsession that it would involve unbearable pain, no matter what was done. He could achieve hypnotic anaesthesia anywhere except his mouth which remained hypersensitive. Erickson suggested that his left hand would become excruciatingly hypersensitive. The patient was then assured the dentist would take extreme care not to brush against his hypersensitive hand.

Erickson said "Note where the left hand is, now turn and let the dentist go to work," after which extensive dental work was accomplished without any direct suggestions of dental anaesthesia or use of chemical agents.[13]

LIFT PHOBIA

Here is a suggested hierarchy for a lift phobia:
1. Entering a tall building and standing at the door of the lift with a friend
2. Entering the lift and going down one floor, to the lower ground, then leaving the lift, still with your friend
3. Pressing the button again and taking the lift up one floor, back to the ground floor, then stepping out

4. Repeating this, going two floors up at a time, still with your friend
5. Travelling to the top floor, leaving the lift and admiring the view
6. Taking the lift back down again to the ground floor
7. Repeating this, without being accompanied by a friend.

Erickson believed that most people are only afraid of going up in the lift, so you might prefer to try this script:

> As you go up in the lift you will experience the feelings that you normally do going down . . . relief that soon you will be able to leave the lift, the pleasant bodily experiences of descending . . . feelings of relief and pleasant sensations will be all that you will be aware of in future whenever you enter a lift.

18
BREATHING, SKIN AND HEART PROBLEMS

Breathing, heart and skin problems often have a psychological component. They can be entirely emotionally induced, or they can be made worse by stress or emotional upheaval. It makes good sense to use hypnosis along with other treatments, even if the problems are apparently of physical origin, as it is becoming clear that we have a lot more potential for control of our autonomic nervous system functions than Western medicine once believed.

ASTHMA

Bronchial asthma is high on the list of chronic diseases. It can be triggered off by allergic reactions, bronchial infections and emotional disturbances. Most studies have shown that even in the presence of allergic conditions some emotional overlay usually accompanies the attack of asthma. It has been established that during periods of extreme emergency or fright asthma will clear up and disappear.[1]

Many believe asthma to be a conditioned response, and bronchial spasm and increased mucus secretion have successfully been induced experimentally in dogs, goats, sheep and guinea pigs. American researchers in 1968 induced asthma in nineteen out of forty chronic sufferers by tricking them into believing they were inhaling allergic substances. They actually breathed air containing a non-irritant salt-water mist, yet they reacted as if the allergic substances were present and most of them developed full-blown asthma attacks. The symptoms were then removed by having them inhale the same salt-water mist they had been told was an effective asthma remedy.[2]

A consultant physician from Royal Hobart Hospital, Tasmania, Dr Paul S. Clarke, has induced asthma attacks with suggestions of anxiety and fear and by suggesting asthma itself; he has also reversed the process with suggestions of relaxation. He says, "One can, in fact, under hypnosis, talk directly to the bronchial musculature and have it obey one's commands." In his opinion the most important problem in asthma is that of hyperventilation (overbreathing).[3]

Hypnosis alone, and hypnosis in conjunction with other techniques such as systematic desensitisation, has been found to be considerably successful in treating asthma. A consultant physician from Sydney reported on 121 asthma sufferers seen over a ten-year period. He treated them with hypnotherapy aimed at ego-enhancement, problem analysis and the emotional expression of repressed experiences. Twenty-five showed excellent results, forty showed good results and fifty-six made little or no improvement. Nineteen out of the twenty-five reporting excellent results were capable of entering a deep trance.[4]

Nine patients in the USA were treated by hypnosis and systematic desensitisation. A hierarchy of feared situations was presented under hypnosis. The time taken for the therapy ranged from four to twenty-three visits, and all patients showed marked improvement, being able to resume normal lives, whereas before treatment they had been repeatedly admitted to hospital.[5]

An eight-year-old Queensland boy was treated with a procedure that included hypnotic dissociation, that is, splitting off from conscious awareness. The asthma usually occurred on the eve of some exciting or demanding event, and he was taught that whenever he felt an attack coming on he would in imagination ride off on his horse Jacko.[6]

BREATHING PROBLEM SCRIPT

From this time forward, whenever your breathing starts to become difficult you will immediately calm down, and relax your body, your mind and your internal organs . . . you will release all tension, and become remote, detached and tranquil.

Your body and your mind will leap into action to combat the problem with your breathing . . . you will relax and be calm, feeling strong and confident of your ability to control your breathing and bring it back to normal . . . you will take a deep, slow breath, filling your lungs with oxygen, hold it for a while, and then release it slowly . . . as you do this you will feel your bronchial tubes opening, expanding, allowing the cool, clean, fresh air to flow through your air passages, feel your rib cage expanding, relaxing . . . feeling comfortable, protected and secure.

Do this right now, breathe deeply, preferably through your nose, hold it for a while, and then release it slowly, also through your nose (*pause*) . . . feeling stronger and healthier already . . . full of confidence that from now on every time your breathing becomes difficult, you will straight away commence breathing more slowly and more deeply . . . very

quickly returning your breathing to normal, filling your
lungs with oxygen, and then releasing it . . . breathing out
slowly.

   From now on the excess fluid in your lungs will gradually
dry up and your lungs will become more and more normal,
with just the usual amount of fluid necessary for normal
functioning . . . as much as is possible the elasticity of your
lungs will become more normal . . . as the secretion of the
fluid returns to normal, the elasticity will improve,
gradually, more and more . . . gradually you will become
less sensitive to those things you are at present allergic to,
less and less reaction will take place until finally there will
be no reaction at all.

I have tried to make the script general enough to cover asthma,
emphysema and bronchitis. If asthma is the problem it is a good
idea to combine this script with the hostility, anger and guilt
scripts in Chapter 19. Asthma patients are thought to suppress
intense emotions that involve threats to their dependent
relationships, and under tension the autonomic nervous system
causes constriction of the bronchi with increased secretions. The
famous physician of Ancient Greece, Hippocrates, said over 2000
years ago that ''asthmatics must guard against strong anger''.

WARTS

Warts are a common skin problem resulting from a viral
infection. The *papova* virus is responsible for all types of warts:
the common wart, which can occur anywhere but more often
appears on the face, hands or arms; the plantar wart, which is
often hard to treat and painful, and is deeply embedded in the
soles of the feet; and the *condyloma acuminatum*, which are
warts of the genital and anal areas. These latter warts can be
sexually transmitted, but can also occur without any such
exposure, and may be related to malignancy.

   Warts may be burnt off or removed surgically, but often recur.
Many weird and wonderful treatments have been proposed
including charming warts away using a dead cat in the graveyard
at midnight, as was tried by Tom Sawyer and Huckleberry Finn.
What these methods do point to is the powerful influence of
belief and suggestion in the cure of warts, which brings about
changes in the blood supply to the wart area, mediated by the
autonomic nervous system.

   With hypnotic induction reinforcing the strength of the

suggestions, clinicians usually report a very high rate of success with wart remission, something in the area of seventy to eighty per cent.

A British physician saw thirty-three patients suffering from multiple warts for treatment periods of up to ten weeks, and suggested under hypnosis that the warts would go away. Fifteen of the thirty-three patients were completely cured, and many improved, but the people who showed little improvement tended to be the least hypnotiseable.[7]

Another British experiment, carried out in 1959, suggested to ten hypnotiseable and four relatively unhypnotiseable patients, while they were under hypnosis, that the warts on one side of the body would disappear. Within five weeks to three months, nine of the ten hypnotiseable patients had lost their warts on the suggested side only while the four other patients remained unchanged.[8]

David Sheehan from Harvard Medical School reported the treatment by hypnotherapy of a large wart which had been removed several times but had recurred. A deep, red vascular bed surrounded it as a result of repeated surgery, and during the hypnotic induction, in which the subject was asked to visualise the wart melting away and disappearing, the bed around the base of the wart blanched. The blanching remained for fifteen minutes after the end of the induction and one week later the wart was gone. Sheehan suggested that changes in the blood vessels at the base of the wart could be a factor in the accelerated remission.[9]

A practitioner who successfully treated four cases of warts of the penis, and described his procedure with before and after photographs, used the following suggestions:

Your body has the capacity to overcome the wart virus and heal this infection. Focus your attention on the involved area and soon you will notice a sensation of warmth in the surrounding skin as the blood vessels dilate to bring in more antibodies and white blood cells to fight the infection, and more protein and oxygen to help build the new and normal tissue when the wart has gone away. When you can feel the increased warmth, your left index finger will rise . . . now your inner mind will lock in on this and maintain this warmth until the warts are healed and your skin becomes normal in every way. You can forget about the warts and turn your conscious thoughts to other things, because your natural healing processes will cure the warts without your having any further concern about them.[10]

WARTS SCRIPT

If you concentrate hard enough, you can redirect the flow of blood from one place to another by conscious effort ... but you have no real need to use such a lot of conscious effort, because from now on your unconscious mind is going to get rid of your wart by cutting off the supply of blood which keeps your wart thriving ... without affecting any other area, the supply of blood will be diverted away from your wart and it will gradually dwindle away and finally disappear altogether.

That suggestion is taken from an article that is described in detail in the section on cancer in Chapter 21.[11]

BLUSHING

Blushing is another embarrassing physical symptom that is amenable to the manipulation of blood flow from one place to another. It is another quite devilish reaction of the autonomic nervous system to a real, imagined or obscure threat.

I have not heard of people blushing when they are alone, so the threat has to involve concern about the opinions of others and is a public admission of a person's insecurity and guilt feelings, most likely unconscious.

Most people who blush are extremely self-conscious about it, more so than it warrants compared to, say, a chronic stutter, but they are right in their perception that it is quite obvious to others. However, other people may react in one of two ways. They may either think, "Hello, hello, what's this one been up to?", or think it is rather disarming, an indication of qualities like shyness and modesty.

You might consider adding extracts to the script below from the assertiveness and rational thinking scripts in Chapter 22, as the only reports I could find in my hypnosis journals of treatment for blushing involved rational-emotive therapy, assertiveness training and imagery of heat and cold.

Dr Kent Welsh, a Texan, was successful in dramatically reducing the incidence of blushing in a twenty-seven-year-old woman by teaching her to flush, with images of a hot shower and other heat images (sauna, sun, etc.), and then getting the flush to disappear by using imagery of cool tubs, ice houses, cold water swimming pools and so on, training her to switch quickly from heat to cold imagery, and from flushing to absence of flushing.

These training sessions utilised hypnosis, but at the same time she attended non-hypnotic group sessions in assertiveness. In discussing the case, Dr Welsh pointed out that it was difficult to say just what had been responsible for the decrease in blushing, but the assertiveness training had been in progress for quite some time before the hypnotic imagery was commenced and only after this did the woman show improvement.

Dr Welsh felt that the change came about mainly because the subject was provided with proof that she could control her internal functions. She had a history of helplessness and feeling out of control, of being self-deprecating, non-assertive and easily manipulated by others, and to her the fact that she blushed so easily was objective evidence that she was unable to control her feelings. When she learned to control the internal sympathetic functioning of her skin temperature, this then led her to believe she could similarly control her feelings.[12]

BLUSHING SCRIPT

From now on, whenever you find yourself starting to blush your unconscious mind will divert the excess blood, which is about to flow to your face, to your right hand instead . . . and as this keeps happening your blush will gradually subside and finally disappear altogether.

Just as soon as the blush starts to rise it will be diverted to your right hand and have difficulty reaching your face and neck . . . your hand will become warm and pink . . . concentrate right now on making your hand warm and pink for a little while by transferring extra blood to it.

This is what will happen from now on every time you start to blush . . . as you start to blush the blood that is being conducted to your face and neck will be converted to your right hand.

From this time forward your unconscious mind will find safe, relevant, alternative ways of serving the purpose that your blush is serving . . . ways that are not so apparent to other people that will achieve the same result . . . your unconscious mind will help you to come to terms with things in your past that cause you to blush . . . it may let you know about it or it may not . . . in dreams you may or may not remember, dreams that will work through these past events and help you resolve them.

Soon, there will be no need at all to blush, no need at all . . . you will feel confident, self assured and any left-over guilts and anxieties will be sorted out by your unconscious mind.

RASHES

Rashes caused by eczema, psoriasis and neurodermatitis are assumed to be connected with the autonomic nervous system and therefore also strongly related to emotional factors. Both the skin and the brain originate from the same embryonic layer (ectoderm), and organisms which attack the skin, such as chicken pox and measles, also involve the central nervous system. As well, the skin is a key organ for expressing emotional states, such as blushing in embarrassment, perspiring with nervousness, becoming pale through shock, having goose pimples with fear, and so on. Rashes are thought to be of similar underlying origin to stammering — repressed hostility — although why the system chooses one way instead of another to express these things is still a mystery.

Treatments have involved uncovering the repressed hostilities, imagery of cool, soothing substances or experiences, assertiveness training and imagery of sunlight and summer warmth for psoriasis. Prolonged periods of sleep, up to six days, under hypnosis (hypnonarcosis) and various images used for pain relief such as glove anaesthesia have also been used to treat rashes.

If psoriasis is your problem, you will use images of strong sunlight or other warming scenes. It is a good idea to avoid suggestions of coldness, as psoriatic lesions are aggravated during winter and the patients themselves are also subject to feelings of chilliness when the psoriasis is extensive, as the disorder permits excessive loss of body heat.

A thirty-four-year-old nun in a hospital in Pittsburgh, USA, was treated by hypnosis for dermatitis she had had for over twenty years. It involved her whole body, which had developed secondary infections in some areas, and she was covered in lesions, lumps, scales and tormenting, itchy rashes. She was referred because her dermatologist could offer her no more suggestions for treatment after the amount of steroids she was taking had reached its limit.

She had a considerable amount of repressed hostility toward her domineering mother, and this hostility had transferred to her religious superiors, especially those who reminded her of her mother: ''That last superior I had, she really *got under my skin*.'' Her passivity and submissiveness were so deeply entrenched that the therapists got nowhere with helping her become more assertive, or helping her experience and accept her anger. They were successful, however, after using trance-induced hallucinations of ocean bathing, having discovered that this was one of the things which in the past had eased her itch. As she had no visual imagery, they had to use different sense modalities:

> *You experience yourself at the beach. Take a deep breath and fill your lungs with this fresh, salty air. Smell the iodine and taste the salt on your lips. You feel the warmth of the sun on your face. Listen, and you can hear the gentle sound of the waves and the sound of the birds. Take a few steps into the water, and feel the coolness of the sea first around your ankles, and your legs. You slowly submerge your whole body. The water is cool and gentle, you feel it on your skin. You wiggle your toes and feel the sifting sand . . . and so on.* [13]

The consulting dermatologist reported, after the treatment These training sessions utilised hypnosis, but at the same time she attended non-hypnotic group sessions in assertiveness. In back.

I have already referred to an oft-quoted case history of the treatment of chronic psoriasis of over twenty years' duration (see page 21). This therapy was carried out by Fred Frankel and Robert Misch at the Harvard Medical School in 1973. The patient was a thirty-seven-year-old man with a long history of treatment for severe psychological disturbances who was referred to Frankel in the hope that hypnosis could be used to treat his psoriasis.

The therapists used imagery of warmth and sunlight under hypnosis and taught him self-hypnosis so he could use these images on his own. The suggestions were simple ones of warmth, relaxation and floating. There was not only an effect on the client in the form of rapid lessening of scaliness and reduction in the redness of the skin, but also in the form of considerable insights into his situation, such as his unwillingness to relinquish his psoriasis because it gave him an excuse to avoid social contact. He also managed a twenty-pound (nine-kilogram) weight loss over three weeks, when previous attempts to lose weight had failed. He described this as an unexpected bonus.

At the end of treatment the lesions had not completely disappeared, and this continued to be the case. The therapists indicated in the text that the patient had had mixed feelings about the success of the treatment.

> *In his own words, which capture the indecision and hesitancy to commit himself, he experienced "a tentative optimism" about what might yet happen. This was indeed, without exaggeration, the first evidence of brightness for over twenty years in a rather gloomy life.* [14]

A practitioner at the University of Idaho projected a female student backward and forward in time, using Erickson's techniques, to remove a skin rash which covered her entire body, and which had made her skin dry, itchy, cracked and inflamed. He asked her to review her life as if she were going back through the pages of a book and report any discoveries that might explain her problem, which brought forth feelings of wanting to achieve goals but being uncertain about her ability to do so, remembering her mother's voice saying, "You're so dumb you'll never amount to anything."

In trance she was told to project herself to a time in the future when the rash was no longer a problem, and to give a history of her life since then, and how she had changed "in thought and feeling and action" to become free of the rash. During the trance she was asked to recall the last time the rash had been a problem and had responded by naming a date a few days after the current therapy session. Sure enough, a few days later her rash had almost gone and soon she was standing up for herself more, letting people know her opinions about controversial things and generally enjoying life much more. She remained puzzled as to how this all came about.[15]

There is no reason you could not construct a self-hypnosis script along these lines. I think the technique is most ingenious, and I have used an adapted version of the hairpulling script.

SKIN PROBLEM SCRIPT

When something is bothering you the autonomic nervous system can produce rashes and other skin problems . . . in future you will combat these rashes because you will become more calm and relaxed and confident . . . things just won't have the power to upset you as much as they used to.

From now on, whenever your skin starts itching, cool sensations will start to flow over your hands and feet the very moment the itch begins . . . over your arms and legs and body and face . . . the very moment an itch commences.

Any redness and itchiness and flakiness of the skin will disappear as the cool sensations drive away the itch . . . it will feel as if the areas which used to be itchy and flaking and red are covered completely in a healing, soothing, non-greasy ointment . . . you are wrapped around in cool, soothing, healing ointment.

Any small amount of left-over rash will be transferred to the back of your right wrist, where it will cover a smaller and smaller area, until finally it disappears altogether.

Your unconscious mind will find ways of getting rid of

your itch that are safe and effective ... it will help you come to terms with past experiences that have not been properly dealt with and are still influencing you ... it will deal with these things and may not let your conscious mind become aware of how it does this, but somehow it will do away with the need for itches and rashes.

Remember, the more relaxed and calm and confident and adjusted you become, the more quickly your itch, redness and flakiness will disappear.

HIGH BLOOD PRESSURE

It is recognised that essential hypertension (high blood pressure) is one of the leading causes of heart attacks and strokes and that ways have to be found of keeping the blood pressure under control. Medication is by trial and error and for many people suffering from mild hypertension, the usefulness of drugs in the long-term has not been sufficiently established.

There is now evidence that both the central nervous system (brain and spinal cord) and the autonomic nervous system participate in the establishment and maintenance of hypertension, and as the autonomic nervous system has only recently been found to be amenable to control by conscious means, the use of psychological means to help lower the blood pressure is also fairly recent. The disciples of yoga and Zen Buddhism have known about control of these processes for thousands of years, and the early Western experiments in increasing and decreasing blood pressure should have alerted medical authorities to their potential for use with high blood pressure victims much sooner.

German neurologist and psychiatrist, the late J. H. Schultz, experimenting in the 1930s with his technique of autogenic training, found that patients could lower and raise their blood pressure substantially.[16] Autogenic training is a relaxation technique based on six mental exercises. The exercises involve focusing on warmth and heaviness in limbs, lowering of heart rate, slow, deep breathing and coolness of the forehead.

In the 1960s experimental psychologist Neal Miller found he could train subjects to control their blood pressure by using various conditioning procedures, including verbal and visual feedback.[17]

Treatments for hypertension have traditionally involved drugs, but treatments involving autogenic training, biofeedback, relaxation training and meditation have all been applied with moderate success. There is general agreement that while these other treatments sometimes produce results, hypnosis (including self-hypnosis) has been found superior in leading to the greatest reduction of the problem.

In 1970 a Sydney physician successfully demonstrated the role of hypnotic procedures in treatment of patients with heart conditions.[18]

American researchers at the Veterans Hospital and University in New Orleans established that hypertensive levels could be reduced through muscle relaxation and completely eliminated through hypnosis. The vast majority of their patients reported increased ease in going to sleep at night, deeper sleep, reduction in frequency and intensity of headaches, decrease in anxiety and greater ability to relax as by-products of their treatment.[19]

In 1980 a team at the Cardiovascular Centre at the New York Hospital–Cornell Medical Centre taught fifteen patients to use Spiegel's method of self-hypnosis (eye-roll, arm floating) and at the end of a four-month period decided that the improvement experienced by all patients in mood, well-being and changed behaviour patterns was likely to be beneficial to cardio-vascular health.

These people were all mild or borderline hypertensives. Oddly, the investigators found that *during* hypnotic sessions the pressure actually *rose*, although between the sessions it tended to become lower. They attributed this to the concentration and narrowed attention that takes place during hypnosis and not necessarily to an indication that hypnosis adversely affects blood pressure.

They also felt that self-hypnosis might be an important factor in preventing sudden heart attacks by changing behaviour and the lifestyle of the coronary-prone "Type A" personality. This person is supposedly a competitive, driving individual, struggling to achieve, impatient and with a continual sense of time urgency, for whom inactivity is a source of much anxiety. They drew attention to the fact that large-scale studies of drugs showed dramatic reduction in incidence of stroke, kidney damage and congestive heart failure but no change in the frequency of heart attack and sudden death. These investigators strongly emphasised their belief that conventional chemical treatments should be used for medium to severe hypertension, but that hypnosis could be used as an adjunct and could well reduce the amount of medication required.[20]

A Sydney medical practitioner carried out a long-term study on a hypertensive fifty-one-year-old male patient with unstable blood pressure. He used hypnosis, psychotherapy and medication over a period of four years. A stable and lower blood pressure was achieved as a result, and medication was reduced from twenty to three tablets daily. The practitioner, Dr J. Arthur Jackson, was of the opinion that control of hypertension is more effective if more frequent measurements of blood pressure are taken. In his treatment the patient took his own measurements twice a day over the four-year period.[21]

People who have already experienced heart attacks have also been helped by hypnosis to allay anxiety and depression caused by the fear of a further attack. As you are a possible walking time-bomb if you are hypertense and therefore cannot afford to take any chances, you should take the medication your doctor prescribes and ask if there is any objection to using hypnosis as an adjunct.

HIGH BLOOD PRESSURE SCRIPT

You have relaxed your muscles . . . now I want you to relax inwardly, your nervous system and your mind . . . relax your mind and your nervous system and descend into a deep inner relaxation, breathing more slowly and more deeply, feeling drowsy, heavy and warm . . . slow down your internal organs, your heart, blood vessels and arteries, slow down the blood flowing through your arteries and veins.

There is a regulatory device in your brain which sets your blood pressure . . . your unconscious mind will influence that device and set your blood pressure at a lower, safe, normal rate from now on . . . soon it will settle down at whatever rate your unconscious mind decides is best and safest for you. Remember, very soon your blood pressure will be reduced to a lower, safe and optimum rate for you.

From this time forward you will gradually change your lifestyle and attitudes . . . you will value your leisure time, and relax without guilt . . . you will find it easy to relax, go fishing or play golf, or go to agreeable social events . . . spend more time with friends and family . . . you won't make such strong demands upon yourself or expect so much of yourself . . . you will be able to organise your priorities better and deal with what is absolutely necessary more quickly and efficiently, leaving time for more and more leisure. As you do this you will find the time you set aside for work will pass more quickly and enjoyably, and your efficiency and creativity will increase.

19

EMOTIONAL PROBLEMS

I recall reading a theory that our descendants could be, in the Darwinian sense of being adaptable and passing on qualities for survival, people with relatively few emotions, phlegmatic types who could have a disaster befall them, accept it calmly and just keep plodding on. And I remember seeing a poor-quality film with that idea as a theme: our descendants some centuries into the future watched unmoved while one of their number drowned.

If you believe that *all* emotions are harmful, as is implied in the Holmes and Rahe stress scale, and will shorten our lives in this world, I suppose it follows that we will diminish the species-prolonging genes for future generations if we are passing on highly emotional dispositions.

As I said before, I find it hard to accept that "good" emotions, brought about by such things as marriage, personal triumph, promotion at work or travelling on a holiday, *can* produce the same wear and tear as "bad" emotions, caused by terror, frustration, hostility, heartbreak, jealousy and so on, even though the same physiological responses take place.

So on the grounds that I question the "dangerous" qualities of pleasurable emotions I would not develop scripts to suppress these. It would be a bleak world if people lost their feelings. However, it doesn't hurt to tamper a *little* with the "bad" feelings.

BROKEN HEART

There are few physically induced pains that hurt as much as a broken heart. It doesn't give much cheer to the person *with* one to say, quite truthfully, that only time will heal it, because it is how they are feeling in the present that is bothering them: bathed in misery and insomnia and quite unable to carry out their normal day-to-day functions. Quite often, the students I see with this problem have been rejected just prior to examination time. A student who was in that situation wrote the following script to help her get through the examination period in one piece, something to take the edge off how she felt.

BROKEN HEART SCRIPT

From now on you will be less able to be hurt, less vulnerable
. . . your feelings will still be there, but they will be less
sensitive, slightly dulled . . . the pain and hurt you feel will
be somehow distant, removed, as if a cushion has been
placed between you and the unhappiness you are feeling . . .
you will find you will be hardier, better able to cope with
being hurt, much stronger . . . you will be able to
concentrate on other aspects of your life, perform your work
with enough efficiency and keep doing your normal tasks
much more easily than usual at times like this.

If you are in that position, try to have a good cry, or preferably
several good cries.

William Frey, a biochemist from the St Paul-Ramsay Medical
Centre in Minnesota, is researching the link between tears and
stress-related diseases such as ulcers. Crying may be a safety
valve for ridding the body of chemicals produced in distress, as
tears wept in anguish have a different chemical composition from
those shed in response to irritants such as cold, wind or dust.

Frey believes that the suppression of tears may aggravate stress-
related diseases by making the body unable to remove some
unwanted chemicals that build up from stress. He found that two
of the chemicals produced by tears wept in anguish (after his
subjects had been shown tragic films) were the hormones ACTH
(the "stress" hormone) and prolactin (which is normally
associated with human milk), generated by the "master gland",
the pituitary.[1]

Thus it is important that people maintain their readiness to
cry, or that they learn to do so.

DEPRESSION

Between eight and fifteen per cent of the community is believed
to be suffering from depression, and most people experience some
brief, minor depression at some stage of their lives. Depression is
classified by the Health Commission of NSW as being one of two
main types, although the distinction is not always clearcut.

One type (called endogenous) happens for no apparent reason —
over a period of a few weeks a person just loses interest in
everything, feels tired and vaguely unwell, can't cope with
normal activities and usually starts waking up in the early hours
of the morning and finding it difficult to go back to sleep. After

treatment with anti-depressant drugs, usually the person gradually makes a full recovery.

The other type (called reactive) generally occurs after a number of unhappy events in the person's life (this is, of course, related to stress). The person copes for a while but then becomes tense and irritable, starts crying or shaking at odd times, smokes, drinks and eats too much and has difficulty in falling asleep at night. It usually takes longer to recover from this form of depression than the other, and the sufferer needs lots of support.

Both kinds of depression are accompanied by a loss of self-confidence and self-esteem, and quite often by suicidal thoughts and plans.

It is very difficult to help someone with depression as they do not seem to have any energy or interest in anything. They are flat, lacking in feelings, hard to converse with, and they do not seem very responsive to hypnosis. Quite often depression is masked by another symptom, such as lower back pain.

Depression caused by hormonal fluctuations, such as pre-menstrual tension and post-natal depression, can sometimes respond to vitamin B6. Severe depressions are usually treated chemically until the person has recovered enough to benefit from psychotherapy.

THE PSYCHOANALYTIC VIEW

Depression comes about in psychoanalytic terms because you did not choose your parents wisely. I am always scolding people for this failure. An unwisely chosen mother, for example, will not allow her child to grow away and become independent, but will encourage the child to cling to her.

Psychodynamic therapists draw attention to the dramatic distinction between depression and sadness. Depression is an *absence* of sadness, a lack of ability to experience sadness and pain. There is an explanation of how this comes about in Robin Skynner and John Cleese's book *Families and How to Survive Them*.[2] A normally developing child learns to cope with a little loss, a little sadness and anxiety as he or she separates from the mother little by little. She encourages this by not rushing in every time the child experiences a setback or some discomfort in the drive toward greater independence and confidence. The unhealthy mother will overreact every time there is a hint of sadness or anxiety on the child's face and will rush in to fix things up, which means that the child is prevented both from learning to experience normal sadness and anxiety and learning to cope with it. Never learning and never coping, the child grows up not being able to handle loss or suffering, not being able to mourn properly

— cut off from feeling — and having instead a feeling of deadness, emptiness, a lack of life and a lack of real emotional connection with other people.

The purpose of depression is, therefore, to enable the person to avoid sadness, and if you cut off sadness you cut off all emotions, and when your emotions go dead, *you* go dead.

According to Skynner and Cleese, the way to deal with this is to get the depressed person to recognise the fact that they are sending out signals for *other* people to change things for them, and instead get them to change things themselves, which is not easy. Three things have to happen simultaneously: they have to be placed in a situation where the sad face does not get the expected payoff (in other words, getting them to accept the idea that they *need* to face up to painful things in life); and in a situation where the reason for the sad-face signal is understood and not condemned; and where emotional support is offered to help them begin to *feel* the sadness.

With severe depression, drugs are generally prescribed to get the patient to the point where psychotherapy may be used to try to alter the family patterns. Skynner and Cleese feel that the severity of the depression depends on the point the child reached in the separation process — the lower the level of separation away from the mother achieved by the person as a child, the worse off they are, and the greater the degree of separation from the mother, the better the prognosis.

At the other end of the scale, a *lack* of love and care in early childhood can also result in habitual depression and stunted self-esteem.

THE BEHAVIOURIST VIEW

Behaviourists view depressed people as people who think there are not many good things to look forward to in life. Whatever they do turns sour and they are not really in control of their lives. Everything happens *to* them.

Another behavioural explanation is that many of the people who seek treatment experience a great deal of personal distress stemming from excessively high expectations and standards of self-evaluation, often supported by unfavourable comparisons with others noted for their extraordinary achievements. This process gives rise to feelings of worthlessness and lack of purposefulness, of "learned helplessness" and futility.

Behaviour therapists have used techniques such as time projection (which involves projecting the depressed person into an imaginary future, engaged in rewarding activities) and also sensory deprivation, on the grounds that after this anything will be better. Sensory deprivation can mean anything from being placed in an isolated room to being deprived of all sensory input (in darkness with ear plugs), or even being suspended in a pool of tepid water, devoid of any stimuli at all.

Another technique is to persuade the patient to *act* happy — to laugh, to smile, to talk with animation even though he or she does not feel like it — on the grounds that playing the role of a happy person will eventually lead to a lightening of mood. It is difficult for patients to do this, however, because their interest and energy level is so low.

Canadian practitioner Dr George Matheson treated a thirty-nine-year-old housewife and mother of four young boys who had been hospitalised for eight months. She had a twenty-four-year history of depressive and suicidal behaviour. She had been the result of an unwanted pregnancy, her mother having tried to abort her using a clothes hanger. She had been undergoing psychotherapy for a considerable time, and although she had gained a lot of insight into her problems, her behaviour had not changed.

Dr Matheson decided to evoke, in hypnosis, a sensation of happiness and then, through post-hypnotic suggestion, associate it with specific activities chosen to move the patient out of hospital. Age regression was used to get the patient to re-experience a happy event in her past, and a hierarchy of activities was drawn up, including going home from hospital for visits, sitting down to dinner with the family and playing with the children. Under hypnosis the patient was told to re-experience the happy feeling and the new activities were "faded in" to the happy feeling. She was told that in future whenever she was in these situations she would experience the same feeling. She was also told that the tune "Whistle While You Work" would enter her mind whenever she was going about her household tasks, and the sensation of happiness would occur whenever this tune was in her head.

The patient's mood and behaviour gradually improved, and soon she was home. Except for a brief lapse she coped well, entering into community activities and good family relationships.[3]

Matheson derived part of this treatment from work carried out by a European team in 1975.[4] They suggested under hypnosis that the same "sense of happiness" which was evoked by imagining a happy event from the past would also occur for fifteen seconds after "a certain number" had been written. The number chosen was one which did not appear very frequently in a long list of numbers the subject wrote. After the hypnotic treatment, when subjects wrote the number that functioned as a signal to release the emotion, they reported an increase in feelings of well-being and a sense of happiness.

Depression has also been treated successfully with rational-emotive therapy (see sections on Rational Thinking in Chapter 22), by having the depressed person recognise their spontaneous negative thoughts and deal with these thoughts. Dr Antony Kidman, Head of the Neurobiology Unit at the New South Wales Institute of Technology, has devised a programme[5] to deal with depression based on the work of Albert Ellis and another cognitive behavioural psychologist, Dr Tim Beck, from the University of Pennsylvania.

Dr Kidman underwent extensive training with Ellis and visited Beck in the USA, having become increasingly interested in the behavioural sciences as a consequence of his work as a neurochemist on the toxicology of the nervous system. In particular he has concentrated on people suffering the effects of chronic stress, excessive anxieties and depression.

The script that follows was developed for a person who had suffered a number of irritations, setbacks and disappointments, nothing terribly serious. I imagine that an improvement in her general situation plus a good break was what put back the sparkle, but perhaps the tape also contributed.

The image of a secret room comes almost unaltered from an article by Dr Diana Elton, a clinical psychologist of the Psychology Department, University of Melbourne, who treats chronic pain patients, and Dr Graham Burrows, from the Department of Psychiatry, University of Melbourne. They use the image with their pain patients, but it is just as appropriate to use it for depression and unwelcome emotions:

. . . Imagine that you are walking along the corridors of your mind. If you can manage this, raise your right hand to show me that you can . . . good . . . Now, imagine that you are looking at a faint outline of a door, which you have never seen before. It is a door to a secret room. If you can see it now, raise your right hand to show me that you can . . . fine . . . Now, open the door and walk in. You now find yourself in your very own secret room. It is absolutely perfect . . . and it is all yours . . . you have designed it yourself for your maximal pleasure, satisfaction, comfort and security. The door is closed now and while you are there nothing can touch you. *Nothing that you do not wish to enter can come into this secret room . . . all your worries, tensions and pains are left behind the door . . . can you feel that? . . . If you can, again lift your right hand to show me that you can. You are still in a deep hypnotic state*

*but you can talk freely. Describe your secret room to me
now ...*

*Yes, it IS a lovely room ... This room gives you strength
... After you have enjoyed its peace for a while, you can
emerge refreshed, more able to cope ... You can accept the
external world better now, since you know that you can
always return to your "secret room" whenever you may need
it ... If you can accept this statement, raise your right hand to
show me that you can ... good ...* [6]

Being a lover of the outdoors, I would probably turn the secret
room into a secret walled garden.

DEPRESSION SCRIPT

When a person is depressed, one of two possible chemicals is
depleted. In future the moment you begin to feel depressed
your internal regulatory system will go into action and
release sufficient quantities of the chemical in which your
body has become deficient and return the levels to normal.

If we take minus five as a very low state of mind, and plus
five as too highly excited, then whenever the state of
depression drops to minus three the chemical systems will
be triggered off by the unconscious mind acting on the
internal regulatory apparatus.

Very, very soon you will recover your sense of proportion
and your sense of humour ... you will feel how good life is
and how lucky you are in many ways ... you will feel
better and more optimistic, with renewed energy for your
various activities ... you will become less and less sensitive
to things that used to upset you and bother you, things you
have no control over, and things which aren't really very
important ... it will be as if you are enclosed in a protective
bubble, safe from distress, within which you are serene and
tranquil ... in this protective bubble the disturbances that
have been upsetting you cannot assail you ... they will lose
the power to bother you.

From now on you will find it easier to distract yourself
from becoming or being depressed by taking immediate
action to do something that you enjoy, that takes you out of
yourself ... perhaps some exercise which aerates the blood,
like swimming or bike-riding, as this acts as an anti-
depressant.

You find you dwell more and more on all the good things
from the past and present that you have to be grateful for, all
the happy memories ... you'll remember all the good things

of the past more and more . . . you'll think about all the
good things in the future to look forward to . . . you'll smile
more, laugh, go out and enjoy yourself, talk with animation
. . . even if sometimes you don't feel like it, the more you
act "happy", the more you will become happy and thus
replace the depression.

From now on when you still feel a little unhappy, you will
find a room where you can be alone and unavailable when
you wish to . . . you can return there when things get more
difficult for you . . . it can be a real room . . . or it can be an
imaginary secret room, your own secret room, where you
can be alone and at peace . . . imagine you are walking along
the corridors of your mind . . . imagine you are looking at a
faint outline of a door, which you have never seen before
. . . it is the door to your secret room.

Now, open the door and walk in . . . you now find
yourself in your very own secret room . . . it is absolutely
perfect . . . and it is all yours . . . you have designed it
yourself for your maximal pleasure, satisfaction, comfort and
security. The door is closed now and while you are there
nothing can touch you . . . nothing that you do not wish to
enter can come into this secret room . . . all your worries,
tensions, miseries, hostility and aggression are left behind
the door . . . you are still in a deep trance . . . this room
gives you strength . . . after you have enjoyed its peace for a
while, you can emerge refreshed, more able to cope . . . you
can accept the situation more easily now, since you know
you can always return to your secret room whenever you
may need it.

Harry Stanton of Tasmania has suggested the image of a laundry
chute in the secret room. Instead of leaving all the "bad"
emotions at the door, they are thrown down the chute: "If you
would like to you can take all your worries, tensions, miseries,
hostilities and aggressions, experience the feelings and sensations
that accompany them fully for a while, then have the pleasure of
throwing them down the imaginary laundry chute in your secret
room."[7]

For a more serious, more deep-seated depression, the script
would have to contain suggestions that in the future feelings of
sadness and loss would be faced up to and experienced, tears of
sadness would flow whenever it is appropriate, and that instead of
expecting other people to make things right the person will start
to take responsibility for making things change *themselves*.

It is important to suggest, too, that they become more

adaptable and not try to cling to things or people that they might have lost, to develop other aims and goals, to find new sources of satisfaction. A depressed person will often cling to the hope of regaining something lost long after it is appropriate, especially if it is a personal relationship, and needs to be helped to let go, give up and start over again.

Suggestions of accepting and experiencing other feelings that have been repressed, such as hostility, anger, guilt and bitterness, would be relevant, but then people should be encouraged to "throw them down the chute" once they have served their purpose and not continue to harbour them.

HOSTILITY, ANGER AND BITTERNESS

Many psychologists believe that pent-up aggressions and resentments are best dealt with by screaming, yelling and banging things. Thumping pillows is quite a practical method of venting these feelings, but as it is hardly socially acceptable to raise the roof publicly I have put together a script that might help. Part of it was taken from an article titled "The Silent Abreaction", by Helen Watkins, an American psychologist.[8] It also includes the laundry chute image to get rid of unwanted feelings.

HOSTILITY, ANGER AND BITTERNESS SCRIPT

From now on you will be able to get in touch with your pent-up emotions and deal with them in some constructive manner. Whenever these feelings are directed against yourself, you will find ways to redirect them, in some acceptable way. Perhaps you could imagine yourself beating a pillow with your fists until all these angry feelings inside you have evaporated, beating it harder and harder until you are completely exhausted, yelling and screaming in your mind until you are too worn out and tired to go on.

Or you could redirect it to some positive constructive purpose . . . something useful and energy-consuming. Or you could climb up, in your mind, into a dusty old attic where all the other outdated things are kept . . . all the things that no longer have a useful purpose to serve . . . take off your past hurts, your anger and bitterness like an old worn-out coat, and leave them behind in the room, locking the door as you leave.

All your hidden personal reasons for the angry, hostile feelings may or may not be communicated to your conscious mind . . . the awareness that is communicated to your conscious mind will be dealt with in a constructive, practical, sensible way.

Whatever still remains of these feelings that is no longer serving any useful purpose will be dumped by your unconscious mind down your laundry chute and will leave you quite free to get on with living your life.

The following passage also incorporates some of Harry Stanton's ideas:

You are entering a comfortable, quiet room where a log fire is burning. See the flames leaping, hear the crackle of the kindling and smell the scent of pine and smoke ... you can dump all of your hostility, anger and bitterness into the fire ... as they are destroyed and disappear as smoke up the chimney, your mind becomes free of all the restricting and tiring influences.[9]

Stanton also suggests that to get at unwanted mental blocks you could incorporate the image of a lift going down into the basement of the mind to see what is there.

It takes a lot of energy to keep pushing away unwanted thoughts and emotions, especially unconscious ones. You cannot grow and develop when too much of your psychological energy is spent fighting unacceptable buried feelings. It is also physically exhausting. It is therefore important to deal with the accumulation of unwanted feelings in a constructive way.

GUILT

Everyone suffers from guilt in varying degrees at various times, with the possible exception of the occasional sociopath (a person who has not formulated an inner moral or ethical code and has no respect for society's rules and regulations. This person usually seeks immediate gratification of whims or wishes with little thought for the consequences.) In the back of our minds lurk shadowy recollections of things we are ashamed of, important tasks we omitted to carry out, times we hurt people either by accident or design, feelings of not measuring up to someone's expectations, and mistakes and blunders of differing magnitude.

Apart from those things we remember, there are many complex guilty patterns established below the conscious level.

Most people's upbringing has a large component of "don'ts", "now look what you've dones" and "if you loved me you wouldn't do thats": punishments for displays of aggression or jealousy, for breaking something valuable or for toilet training mishaps. Punishments may range from a sad look or a light smack to harsher methods, but when an exaggerated fuss is made of something then the guilty feelings are likely to be permanently etched in the psyche. There is always the fear accompanying the guilt that if you don't do what is wanted your parents may cease to love you.

Sex and religion are two major areas in which guilt tends to thrive.

Among a tongue-in-cheek list of evening courses I somehow acquired, there are two that are more painful than funny: "Moulding Your Child's Behaviour Through Guilt and Fear" and "Guilt Without Sex".

Small children found masturbating (they *all* seem to do it) can bring a furrow to the brow of quite liberal-minded parents and very strong reactions from the more straight-laced individual. One can only guess what complex guilt patterns are established while children are busily trying to obtain the opposite-sex parent's affections for themselves (see Chapter 20, Sexual Dysfunctions). This is especially so if the same-sex parent dies or the marriage breaks down and the "rival" moves away from home, leaving the child with the impression that his or her secret wishes were responsible.

Many religions make it almost impossible for a person to be anything *except* riddled with guilt.

I remember reading at a young age a book called *The Importance of Living*, written by the Chinese philosopher Lin Yutang who compared the Christian theological view, the Greek pagan view and the Chinese Taoist–Confucianist view.[10] He said of the Christian view: "All in all there is still a doctrine of sin and the wickedness of human nature; that enjoyment of life is sin and wickedness, that to be uncomfortable is to be virtuous, and that on the whole man cannot save himself except by a greater power outside."

He said that the Greeks made their gods like men, while the Christians desired to make men like the gods. The Greek gods were a jovial, amorous, loving, lying, quarrelling, vow-breaking and petulant lot, "a marrying lot, too, and having unbelievably many illegitimate children".

In contrast the Confucianists had a *"forgiving* kind of philosophy" which could be summed up in the phrase "let us be reasonable". Men and women have passions, natural desires and noble ambitions, and also a conscience. They have sexual desires, hunger, fear, anger and so on, but these are neither good nor bad, just something given and inseparable from characteristic human life. They expect neither too much nor too little from man. One has only to live reasonably, according to his or her best lights, and one will then have peace of conscience.

After saying all this, and making the other two religions sound much more attractive and easy to live with, he rejoined the Christian faith on his deathbed. However, I still think back to his writings when I see students tormented because they can't live up to the high standards and ideals their particular religious faith has set them.

Even if we have been spared guilt feelings as a result of our upbringing, sex or religion, some of us may feel even more guilty when we dwell on what our personal role should be in taking a stand of conscience against the arms race, the development of nuclear weapons, and war and injustice in general, or what we should try to do to help those less fortunate than ourselves — in our own country or elsewhere.

Women, in particular, have additional guilt thrust upon them nowadays. The woman who chooses to work feels guilty that she is not at home looking after her "latch-key" children and crumple-shirted husband, whereas the married woman who remains "only a housewife" is just as apt to be made to feel guilty that she is not out expanding her horizons and making a contribution to society that can be more easily quantified.

GUILT SCRIPT

The previous scripts are fine for guilt as well as the other more negative emotions, but here is a script that is more specific:

From now on your mind will at all levels start to process all your guilt feelings.

It will gradually accept that because you are only human you have human failings ... that you have made mistakes and done things you should not have done, and not done things you ought to have done ... that at times you have been careless or irresponsible, that at times you have hurt others and yourself.

Your unconscious mind will dwell especially on ways of safely dealing with the guilt that has been repressed from an early age, about jealousy and anger against other children, about childish sexual fantasies and behaviour.

Your unconscious mind will find ways of accepting these things and assimilating them and seeing they are of no importance ...

At all levels of your mind you will begin to discard and come to terms with those guilty feelings you have no control

over, those in the past that nothing can be done about . . .
you will shake them off completely . . . and at all levels,
your mind will work on ways you can get rid of other guilty
feelings by taking some action . . . to change what can be
changed . . . to make up somehow for what you have done
or left undone in the past or the present.

FEELING LOW AND VULNERABLE

Here is a script to perk you up a bit when you are feeling a little
depressed or thin skinned:

From now on when you start to feel low, you will
immediately distract yourself with plans or ideas or
activities . . . quickly you will recover your sense of humour
and your sense of proportion . . . you will feel better and
more optimistic, with renewed energy . . . you will dwell on
the things you have to be grateful for, and happy memories
and things to look forward to.

From now on you won't get nearly so upset about teasing
remarks or hurtful incidents . . . these will have less and
less effect on you . . . you will realise that they aren't really
intended to upset or hurt you . . . they just won't bother you
any more.

When you are slighted or rejected from now on your
feelings won't be nearly so hurt . . . you will be far less
affected . . . things just won't be able to get under your skin
so much . . . you may be a little sad, but you won't be
devastated . . . inwardly you will be much stronger, much
better able to withstand hurts and disappointments . . . far
less vulnerable than before.

EXCESSIVE WORRY AND
STOMACH PROBLEMS; MOOD SWINGS

Here are some other scripts connected with feelings that were
written for students and might give you some ideas for your own
scripts:

EXCESSIVE WORRY AND STOMACH PROBLEMS
SCRIPT

From now on you will be able to assimilate and process far
more ideas, problems and information than before . . . you

will be able to sort out priorities and deal with the most important things first, leaving the least important things till last . . . wherever possible you will resist taking on duties and obligations that will overload your coping capacity.

Remember, conflicting ideas and problems will be assimilated and processed far more easily, priorities will be set and wherever possible new pressures will be avoided.

From now on you will worry less and less about things you have no control over, or things that are not important . . . you will set aside a relatively small amount of time each day for constructive planning rather than useless worrying.

As you learn to relax, and become calmer and more tranquil, and learn to cope better with all the pressures on you, you will find that very quickly your stomach problems will ease and eventually disappear . . . the minute your stomach begins to hurt, your unconscious mind will release a chemical to counteract the discomfort . . . it will feel as if a cooling, soothing liquid is taking away all the pain, flowing gently over your acidic stomach lining . . . bringing it back to the relaxed, healthy, comfortable state it should be in.

MOOD SWINGS SCRIPT

I am going to create for you an internal regulator, just like a thermostat . . . if you begin to feel a little too "high" it will work to prevent you from going "higher" . . . if you feel too low, it will prevent you from going "lower".

Imagine a scale of minus ten to plus ten, minus then is the lowest you can go and plus ten is the highest you can go without serious disturbance . . . from now on you will find that the maximum you will go will be as high as plus seven, and the minimum you will drop down will be minus seven.

LACK OF FEELINGS AND SENSES

The other side of the coin from that of harbouring a lot of negative emotions is that of not feeling *enough*. Most of the therapies are aimed at getting you to be a fully functioning person, alive and aware in the present, realising as much of your potential as is possible. Many of them emphasise awareness of senses and feelings as an important part of this process. "Getting in touch with your feelings" is an intrinsic part of the Gestalt approach, as is concern with being aware of what is going on around you — sights, smells, textures, impressions.

The other important idea is that of *living* in the present. It is a waste of a life to constantly refer to the past or to live your life on plans for the future.

So if you have no plans to undertake therapy, then *do* embark on a deliberate, conscious programme of awareness and appreciation of all the things going on around you now and the feelings they generate inside you. Force yourself to come back to the present, if you find yourself too often unaware of it.

There is a great deal of interest currently on the theme of the importance of the process, and not the product, it being better to travel than to arrive. It did not strike me how important this approach was until I met a man at a conference who said that twelve years of his life had gone missing. He had lived all this time looking forward to getting his PhD. He gained very little in these twelve years, but did not realise what was happening until he finally reached his goal and found that he felt quite empty. Of course this does not mean you can't make plans for the future, or reminisce about the past, just that it is wiser to concentrate mainly on the present.

LACK OF FEELINGS AND SENSES SCRIPT

From this time forward you will be more and more consciously aware of your feelings, joy, affection, contentment . . . more aware of your mental states and body sensations, memories and emotions . . . you will be more and more alive, and will experience your emotions . . . more and more aware of things around you, colours, textures, scents, sounds and tastes . . . you will have the ability to notice these things, both inside your body and around you . . . you will keep in contact with these sensations and emotions and really feel and really experience them . . . flow with them and permit them to be felt and experienced.

Your senses will be sharper, acutely aware . . . you will be far more sensitive and aware of your own feelings and values, and far more sensitive and aware of other people's feelings.

From now on you will live for the most part in the present, you will appreciate and enjoy the present and not yearn for the past or long for the future . . . you will concentrate on making the most of the present.

Things that once used to irritate and annoy you will have very little power in the future to irritate and annoy you.

20
SEXUAL DYSFUNCTIONS

Although there are quite a number of problems associated with sexual functioning I will deal with only four of them — vaginismus, frigidity, premature ejaculation and impotence.

An explanation of these problems in psychoanalytic terms, although greatly simplified, appears in *Families and How to Survive Them*.[1] According to authors Skynner and Cleese, at times during the course of normal development, children become seductive towards the parent of the opposite sex, and it is how this is handled by the parent that determines whether sexual development proceeds normally or otherwise.

They explain frigidity by the fact that the father is embarrassed or made nervous or frightened by his little daughter's romantic feelings, or else comes on too strongly, so she switches off the feelings. Or else there is a strong community attitude against showing sexual feelings, or some trauma occurs.

With impotence, a similar situation arises with the mother. This type of impotence is distinguished from temporary impotence due to stress, illness or alcohol. The worry caused by poor performance can lead to a more persistent kind of impotence unless an understanding woman, or therapy, or plain good luck breaks the vicious circle.

Premature ejaculation is attributed to different causes: the man is not allowing himself to *feel* sufficiently and needs to become far more aware of the physical sensations of pleasure. His sexual excitement runs away with him in the absence of these feelings and he ejaculates too quickly. The reason he has turned off his feelings is also because of family attitudes — it is "not nice" to be highly sexually interested and involved. Old-fashioned sex manuals actually made this problem worse by recommending ways of reducing excitement by thinking of other things — reciting multiplication tables, for instance.

Treatment of sexual problems has been revolutionised in the last fifteen years by the work of Virginia Johnson and William Masters in the USA.[2] Apart from their valuable research into normal sexual responses, they also treated people, mainly couples, who had various sexual dysfunctions. The couples were treated over a two-week period, Masters and Johnson working with them as a team, discussing the problems and how they had arisen and then giving them specific tasks to perform.

A standard part of the treatment method that Masters and Johnson used is called sensate focus. Fundamental to this is the idea that touch is vital to personal communication. So for a few days of the programme the couple is told to spend periods exploring sensory experiences, expecially touch, with each other. They take off their clothes, and massage and fondle each other, all the time giving feedback and instructions. At this time there is to be no sexual stimulation, no touching of breasts or genitals, and they are to aim at creating sensual feelings. As the treatment progresses, touch extends to the genital areas but not to the point of sexual release, and only further into the programme are couples encouraged to have orgasm.

While these ideas were formalised and systematised by Masters and Johnson, they were originally put forward by earlier behaviour modification therapists.

VAGINISMUS

Vaginismus is a psychosomatic disorder in which any attempt at sexual intercourse causes an involuntary spasm of muscles in the vagina. This can be so severe that it becomes physically impossible for the woman to have intercourse.

Women with vaginismus tend to be tense, anxious, more neurotic and less extroverted than normal women. It usually occurs in young women and a marriage may be consummated prior to the onset of vaginismus.

A psychodynamic explanation is that vaginismus is a hysterical conversion: these women are either fixated to their fathers, which is relatively easy to treat, or else they are fixated to their mothers. The latter condition is difficult to treat and very time consuming. Alternatively, as the Freudian psychiatrist Otto Fenichel believed, vaginismus is a symbol of repressed fantasies of castrating the male due to unresolved Electra conflicts.

A behavioural explanation is that vaginismus is a result of fear and anxiety: that it can be viewed as an avoidance reaction to an anxiety-producing situation.

Masters and Johnson treat vaginismus by gradually introducing vaginal dilators of increasing size into the vagina while the woman is relaxed. You can do this yourself by obtaining dilators from a chemist, or you can simply use objects of increasing size, including fingers, while concentrating on relaxing. Sometimes treatment involves more formal systematic desensitisation ranging from simply looking at the vagina to actual intercourse.

Greta Goldberg, a Sydney clinical psychologist who has treated several women with vaginismus, writing in the *Australian Journal of Hypnosis*, makes the point that vaginismus has been medically documented for a long time.[3] The Anglo-Saxons thought it was caused by an inadequately sized vagina and used a stretching device similar to a modern dilator.

Goldberg refers to three types of vaginismic women as described by European psychiatrist M. Balint in 1968[4]: (a) the "Sleeping Beauty", an infantile woman who lives with her husband in a fraternal relationship; (b) the "Brunhilde" type, who experiences sexuality as a battle of the sexes and fears that femininity might be a sign of weakness and passivity; and (c) the "Queen Bee" type who wants to have a child from her husband but refuses sexuality; sex is considered a humiliating, unpleasant necessity for motherhood. Goldberg quotes literature claiming that the typical husband of a vaginismic woman is timid, gentle and compliant.

Her treatment programme emphasises that the goal of vaginismus therapy is for the client to enjoy arousal during penetration, which is, she points out, rarely emphasised in the research literature. She feels that unless enjoyment is made a therapeutic goal, the long-term maintenance of coitus is not at all certain.

Her therapy is in two stages, initially the female alone and then with her partner, because, she explains, "Vaginismus also exists at the relationship level and in a way you and your partner are both afraid of penetration hurting you and are co-operating to avoid it, otherwise you might be sitting there complaining about rape and not vaginismus." The maximum number of sessions required is between ten and twelve. Treatment consists of education about sexual responses, relaxation training and a gradual programme of finger insertion carried out in a warm bath and a great deal of reassurance and encouragement with homework involving trance and imagery.

In contrast to this behavioural treatment, New York therapist Mary Gottesfeld treated a twenty-year-old woman with an unconsummated marriage of one year's duration with a long-term psychoanalytic approach. Sexual relations consisted of her twenty-two-year-old husband ejaculating outside her vagina and then masturbating her to orgasm. Her husband did not seem overly concerned about her sexual problem; he not only did not complain but seemed satisfied with their sexual life. It was the patient who sought help.

Originally the patient had been to see a gynaecologist who

made the recommendation that her husband rape her, which resulted in her avoiding another treatment attempt for quite some time. Finally she was referred to Gottesfeld for treatment. An investigation of her background revealed that when the patient was fourteen, her mother had died from complications of severe diabetes, including obesity and the amputation of a limb. She had persistently neglected her sores and tumours and refused to have a much-needed operation until it was too late. The patient described her relationship with her mother as a good one, and satisfactory in all respects.

Hypnotic treatment sessions revealed a series of painful early memories, among them those of being brutally beaten by her mother throughout her childhood, with whatever was available, inexplicably and on impulse. In the first two years of therapy she broke up the relationship with her husband and worked through her past. Therapy was finally terminated three years after it had commenced, when the patient was better adjusted and had formed a healthy relationship with a young man she was about to marry.[5]

I used the following script with a twenty-three-year-old girl who was unable to have intercourse with her fiancé:

VAGINISMUS SCRIPT

From now on you will be completely relaxed in the area in and around your vagina when there is a possibility of intercourse ... you will no longer feel tense and anxious, or guilty or afraid ... you already know in your conscious mind that intercourse is natural and normal and enjoyable, and that you have nothing physically wrong with you ... that there is nothing whatever to be afraid of ... from now on you will realise these things at an unconscious level ... that there is no reason at all to prevent you having intercourse ... your vagina will no longer produce contractions when intercourse is imminent ... there will be no more spasms as you continue to relax more and more deeply.

FRIGIDITY

Frigidity is a disparaging term for anorgasmia, or failure to achieve orgasm. Orgasm is the release of muscular tension and congestion of the veins produced by sexual stimulation, and the experience varies considerably from person to person. Generally, it is a feeling of increasing arousal to a peak of physical pleasure, followed by a feeling of relaxation throughout the body. Anorgasmia is likely to be a peak of physical pleasure which is *not* followed by relaxation, quite often leaving the woman frustrated and experiencing some degree of discomfort. Some women fail to become aroused to any degree and therefore do not experience the feelings of frustration and discomfort at all.

Dr David Cheek, a gynaecologist and obstetrician in San Francisco, worked with 255 frigid women and found that some of them could be helped substantially after treatment for a total of only two hours. His therapy was based on research he carried out on women capable of multiple orgasms. Using hypnotic age regression, he found that all of these women had a sense of total acceptance by their parents from the moment of birth and that orgasm frequently occurred under circumstances associated with displays of loving attention in nursing, being bathed and having diapers changed. They had all seemed to have escaped punishment for exploring their genitals and had experienced orgasms in dreams when between six and ten years of age. They had also discovered that thoughts could lead to orgasm in an environment of love and acceptance.

Cheek divided the group of frigid women into two classes. Class A were those women who had experienced some form of orgasm, and Class B were those who had never had any kind of orgasm, or at least no conscious memory of such.

Class A had subgroups. A-1 comprised women who had had orgasms in sleep, or with petting or masturbation, but never with a male sexual partner during intercourse. Those in A-2 were experiencing orgasms of some sort with their current sexual partner (with clitoral stimulation, oral sex or during sexual intercourse), but were expressing some sense of dissatisfaction, and A-3 had experienced orgasms in the past with another sexual partner or with their current partner, but were no longer responding in this way. Cheek found that some A-3 women were suffering from some gynaecological misconception, or guilt, or fear of pregnancy, but most commonly they had realised they were with the wrong man. The majority of treatment failures came from this group.

Usually the sexual feelings of Class B women had been stopped when masturbatory experiments in early childhood drew expressions of disgust, shame or anger from a parent.

Cheek explained to the women that hypnosis was to be used as a means of understanding unconscious sexual attitudes and of improving self-confidence and related the steps of early learning about orgasm. He used a variety of techniques to discover information, which was not known to them consciously, about relations between the patient and her sexual partner, and birth experiences and later sexual feelings. He regressed them to early childhood and explained the healthiness and importance of sexual feelings, saying that if mammals did not enjoy sexual intercourse their species would die out, and talked to the "inner part" of the mind by finger signals, asking, "Does the inner part of your mind know that you can have orgasms with intercourse just as well as or even better than other normal women?" He attested to the importance of breast-feeding in establishing a feeling of love; he said it was an apparently biological need, something which demanded more attention than it currently received by obstetricians and pediatricians.

He reoriented the patient to the earliest times she had experienced orgasm, and pointed out that genital exploration was normal when she was a baby and continued to be until someone in authority made her feel self-conscious or guilty. Next the patient was asked to go back over old and more recent experiences and dreams, having the sexual feelings she would have had if she had not been made to feel guilty or ashamed. Cheek would then describe to the patient how she could expect to feel from that time onwards when having sex with her partner.

He found that, of the 255 women he treated for frigidity, eighteen dropped out before completion of treatment, 124 could not be satisfactorily followed up, and of the remainder, sixty per cent reported some improvement in sexual performance with the current partner.

He decided he would have obtained more favourable results if he had applied the criteria for selection for treatments to all patients that he later adopted: that is, that they were able to form some meaningful relationship with a man. He felt the others needed much more comprehensive therapy than was feasible in such a short time. Some of the "improved" women moved from Class B to Class A, and some shifted from Class A-1 to A-2. These latter women, he notes, were all Catholic. The best results were demonstrated in the improved subjective satisfaction of Class A-2.[6]

Doctors Lorraine Dennerstein and Graham Burrows from the Department of Psychiatry, University of Melbourne, report that anorgasmia can often be understood and treated using behavioural techniques. They say the woman who has never climaxed in any situation is often unaware of her own sexual needs and is frequently ignorant of her own anatomy, the female sexual response and orgasmic techniques. They recommend individual therapy, emphasising education by book and film, reassurance, and behaviour modification techniques such as systematic desensitisation. The woman is then taught orgasmic techniques and encouraged to take responsibility for learning her own sexual response pattern and teaching it to her partner. She is encouraged to masturbate, and is taught how. She is told, for example, that direct stimulation of the clitoris is not recommended, and that it may take thirty minutes to one hour before she begins to feel pleasurable sensations at her first attempt. She is also cautioned against "spectatoring" her own performance but is urged to absorb herself in these experiences.

The next phase is to teach the woman to communicate her sexual needs to her partner. Reluctance to do so, because of embarrassment or not wishing to seem sexually aggressive, is a common cause of a second type of anorgasmia: being able to have an orgasm with self-stimulation, but not with the partner. Here the couple are usually treated together, often with a structured programme of physically touching and exploring one another (sensate focus).[7]

FRIGIDITY SCRIPT

From now on your unconscious mind will find ways of dealing with the issues in your past or your childhood which have contributed to your problem ... it will find safe ways of solving these issues, of coming to terms with them, and it may or may not let your conscious mind know. Whether it does or not, it will find ways to help you lead a normal, healthy and enjoyable sex life.

From this time forward you will be far more sexually aware and interested ... sexual feelings that have been pushed away, perhaps for a long time, will rise to the surface ... you will find that thoughts of engaging in sexual intercourse and self-stimulation will enter your head spontaneously, sexual fantasies will occur to you and sexual films and magazines will interest you more and more.

In future when you are involved in sexual activity you will become lost, completely absorbed and involved, in the sensual and sexual feelings and experiences ... you will no longer be self-conscious or monitor your own performance ... you will be completely immersed in the sensations and the feelings and the experiences ... interested only in giving and receiving pleasure.

PREMATURE EJACULATION

Fred Belliveau and Lin Richter, in their book *Understanding Human Sexual Inadequacy*, say:

> *Most men who have premature ejaculation give the same
> history. All their early heterosexual attempts were hurried. A
> prostitute may have congratulated her client on his speedy
> performance because it meant she could go on to the next
> customer. A young man having intercourse in the back seat of
> a car at a lovers' lane may have been worried about being
> caught in the act.*[8]

And this unfortunate early behaviour is often there to stay. If a
man is capable of more than one sexual performance in a
reasonably short space of time, then a fairly dismal performance
the first time is probably neither here nor there, but this is not
always the case.

Masters and Johnson define premature ejaculation as inability
to delay ejaculation long enough for the woman to have orgasm
fifty per cent of the time. Others define it as inability to delay
ejaculating for thirty seconds to a minute after the penis is in
the vagina, and some prefer to define it by the stated satisfaction or otherwise of the people involved. It has also been
defined as consistent inability to exert voluntary control over
ejaculation.

Various treatments have been proposed. One is the "stop-
start" method, which is simply to stimulate the penis outside the
vagina until ejaculation is imminent, then stop for a while until
the sensation has disappeared, then start again, until the male
has learned to postpone ejaculation indefinitely.[9] Another is the
"squeeze" technique, whereby the female controls ejaculation by
squeezing the male near the head of the penis, which makes the
man lose his urge to ejaculate and also lose some of his erection,
and repeating this until he learns more control.[10]

Milton Erickson described his treatment of a thirty-eight-year-
old patient who had suffered from premature ejaculation for
eighteen years. This had begun with his first attempt at sexual
relations at the age of twenty, and the experience had frightened
and humiliated him so much it had deterred him from another
attempt for several years. He then visited a brothel, thinking that
he would be less humiliated if he failed there, and he did fail.
Shortly afterwards he revisited the brothel, selecting the least
attractive prostitute, thinking for some reason that this might
help, but it did not.

He tried casual pick-ups, and liquor to calm him down, but
nothing worked, and then he decided his problem was due to an
overactive conscience. He then sought out an attractive young
woman and began a chaste courtship, and after about six months
he decided he wished to marry the girl, and asked her for a kiss.

As he kissed her he ejaculated, and after that did so upon just meeting her.

Discontinuing this relationship he cultivated a relationship with a woman who was socially and educationally inferior to him and who he knew was promiscuous. When the same thing happened he embarked for many years on a search for a physical or mechanical cure for his problem, insisting that his trouble was organic and certainly not in his head.

Finally he approached Erickson, who realised that by then the patient was firmly convinced that he was past help and was now merely trying to prove this beyond any shadow of a doubt. Prior to commencing treatment Erickson paid a secret visit to the apartment where the patient had failed so many times, which was reached by a long outdoor walkway, a stairway and another long walkway indoors.

After putting the patient in a deep trance, Erickson suggested amnesia. He then insisted that the patient *must* get a wristwatch and it was imperative that the watch should have a second hand. It was also necessary that he obtain a night light and sleep with it on so he could tell the time to the very second at any time during the night. He was then told he would continue his "useless inviting of girls to spend the night with him", that only in this way could he find out what he "really really really would want to learn".

The next suggestion was a "medical explanation" of future developments of his total problem, on a physiological basis. This was that his premature ejaculation, by virtue of body changes from ageing processes, would be completely changed. The suggestion was as follows:

Do you know, can you possibly realise, can you genuinely understand, that medically all things, everything, even the worst of symptoms and conditions, must absolutely come to an end. But not, but not, I must emphasise, not in the way a layman would understand! *Do you realise, do you understand, are you in any way aware, that your premature ejaculation* will end in a failure, *that no matter how long your erection lasts, no matter how long and actively you engage in coitus, you will fail to have an ejaculation for 10, for 10 long, for 20 long minutes, for 20, for 25 minutes! Even more! Do you realise how desperately you will strive and strive, how desperately you will watch the minute hand and the second hand of your wristwatch, wondering, just wondering if you will fail, fail, fail to have an ejaculation at 25 minutes, at 25½, at 26, at 26½ minutes! Or will it be at 27½, at 27½ minutes — at 27½, at*

27½ minutes! [this last said in tones expressive of deep relief]. [11]

The session continued in much the same vein, suggesting that the same thing would happen the morning after; but that he would fail to have an ejaculation until thirty-three, thirty-four or thirty-five minutes had passed. Erickson next instructed his patient to find one of the girls he was used to and take her to his apartment, and as he did so he would not be able to help counting the cracks in the sidewalk, then the boardwalk, no matter how much he tried to keep his mind on the conversation, he would keep desperately counting all the cracks on the way to his apartment ... it would be such a relief to reach his apartment and feel comfortable and relaxed, but all the time after he reached the apartment his mind would be on the wristwatch.

Erickson then told him to forget all he had said, but to come back and tell him that the wristwatch was right when it read twenty-seven and a half minutes and when it read thirty-three, thirty-four and thirty-five.

That obscure piece of rhetoric was all that the therapy comprised, but yes, you've guessed it — there were no further problems.

PREMATURE EJACULATION SCRIPT

More and more your growing calmness and confidence will decrease your anxiety about your sexual performance ... you will find it much easier to delay ejaculation ... from now on it will become more and more easy to delay ejaculation until the right moment ... as your performance improves your anxiety will disappear ... you will find it easier and easier not to get too excited too early ... you will become more and more aware of how to satisfy your partner ... knowing that mutual satisfaction is your goal.

If you find that you still want to ejaculate too soon, you will be able to delay it by becoming more and more immersed in the sexual experience you are having, submerged in pleasure ... you will be able to lose yourself more and more in the experience, in the sensual feelings ... you will become so absorbed that the experience itself becomes the important thing ... you will enjoy it more and more, so much so that you will delay ejaculating as long as possible in order to prolong the pleasure of the sexual experience ... from this time forward, more and more time will pass before ejaculation occurs.

Remember, from now on you will be completely absorbed

and involved in the sensual and sexual experience and you will be able to get these feelings and experiences to last longer and longer ... you will channel much of your creative capacity and your capacity for enjoyment into your sexual experiences.

As you find it becoming easier to delay your ejaculation, you will be increasingly aware of the improvement this brings to your relationship ... you will open up your mind to new ideas and methods, knowing that anything agreed upon together is acceptable ... as you become more and more confident and adventurous, your nervousness will disappear and you will find it easier and easier to satisfy your partner and yourself.

IMPOTENCE

Masters and Johnson define primary impotence as a disorder in which the male has *never* been able to achieve and/or maintain an erection sufficient to accomplish sexual intercourse. A man with secondary impotence has succeeded in intercourse at least once and mostly quite often, before impotence occurs. Masters and Johnson classify a man as secondarily impotent if he cannot achieve or maintain erection in twenty-five per cent of his sexual encounters.

The assignment of a single cause to impotence would be an oversimplification. Most of Masters and Johnson's impotent patients had many family and social influences destructive to the personality development of a young boy. These included:

• Seductive behaviour on the part of the mother, though not to the point of actual intercourse.

• Religious taboos or restrictions, equating sex with sin. Masters and Johnson found that the single most common factor in the backgrounds of sexually dysfunctional people is rigid adherence to religious restrictions. They comment: "There can be no appreciation that sexual functioning is indeed a natural phenomenon, when material of sexual content is considered overwhelmingly embarrassing, personally degrading, and often is theologically prohibited." They point out that the problems of couples from restricting and controlling religions often multiply when they seek help from their religious advisers. Most often they are told that their sexual problem is not important.

• Traumatic initial experiences, such as degrading and unsuccessful experiences with prostitutes.

Often impotent men have an internal conflict about their sexuality or even know they are not interested in women. They marry for social or financial reasons or because they wish to have a family.

Treatment in Masters and Johnson's approach begins with the injunction that the couple *not* participate in any sexual activity without specific instructions, which takes the pressure to perform off the male partner. Then follows exploration of the marriage relationship, information about natural sexual responses and discussions about religious problems, excessive drinking or homosexuality, and value systems. On the third or fourth day of therapy the couple then begins a graduated sensate focus programme.[12]

Dr Herdis Deabler, at the Veterans' Administration Hospital in New Orleans, describes how devastating impotence can be to a male's ego and self-image, and how humiliated and depressed he may become. In 1976 he treated a thirty-two-year-old whose first marriage had failed because of his inability to perform sexually and his performance was even worse with his second wife. Analysis under hypnosis uncovered three layers of inhibitory factors, including early vivid memories of severe punishment for masturbation, early adolescent memories of his mother lecturing him about the evils of sex and the need to be cautious of girls, and adolescent fantasies of his mother, naked, while he masturbated. The realisation came that he was not able to complete sexual intercourse with either his first or second wife, both of whom resembled his mother, because unconsciously this meant having intercourse with his mother.

After further hypnotherapy sessions, fears and anxiety about sex were allayed, disidentification of the wife with the mother was clearly made and his impotency ceased.[13]

Steve de Shazer, a therapist from Milwaukee, Wisconsin, developed an indirect method of treating impotence based on a more complex method of Milton Erickson's. A client approached him at the request of his wife because he had suddenly become impotent about six months previously. The therapist denied having any magic, and denied that hypnosis could work any magic; that a quick resolution to the problem was unlikely and that one session could achieve very little except act as a good foundation. The client said he understood this as he was an architect and knew about foundations.

Asking the client to focus on his key ring, and counting from one to twenty the therapist suggested that the client imagine the construction of a tall, erect, cylindrical building, on a firm foundation — a building that was fully functional. Slowly, one floor was added to another. As each floor was added, so was the necessary plumbing and wiring that made the building totally functional. The suggestions were elaborately repeated in various forms. The client went off on vacation two days later and at the end of the first week resumed normal sexual functioning.

With another client de Shazer used similar symbolic imagery, that of riding in an elevator to the top of a very tall building, counting off each of the floors, and instructing the client to pay close attention to the feelings caused by rising to the top of the elevator.[14]

Dr Harold B. Crasilneck is a clinical professor in the Department of Psychiatry at the University of Texas Southwestern Medical School in the USA. Writing about psychogenic impotency, he said that while there are many reports of impotence being successfully treated with the use of hypnosis, it should not be used by anyone with severe depression, masochistic tendencies or on medication for diabetes. Here is a script he uses:

> Make a fist with your right (or left) hand. The tighter you clench your fist, the harder your arm and hand will become . . . harder and stiffer . . . feel your arm stiffening, stiff and rigid, see how hard it is to bend, stiffening even more.
>
> From now on your unconscious mind will make your penis just as stiff as this, just as hard to bend or soften, stiffer and stiffer, and staying that way for as long as is necessary . . . the blood will flow easily into your penis, creating this hardness, and your unconscious mind will make sure it stays this way, hard and stiff and rigid, for as long as is necessary . . . for as long as is needed for a satisfactory performance . . . you will enjoy your sexual experiences, they will be natural and pleasurable.
>
> Now your arm and hand are returning to normal, no longer stiff, no longer hard, quite relaxed and normal . . . but remember, from now on your penis will be stiff and hard as your arm was for as long as is necessary.[15]

Here is the script we have used in our Unit for some time, with satisfactory results:

IMPOTENCE SCRIPT

> More and more your growing calmness and confidence will decrease your anxiety about your sexual performance . . . you will find it much easier to obtain an erection . . . from now on you will have erections more and more frequently at the appropriate times . . . more and more easily . . . you will find you become more excited, more easily . . . you will

become more and more aware of how to satisfy your partner
... more and more aware of the good influence it is having
on your relationship ... relaxed and calm and confident at
all times about your sexual performance.

21
PAIN AND SUFFERING

Hypnosis can block pain, even of a severe kind, but we do not know how. Theories range from the sceptical, explaining-it-all-away type theories (such as people pretend not to notice the pain in order to please the therapist) to the credulous, altered-state-of-functioning type theories. Two researchers have written, "Perhaps the only conclusion on which all authorities agree is that we do not know how or why hypnosis controls organic pain".[1]

Hypnosis was frequently used as an anaesthetic in surgery during the first half of last century until the discovery of chemical anaesthetics. Sadly, most of those continuing to use hypnosis risked the hostility and disapproval of their colleagues, and some were even dismissed from their professional posts. As soon as ether, chloroform and nitrous oxide were discovered, hypnosis was rejected as a means of producing analgesia for over a hundred years, even though it had a much lower mortality rate during and after operations than did the chemical anaesthetics.

Our bodies have their own inbuilt anaesthetic systems: so far, three chemical pathways have been located in the brain and nervous system. These are an endorphin system and two enkephalin systems, sharing the same chemical properties as morphine, a very efficient painkiller. Investigations to date have shown that there is no connection between these particular systems and hypnosis, as there is with acupuncture. Perhaps hypnosis triggers off similar painkilling systems, and as the locating of these systems is relatively recent, as research continues it should not be too long before links are found between hypnosis and painkilling systems.

According to three anaesthesiologists from the University of California and Los Angeles, the best hope for pain therapy in the years to come lies in finding "non-invasive" ways of triggering off these analgesic systems.[2] What better non-invasive way than self-hypnosis?

We know that with the use of hypnosis we have much greater control over pain perception, our auto-immune system (the body's internal system for resisting and overcoming infection) and our autonomic nervous system, but the question of whether everyone is able to make use of hypnotic techniques to control pain has not yet been satisfactorily answered. People who conduct experimental work on pain in laboratories generally feel that only those who are moderately to highly hypnotiseable can make successful use of these techniques. In contrast, many users of clinical hypnosis treating pain patients would agree that "anyone who walks through the door, especially in regard to the problem of pain, is usually hypnotiseable and treatable by hypnosis".[3] But the most common belief is that five per cent of the population is not in the least susceptible and therefore it is useless in their case to try hypnosis for pain removal.

One of the earliest reports on the use of hypnosis as an anaesthetic came from France in 1829, when Dr Jules Cloquet removed the breast of a sixty-four-year-old female while she was mesmerised. Surgery took twelve minutes without incident in terms of movement or complaints of pain. In 1842 M. Squire Wood, an English surgeon, performed a mid-thigh amputation while the patient was hypnotised. By 1851 James Esdaile, the Scottish surgeon mentioned in Chapter 2, had conducted over 300 major surgical operations in India, using hypnosis as an anaesthetic, to reduce post-operative complications and to reduce operative mortality. In answer to the sceptics of his day he wrote:

> I have every month more operations of this kind (for scrotal tumour) than take place in the native hospital in Calcutta a year, and more than I had for the six years previous. There must be some reason for this and I see only two ways of accounting for it: my patients, on returning home, either say to their friends similarly afflicted, "Wah, brother! What a soft man the Sahib is ! He cut me to pieces for twenty minutes, and I made him believe that I did not feel it. Isn't it a capital joke? Do go and play him the same trick; you have only to laugh in your elbow." Or, they say to their brother sufferers, "Look at me; I have got rid of my burthen (of 20, 30, 40, 50, 60, or so pounds, as it may be), am restored to the use of my body, and can again work for my bread; this, I assure you, the doctor Sahib did when I was asleep and knew nothing about it; — you will be equally lucky, I dare say; and I advise you to go and try; you need not be cut if you feel it." Which of these hypotheses best explains the facts, my readers will decide for themselves.[4]

Since the 1950s there has been a revival in the use of hypnosis in surgery for people who are allergic to anaesthetic, or nervous due to adverse experiences under anaesthetic, or where an EEG is used to monitor condition (anaesthetic affects EEG patterns), and in casualty departments for speed or risks due to full stomachs, or where there is a possibility of heart attack.

One of many examples was an operation to remove both breasts of a twenty-four-year-old woman, carried out in 1955. The first stage of the operation was carried out using chemical anaesthetic but it caused too many problems, so the second stage was carried out under hypnosis. First, a "trial run" was conducted by the removal of two wisdom teeth by hypnoanaesthesia to see if she could tolerate the procedure. After both teeth were removed without pain the second stage of the breast operation was carried out. While the incision was being made the patient did not flinch or withdraw, although she reported pain when the surgeon went too far laterally, apparently beyond the area of the suggested anaesthesia. The patient was talkative during surgery and did not show anxiety or pain. The whole procedure took seventy minutes. When the operation was over, the patient said, "Good show," and asked to sit up. Blood pressure was the same after surgery as before.[5]

There is a fascinating report of the use of self-hypnosis in surgery by a Canadian dental surgeon, Dr Rausch. In preparing for a gall bladder operation, Dr Rausch had no premedication or anaesthetic. After preparing the surgical team for the unusual procedure, he underwent a fifty-minute operation. He points out that he should not have been able to undergo such a procedure, as he is not a highly hypnotiseable individual as measured by standardised tests. To enter hypnosis, in addition to relaxation he concentrated on the memory of a film he had seen in which Chopin's "Nocturne in E Flat" was played, visualising the scene and hearing and feeling the music. He also found it helpful for much of the time to focus on the eyes of an operating room nurse:

> At the precise moment the incision was made several things happened simultaneously. I felt an interesting flowing sensation throughout my entire body ... I felt as if my consciousness expanded and merged ... my eyes were open and according to the operating team there was no visible tensing of the muscles; no change in breathing, no flinching of the eyelids, and no change in facial expression ...[6]

One of the nurses later commented that he turned a strange colour, as if he were dead. He found he could mentally direct the flowing sensation he had experienced at first incision to any area, achieving complete control while still being totally aware of every step of the operation. He even chatted and joked with the anaesthetist and the nurse:

> Throughout the procedure I perspired profusely yet my pulse and blood pressure remained steady. After the final sutures

were in place, the anaesthetist asked me if I might care to walk back to my room. I enthusiastically agreed, climbed off the operating table and walked around the operating room. I felt no pain and no discomfort. I felt only pure elation. The anaesthetist sent for my robe and slippers. We all linked arms, walked into the hall and proceeded via the elevator to my room. [7]

Many of the ideas in the following script have come from a book by Ernest and Josephine Hilgard, *Hypnosis in the Relief of Pain*.[8] Instead of putting a variety of images in your script, you may prefer to concentrate on one and elaborate upon it fairly extensively:

PAIN SCRIPT

Hynosis can block pain, even of the more severe kind . . . we know that the body has its own painkilling systems and that, somehow, using hypnosis triggers off these systems.

We can trigger off these painkilling systems by a variety of methods . . . let your unconscious mind decide which method it will select for you. It may imagine that your nervous system is controlled by switches in your brain . . . the brain cannot conduct the pain unless the switches are turned on . . . all your unconscious mind has to do is to choose to turn off the switches . . . turn off the switches and the painful area will be insensitive, without feeling . . . the nervous system can no longer conduct the pain.

It may choose to allow the painful areas to gradually become more and more numb and no longer feel pain or other sensations, as if a local anaesthetic has been placed on the area and is beginning to take effect . . . feel the painful areas starting to feel numb . . . more and more numb.

Your unconscious mind may decide instead to pull an imaginary anaesthetic glove on to your right hand . . . it may choose a gardening glove, or a leather glove for driving a car, or a long evening glove . . . as the glove works on to your hand the areas it covers become numb and insensitive, first the fingers, then the hand . . . wherever you place this numb hand, that part of you will also become numb and insensitive.

Or, the painful area will begin to shrink, it will become smaller and cover a smaller and smaller area, then it will transfer itself to your hand, and gradually convert to a tingle in your hand.

It may decide to confuse the pain signals that are being

transmitted so that they will be received as signals other than pain ... warmth or discomfort or slight dizziness, perhaps.

Whatever your unconscious mind decides to do to get rid of the pain, it won't do away entirely with your ability to perceive the pain ... it will leave a small residue of pain so you can monitor your condition, and it will take away any suffering so that you are aware the pain is there, but it won't bother you any more.

Remember, your unconscious mind will select one of the methods to get rid of your pain, or it may select combinations of them, or it may choose different ones at different times, but whatever happens, it will find safe ways to eradicate your pain.

Instead of an on/off switch you could use the image of a dimmer switch, turning the pain off slowly, like a tap.

Diana Elton, a psychologist who treats chronic pain patients in a Pain Clinic at the University of Melbourne, aims her treatment during hypnosis at a reduction of anxiety, improvement of self-concept and assertiveness training. She suggested the following imagery during a lecture to the NSW branch meeting of the Australian Society of Hypnosis:

• A pain thermometer — shake the thermometer registering the pain, and as you shake it the pain goes down.

• A red balloon — as the pain increases imagine it is a balloon; take a huge hat pin and pierce it, and watch it shrink to nothing.

• An audio-tape being cut and repaired: "Viciously cut the pain out ... it is a self-repairing cassette so you must cut it again and again ... when it is cut often enough the cassette may not be as loud, as clear or as persuasive."

• "Play billiards in your imagination ... play only the red ball and you will pretend that the red ball is the ball of pain."

When treating pain Diana and Graham Burrows make frequent use of their "secret room" image I referred to in the Depression section in Chapter 19. You can build in a suggestion that the time span in the secret room differs from objective time (see Time Falsification in Chapter 25).

Milton Erickson, when talking about the auto-hypnotic experiences he had when dealing with the pain he suffered from arthritis and the after-effects of poliomyelitis, said that, at least for him, physiological sleep caused ordinary hypnosis to disappear. He suggested therefore that pain patients should be put in trance with instructions to remain in a trance until morning.[9] Other things you should know about pain are:

• Fear and anxiety are of major importance in the sensation of pain. Reduce the anxiety and fear and you lessen the pain.

• Hypnosis reduces the conscious perception of the pain, but the physical indicators are that pain is still being registered at some level.

• Some chronic pain is believed to have a high psychological component, especially lower back pain and pain in the neck. It can be a conversion from anxiety, fear, guilt, depression or anger. Ask yourself, "What is this symptom doing for me?" Is it getting you attention, punishing someone, pacifying guilt feelings or making it possible to avoid doing something you do not like?

According to Deirdre Cobbin, a psychologist and pharmacologist who conducts a Pain Clinic at Macquarie University, the emotional aspect of pain (that is, the suffering) can be just as intense as the sensation of pain. She also points out that drugs are only efficient in short-term use. People become tolerant of them and dependent on them, and they interfere with normal functioning. She thought the most useful drugs were probably the antihistamines, which are sedative and may have an analgesic effect, but which do not have any addictive or tolerance problems.

MIGRAINE AND TENSION HEADACHES

For about five per cent of the general population, headache, either migraine or tension, becomes a chronic problem that can seriously interfere with the enjoyment of living.

Migraine differs from tension headache in that it is often accompanied by an odd feeling, warning of the onset of the headache (the "aura"), and by nausea and vomiting. All the migraine sufferer wants to do is lie in a darkened room.

It is thought by many that there is a "migraine personality", that sufferers are often hostile, compulsive, rigid and perfectionistic. Others believe there is a connection between hysterical personalities and migraine.

With tension headache people usually feel as if there is a tight band around their brow or a heavy pressing weight as a result of chronic muscle contraction. Headaches usually develop when there is relaxation after stress, or after sudden changes in your external or internal environment. For example, many women have migraine headaches when the oestrogen and progesterone levels drop just before their periods. So, you can prevent headaches only if you can remain on an even keel emotionally, mentally and physically. Other factors associated with headaches are heredity, electrolyte imbalance, histamine sensitivity, vitamin and hormonal deficiencies, and chronic intestinal disorders.

It is *most* important to rule out the possibility of any physical factors such as brain tumour or sinusitis before you attempt hypnosis.

A highly technical description of the headache points out that it usually begins on one side of the head and may become generalised, and it is associated with irritability, nausea and other physical symptoms. There is an excess supply of blood and subsequent swelling of the blood vessels in the head, which results in:

> ... *accumulation of pain-threshold-lowering material in the subcutaneous tissue of the scalp. There is thus present in the tissue in greater amounts than normal a substance postulated as "headache stuff". Dilatation and distension of large arteries coupled with accumulation of this pain-threshold-lowering substance result in headache.* [10]

With regard to migraine headache, it has been pointed out that there is constriction of the veins prior to the dilatation. This produces the visual, motor and sensory experiences of the "aura", which warns the person of the approaching headache. Since the research showing that we are capable of substantial control over blood pressure and blood flow, several techniques making use of this capability have been employed in trying to get the swollen blood vessels back to normal — autogenic therapy, biofeedback, relaxation training and hypnosis.

In 1973 a team of three investigators observed a temperature increase in the hands of a patient experiencing a spontaneous recovery from a migraine attack and investigated further. They trained patients to tell the difference in temperature between mid-forehead and index finger and had the patients practise "autogenic phrases", suggestions for relaxation and increase in hand temperature. They found a sixty-three per cent improvement rate in migraine patients, a reduction in both frequency and severity of migraine headaches and a significant decrease in the use of medication to control migraines. They suggested that warming the hands increases the flow of blood to the hands and that this is associated with a decrease of flow in and around the head, thus relieving the migraine. [11]

Two New Zealand researchers from the University of Canterbury compared biofeedback, relaxation and hypnosis with suggestions for hand-warming, and found that biofeedback, false feedback information and relaxation training had no effect on skin temperature, whereas hypnosis had considerable influence in warming the hands.[12]

Other researchers, comparing the relative effects of chemical treatments — analgesias and sedatives, ergotamine and methysergide — and biofeedback, relaxation and autogenic and hypnotic treatments, found that only auto-hypnotic anaesthesia treatment produced significant remission over one-month and eight-month follow-up periods. They decided that relaxation therapy was useful when practised during the "aura" period which preceded the migraine attack, but was ineffective once the tension had progressed to the point of pain.[13]

Generally speaking, biofeedback with hand-warming suggestions and hypnosis with similar suggestions have been found to be equally effective, and more useful than the other treatments. It is not always possible to obtain access to expensive biofeedback equipment, so hypnosis aimed at pain reduction and returning arteries to normal size remains the treatment of choice.

The late J. Clagett Harding, an American medical practitioner, treated migraine sufferers using hypnotic techniques over a period of many years, and in a published report stated that of the 194 patients he treated, forty per cent reported complete relief at follow-ups ranging from six months to eight years. Forty-five per cent of the remaining patients were from twenty-five per cent to seventy-five per cent relieved. In other words, of those patients who were successfully followed up, about eighty-five per cent reported complete or partial relief from migraines which had been resistant to medical treatment.[14]

Harding gave a talk to the Australian Society of Clinical and Experimental Hypnosis a few years ago and I was quite taken aback by the difference in style compared to Australian speakers. It was more like an amusing after-dinner speech with cartoons, jokes and anecdotes to illustrate his talk. Australians are used to more "hard facts" in their addresses, with research findings, figures, and so on — a much more scientific approach. Apart from hand-warming Harding used images such as: "Your head is covered with a plastic dome — see into your brain through the top of it, see the veins and arteries swelling, now see them shrinking back to normal size."

HEADACHE SCRIPT

We know that hypnosis can block pain, even of the more severe kind . . . somehow, hypnosis triggers off the body's own painkilling systems.

From now on you will find it easier and easier to turn off the pain . . . it will be as if a tap has been turned off in your brain and the brain and nervous system can no longer conduct the pain.

As soon as you say to yourself "Stop, pain!", it will feel as if you have taken a very powerful painkilling drug and the painful area will become more and more numb and insensitive.

Add for migraine:
As soon as you become aware of the warning signal which precedes a migraine attack your body will take action and divert the excess blood which is about to swell the arteries and veins in your head, to your dominant hand, then your other hand . . . as this happens, your hands will become increasingly warm, and your head will become cooler . . . picture it now, the arteries in your head shrinking back to normal size.

If there is no warning of your migraine, or if you have tension headaches:

As soon as your headache commences your body will take action and divert the excess blood, which is starting to swell the arteries and veins in your head, to your dominant hand and then your other hand . . . the excess blood will drain away to your hands, and as it does your hands will become increasingly warm and pink, and your head will become cooler as the arteries in your head shrink back to normal size . . . picture it now, the arteries in your head shrinking back to normal size.

Remember, whenever an artery in your head expands to start your headache, your unconscious mind will immediately contract this artery and prevent the headache.

Add for tension headache:
If you feel there is a tight band clamped around your forehead imagine it is a steel band, and as you concentrate it starts to loosen and soften and takes on the qualities of a cotton sweat band, a slight pressure, but quite, quite, comfortable.

If there is difficulty in achieving a warm hand, these suggestions might help:
• Visualise your hand under a ray lamp; now feel the heat in your hand.
• Picture yourself warming your hands over a roaring fire; become especially aware of the warmth in your dominant hand.
• Feel the heat in your hand as if it were in a tub of warm water.

• If that isn't successful, swing your arm around rapidly in a clockwise direction until the blood starts moving to the extremities.

DENTAL TREATMENT

I have noticed that the most involved and committed people practising hypnosis are those dealing with pain and suffering directly and continuously: anaesthetists, cancer specialists and dentists.

It must be heartening for a dentist to be able to change his patients from being ultra-tense to calm and smiling, willing to pass the time of day casually whenever the objects in their mouths permit. And this does happen. In 1979 I witnessed root canal therapy on a dental phobic patient under hypnosis. This is said to be one of the most painful dental procedures as it involves removal of live nerve pulp. Quite often anaesthesia that is adequate for normal dental surgery is inadequate for this purpose. Throughout the procedure the patient behaved as calmly as if she had made an appointment for a dental inspection.

The uses for hypnosis in connection with dental work have been listed thus: (a) patient relaxation; (b) elimination of patient's tension, anxieties and fears of pain and discomfort; (c) maintenance of patient's comfort during long, arduous periods of dental work; (d) control of salivary flow; (e) control of bleeding, swelling and shock; (f) postoperative anaesthesia; (g) dental phobias and such conditions as pain in the face, jaw and head.[15] Many dentists use hypnosis as an adjunct to local or general anaesthetics or together with a combination of nitrous oxide and oxygen to allay fears and anxiety.

Dr N. Bruce Litchfield, a Sydney dental surgeon, compared 508 patients requiring intravenous diazepam who were also given five to ten minutes' hypnosis, and 2470 patients who received the intravenous diazepam but no hypnosis. The dose required to achieve adequate operating conditions for the necessary dental procedures was significantly lower for the hypnosis group, and in this group adverse psychological reactions were reduced.[16]

The relevant literature is thick with reports of hypnosis being used successfully for a variety of dental procedures, but one that is rather more ingenious than most is the case of a forty-eight-year-old woman with multiple sclerosis who became paraplegic. She was extremely depressed and suicidal because, on top of all her miseries, she developed trigeminal neuralgia (pain in the face and head), which was so severe that she could neither eat nor talk.

The patient was told to assign a number to the pain she was experiencing, and chose number five. She was then told to assign numbers to other things that influenced her perception of the pain, and assigned the number ten to the muscle tension of her jaw, and appropriate numbers to anger, depression, frustration and so on. She was then told to multiply them, and she reached several thousands. It was then explained that just as she was able to multiply her pain she could reverse the process and diminish the pain by decreasing the effect of those factors she could control, by whatever amount she wished. After hypnosis she was able to open her mouth, and speak freely. She actually smiled and appeared happy. Soon she was able to go an entire day without pain, and after a few weeks the pain went away. The patient was also given relaxation exercises, ego-strengthening suggestions and other therapeutic attention, so it is not entirely clear-cut just what part of the treatment was responsible for the disappearance of the neuralgia.[17]

In his book *Relief Without Drugs*, Ainslie Meares describes how he persuaded a dentist friend to extract a decayed tooth while he used self-hypnosis. His friend expressed amazement at the patient's ability to relax while the gum was cut and peeled off the bone, the bone was chiselled away to the end of the root, and the tooth extracted obliquely.[18]

As far as my own experience is concerned, I wrote the script below when I was about to have a wisdom tooth extracted. Convinced of the anaesthetic-producing qualities of hypnosis I suggested to the dentist that I have it out under a local anaesthetic. However, he said that it would be a gory and lengthy process as the tooth had to be extracted in three stages. The roots were pointing in different directions and one was wound around the root of the tooth next door.

So I concentrated on relaxing my anxiety about the general anaesthetic and suggestions that operative and post-operative complications such as swelling, bleeding and pain would be kept to a bare minimum. I remember smiling and chatting to passers-by in the corridor (it was a small private hospital) prior to surgery and when I woke up a few hours later I felt really good, and hungry. There was a whole ward full of dental patients and no-one else could face food — they all looked and felt decidedly the worse for wear.

I had no pain, very little swelling and no bleeding! The dentist came in early next morning, looked at me a little oddly and sent me home. I went to a barbecue that afternoon and felt no ill-effects. However, a couple of weeks later my jaw became a little tender, and more tender still as the week passed.

I finally returned to the dentist, who identified my condition as dry socket, and exclaimed "You must have been in agony!" I said, "No, I barely noticed it," and he looked at me even more oddly. For some reason I hadn't told him what I was up to. However, I can vouch for the efficacy of hypnosis in that situation, and my experience does underline the need to leave a residue of pain behind to monitor the condition.

DENTAL TREATMENT SCRIPT

From now on you will feel calm and detached about a visit to the dentist . . . and the anxiety and discomfort you have previously experienced will flow over and away from you and completely disappear . . . from now on your body will release its chemical painkilling systems whenever your teeth are being attended to, and you will feel no discomfort whatever . . . even when the procedure is complicated . . . you will feel no discomfort . . . very little blood will be lost from an extraction . . . swelling will be reduced to a minimum . . . and any post-treatment discomfort will be almost non-existent.

You will wake up feeling energetic and ready for a normal day . . . remember, you will feel very little discomfort, very little post-treatment discomfort, little blood will be lost and swelling will be reduced to a minimum, and you will wake up feeling energetic and ready for a normal day . . . the operation will be a complete success, no complications whatever, a complete success . . . and afterwards you will recover in minimum time . . . as quickly as possible you will be back to normal.

PREGNANCY AND CHILDBIRTH

One researcher into the advantages of hypnosis in obstetrics said that in twenty per cent of patients episiotomy, forceps delivery and repair can be carried out without analgesia, and that the balance of deliveries can be performed with a combination of hypnosis and drugs. [19]

The main advantages are:

• Reduction of fear, tension and pain before and during labour, with a consequent lowering of sensitivity to pain.

• Reduction of the use of analgesics, or even their complete elimination in good hypnotic subjects.

• Control of much of the discomfort from uterine contractions, delivery, episiotomy and suturing of the perineum.

• A minimum of fatigue, blood loss, shock and undesirable postnatal effects, and a shortening of the average time of labour.

There is some evidence that the neck of the vagina is swarming with endorphins (the body's own painkilling system) at the time of delivery and the foetus is also surrounded by endorphins coming from the umbilical cord, which lends support to the idea that the actual birth should not be as painful as is often the case. That is, the pain may in part be psychological, a function of what people are led to expect.

Although there is no such palliative for contractions, perhaps that is as it should be, since it is known that normal analgesics and anaesthetics tend to increase the length of labour by making contractions less effective.

Barbara Davenport-Slack, researching various methods of preparing for childbirth, found no difference between the beneficial effect of antenatal childbirth training (Reed's Natural Childbirth, the Lamaze Method, the Psychoprophylactic Method and Jacobson's Progressive Relaxation) and hypnosis. However, she said they were both much more effective than no childbirth preparation at all, since they led to less medication, calmer behaviour and more positive childbirth experiences.

She examined the three common features of antenatal childbirth training and hypnosis, which were relaxation, breathing and verbal suggestions for pain reduction. Her conclusion about relaxation training was that although it is a central feature of childbirth preparation, precisely how it works is still unknown. "We do not know whether relaxation actually reduces uterine and cervical muscle tension or whether it shifts the focus of attention away from the pain. Furthermore, we do not even have a clear definition of the term 'relaxation'." And of breathing she said, "Again, concentration on breathing may serve to direct attention away from the pain without actually reducing the subjective experience of pain."

As to the role of verbal suggestions, she was a little dubious about the claims made for shorter labour and pain reduction as she thought there were too many flaws in the research methods used to come to these conclusions. She suggested that the important factor might not be antenatal preparation or hypnosis, but being allowed the opportunity to participate more actively in the birth, to exercise some degree of control over what goes on.[20]

Excessive morning sickness has been successfully treated with hypnosis by normal trance induction using relaxation, arm levitation or eye fixation and suggestions of calmness, comfort and general wellbeing. Suggestions were made, such as: "You are happy to be pregnant . . . your pregnancy is progressing well . . . watch your breathing . . . in and out . . . relax . . . count your breathing . . . that is right, you are going deeper and deeper . . . you are looking forward to your delivery . . . it will be a beautiful experience."

CHILDBIRTH SCRIPT

More and more your increasing calmness and confidence will prepare you well for the birth of your child . . . you will be ready to relax when the contractions commence and will go along with each contraction, calm and relaxed . . . breathing slowly and deeply.

You will find that the discomfort becomes less and less, any pain you feel becomes more and more remote, while it is still perceptible, it doesn't bother you any more.

Relaxing all the while the contractions are happening . . . if you wish you can make your hand and arm numb and transfer this numb feeling to your midriff by touching it . . . imagine you are drawing on a long evening glove, or a gardening glove, or a rubber glove for washing up . . . as you slowly pull on the glove over the fingers and hand and wrist, first the fingers, then the hand, then the wrist become numb, as if a powerful anaesthetic has flowed through them . . . as you place your numbed hand on your stomach, the contractions will feel even more comfortable than before, no matter how strong they become.

Although the contractions will continue to be as strong, you will not perceive them as being so uncomfortable or painful as you would do normally.

During the whole birth process you will be energetic and strong and healthy and powerful, in control of the situation . . . you will have far greater powers of endurance and strength than ever before.

BURNS

There are many reports of hypnosis being used successfully with burn patients as an adjunct to conventional treatment and medication. A team of practitioners in 1955 used hypnosis with burn patients, claiming it was highly valuable, even life-saving, for severely injured and toxic patients. Pain was relieved and hunger and thirst were promoted among patients who needed these responses for maintenance of life as well as for healing. It also helped with exercise of painful parts and improvement of morale and attitude.[21]

In 1959 Dabney M. Ewin, a medical practitioner at Tulane Medical School, New Orleans, demonstrated that the inflammatory reaction and tissue damage caused by a standard burn could be increased or decreased by hypnosis. Ewin had had eighteen years of experience with burns at a local aluminium plant (the burns were caused by spillage of molten aluminium at 960 degrees centigrade). These were invariably third degree burns requiring skin grafting. In one case a man had slipped and fallen into a pot of molten aluminium up to his knees. A good hypnotic subject, he developed, with the help of hypnosis, only second degree burns. He was out of hospital in three weeks, and returned to work in two and a half months.[22]

Children with burns have been helped by hypnosis to deal with depression, regression and anxieties[23], and successful use of prolonged hypnotic sleep (narcohypnosis) has been made with burn victims.[24]

In 1975 a practitioner from the University of California used hypnosis with twenty severely burned patients, and found that hypnosis was of help with the pain of the burn itself, the changing of dressings and other painful treatment procedures, and for reducing the intake of possibly addictive drugs. It was also used to promote an interest in food and drink and to prevent nausea.[25]

R. John Wakeman and Jerold Z. Kaplan of the Brooke Army Medical Centre in Texas treated forty-two burn patients using various hypnotic techniques, including descending escalators, hand levitation, glove anaesthesia and personally tailored images such as boat races in San Diego. They also taught patients how to use self-hypnosis. Medication was reduced considerably and children benefited much more than adults, making use of imagery such as television screens and dissociation to a favourite place. Wakeman and Kaplan also dealt with the psychological crises the severely burned patient undergoes over how much they have changed and what faces them in the future. They used ego-strengthening techniques and suggestions to improve self-esteem, acceptance of body image, optimism and coping skills.[26]

The script they used for this, with some adaptations, follows:

BURNS SCRIPT

As the days go by you will find that your attention is less and less focused on your liabilities ... your disabilities ...

or your changes of appearance . . . and more and more
focused on your assets . . . your strengths and your inner
resources . . . such as appreciation and pride in your self-
control . . . co-operation . . . and inner fortitude . . . never
allowing yourself to quit or give up . . . and becoming more
and more fully aware in attitudes, beliefs and feelings . . .
that despite your body being different from the way it was
. . . you are still, and will continue to be, as worthwhile as a
human being . . . you will be driven to find new strengths
. . . new abilities . . . new interests . . . you will accept that
you are the same person as before, but stronger and with
new interests . . . you will seem less and less concerned
about how you have changed . . . and more and more
interested in what new and exciting experiences lie ahead
. . . more and more hope and optimism . . . about your
return home . . . about seeing friends . . . and you will get as
much out of life as possible in the years to come.

A severe burn case would need an elaborate script, including
suggestions for pain control, quicker healing, reduction in
swelling and elimination of infection, and lack of discomfort
during treatment. It should also include assistance with sleeping
soundly, promotion of hunger and thirst, and suggestions (as
above) for improving self-esteem and optimism for the future.

For relatively minor burns the following should suffice:

Your unconscious mind will take swift action and trigger off
the chemical painkilling mechanisms in your brain and
nervous system . . . pain and discomfort will be reduced to a
bare minimum, almost unable to be perceived . . . healing
will be swift, much quicker than ever before, and there will
be very little scarring and swelling.

When the wound heals, ever so quickly, there will be
hardly any sign at all that it was ever there . . . remember,
from now on you will be aware of very little pain or
discomfort, healing will be extremely swift and scarring will
be kept to a bare minimum.

It has made quite a difference to me knowing that a large part of
the perception of pain is anxiety and fear, and that we can
influence the way we perceive and react to pain. I used to have an
extremely low pain tolerance; the slightest hurt was multiplied
in my mind. I had a full-blown dental phobia which kept me away
from dentists for years. Somehow, knowing a lot more about pain
has increased my conscious control over it considerably.

One day while I was hastily ironing a frock for work, without any clothes on, I swished the iron across the length of my stomach below the navel (serves me right for having it protruding over the ironing board!). I commanded, "Stop, pain!", in my mind and quite successfully turned the pain off. It was quite a nasty burn, but it cleared up very quickly, with a minimum of scarring and very little discomfort. I could not have done that had I not understood a lot about pain. Somehow, being convinced by all the evidence gave me the power to control it.

POST-HERPATIC NEURALGIA

I constructed the following script for my father when he developed shingles (herpes zoster virus) after an operation and for quite some time was in dreadful pain. We accepted the statement from his GP that absolutely nothing could be done about the pain emanating from his damaged nerve endings, that it was permanent, until I could stand it no longer. Feeling a bit foolish but prepared to clutch at straws, I arranged an appointment for him with a neurologist.

After a comprehensive interview and examination she pronounced that his nerve endings had not been damaged beyond repair, that they were in the process of recovering. She said that in six months' time he would have only half the pain he was suffering at that time, and in a year from then he would be completely free of it. This was of enormous importance, as one of the worst features of the pain was that it was supposedly there to stay.

The neurologist also prescribed tablets which were not actually painkillers, but which would confuse the pain signals that the brain was transmitting. She thought it was likely that these signals would then be perceived as other signals, apart from pain. That is apparently what happened. My father sometimes felt sick and dizzy and disoriented and lost his balance every now and then, but he had no recurrence whatever of the pain from that time onwards.

At the same time I recorded the following script, as he was not well enough to do so himself. I have no idea whether the tape helped at all, or whether it was solely the effect of the drugs, but the pain disappeared.

POST-HERPATIC NEURALGIA SCRIPT

Your damaged nerves have been sending out pain signals in the past ... from now on they will send out signals other

than pain, they will become confused about what they
should be conveying . . . they will send out some other
signals instead . . . just as the pain signals were irrelevant
and irrational products of the damaged nerves, so will the
new signals be . . . perhaps a very slight nausea, perhaps
some mild dizziness or a slight difficulty in walking straight
. . . not the signal of pain any more . . . a signal of
something else not very hard to deal with.

PHANTOM LIMB

As far as I can ascertain, phantom limb pain exists because the
nerves keep transmitting signals at the site of the amputation just
as if the limb were still there. It is a fairly common occurrence,
and produces extreme discomfort and annoyance. Treatment
usually involves relaxation training and muscle and brainwave
biofeedback.

Dr Eleanor Siegel, formerly of the John F. Kennedy Medical
Centre in New Jersey, treated a fifty-four-year-old woman who
underwent a left above-knee amputation because of circulatory
problems. She expressed feelings of depression, isolation and high
anxiety as well as considerable pain in the missing leg. So
hypnotic induction with eye fixation was used and she was
instructed in the use of self-hypnosis. Her attitude improved, but
she was still experiencing pain, so the hypnotic procedure was
augmented with glove anaesthesia suggestions. An image was
used[27] of a mountain cabin scene in which suggestions were given
of numbness and chill, and the patient made use of these to
control the pain in her stump, and later applied it to her phantom
limb pain. She reported after several sessions that she could
control the pain any time and cut her pain medication in half.
The staff also noticed a general improvement in her mood and her
participation in activities.[28]

In an article on phantom limb pain[29] the authors, Solomon and
Schmidt, report that hypnosis was successfully used in a case of
burning pain perceived in the patient's "legs", which had been
amputated. The use of hypnotherapy uncovered the fact that the
patient had feelings and fantasies about incineration of the
removed limbs. The authors discussed the importance of
preparing the patient for amputation, taking into account the
patient's concern about the disposal of the amputated limbs, as
this may help prevent pathological limb sensations.

Here is an excerpt from an article by Erickson on the subject:

I was asked yesterday by someone about the problem of phantom limbs. "How do you handle that in hypnotherapy?" A friend of mine who had suffered an amputation had a discussion with me one night. He was also a psychiatrist and psychologist. He had written out his ideas, and he started quizzing me on the subject because he had experienced a great deal of difficulty with his phantom limb. We both had worked out essentially the same method. I suppose you would call it reconditioning. I will give you an illustration. The amputation is here on the arm, and the index and second fingers get crossed, you can't straighten them out, and they are painfully tired. How are you going to approach that sort of thing hypnotically? The thing I do is to put the subject in a trance and try to reorient to a time previous to the amputation, which is a very difficult thing. He has only got one arm, and he can't balance his body properly. You reorient, however, certain memories, then you raise this question of crossed fingers. "Now, where do you feel that? Do you feel pressure here, or do you feel it in the joint? Or perhaps your wrist gets tired?" I am speeding the procedure up; but you discuss such matters and you slowly move up the locus of the feeling to the stump. Get the patient to understand the progressive upward movement, so that they can't be certain it's their fingers, or just exactly where it is.[30]

I helped a courageous young man to construct this script for an uncomfortable and painful itch on the bottom of the foot of his missing leg. He said he gained great relief from the tape that he made:

PHANTOM LIMB SCRIPT

The next time the pain in your foot starts to become apparent, the body's analgesic systems will go into action and turn off the pain . . . it will be as if the nerves conducting the pain were controlled by switches, and you have just turned off the switches, turned off the switches completely.

Any left-over pain will be converted into a tingling or twitching in your right arm and hand, and all you will notice from your missing limb in future will be a vague feeling of discomfort from time to time, very, very rarely.

Remember, from now on the pain and discomfort in your missing limb will disappear as if you have turned the switches from on to off . . . any left-over pain will become a mild tingling or twitching in your right arm and hand.

CANCER

Hypnosis is extensively used with cancer patients for increasing food and drink intake, increasing rest periods, making sleep easier, and making it easier to tolerate spinal taps, bone marrow aspirations, and radio- and chemotherapy. Patients are also made less anxious and depressed, and less apprehensive prior to treatment. All of these applications are aimed at lessening the suffering.

Usually patients are taught self-hypnosis so they can use the techniques in the absence of the therapist, and to give increased feelings of mastery and control. Ernest and Josephine Hilgard in their book *Hypnosis in the Relief of Pain*, said that hypnosis is a way of "helping people die with their boots on".[31]

While hypnosis has undoubted uses for alleviating pain and anxiety, producing general feelings of greater wellbeing and improving the "quality of life" as an adjunct to therapy, it may have curative as well as therapeutic value. There is a growing body of evidence to support a psychosomatic view of cancer in humans. Besides a probable inherited potential, and known cancer-causing agents, there also seems to be a strong connection with early childhood, developmental and emotional experiences.

Dr Carolyn Thomas of Johns Hopkins University carried out a project with male medical students, lasting from 1948 to 1973. Of 914 males seen over this period, twenty eventually developed malignant tumours. Sixteen of these were found to be emotionally distant from their parents and had parents who were perceived as being colder than those of the control group. They also scored highly on depression in personality tests many years before the cancer developed.[32]

At a conference on holistic medicine in America in 1978, attended by highly respected psychologists, psychiatrists and medical practitioners, the emphasis was on mind–body interaction. Many of the addresses were about cancer and the influence of mental states on its formation and elimination. One of the delegates, Dr James Walt, a clinical and counselling psychologist, outlined the results of his research.

Most of us have cancer thirty or forty times a year, but the immune system sends out surveillance units which identify and code anything alien, and then the white blood cells destroy the strange cells. We do not get cancer until the immune system breaks down at the same time as we are in contact with cancerous agents.

The limbic area in the brain governs the immune system and also the prime emotions — fear, hate, rage — *and it operates as one unit*: if the person is upset the immune system is upset; when the person is depressed, the immune system is depressed. So under prolonged stress or with a sudden shock the immune system breaks down and we get colds, arthritis, aches and pains, TB, cancer, or whatever. It takes six to eighteen months for cancer to develop.

Dr Walt expressed the belief that just as there is a specific cancer for every cell in the body, there is also a specific cancer for a certain personality. He said women who get breast cancer quite often have a lot of turmoil with mother images, either problems about being mothers, or problems related to whether their mothers loved them. Cervical cancer tended to appear in those with problems related to sexuality. Lung cancer appeared more in men than in women, and these were usually men who do not express their emotions. He pointed out that nurses in cancer wards have known for years that the nicest people in the world have cancer, people who try not to let you know that they are in pain, or are very depressed: they are stoic and bear the burden.

He spoke about the work of Carl Simonton in Fort Worth, Texas, an oncologist (cancer specialist) and radiologist who became interested in the idea of using visual imagery after seeing psychologist friends experimenting with biofeedback. Simonton and his wife Stephanie began to treat advanced cancer patients with meditation, imagery and exercise, also taking nutrition into account. He found that symbols worked better than imagining the cancer as flesh and blood, such as picturing the cancer as a big mound of some horrible substance, or a large rat. Patients visualise the immune system's white blood cells as knights in shining armour fighting the cancer symbol and visualise the treatment (chemotherapy or radiotherapy) as fighting alongside the immune system and not harming surrounding tissue. He asked patients if they wanted the disease to win or lose and found it was important that they were able to visualise the immune system forces as more powerful, intelligent and numerous than those of the disease.

Reports of Simonton's successes are included in his book *Getting Well Again*, published in 1978.[33] Of 159 patients who were treated in this manner, sixty-three were still alive four years later. Of these, fourteen had no evidence of disease, twelve had regression of their tumours and seventeen had stabilised. As these were patients initially diagnosed as incurable, these are remarkable results.

Simonton himself addressed the conference, putting his overall results in a less dramatic light. He said that the type of person he had been seeing usually had a life expectancy of less than twelve months, but his patients had in fact lived an average of two years. He said this was nothing to get excited about, it simply pointed to the fact that what he was doing was worth exploring. What he did get excited about was that people who threw themselves enthusiastically into the treatment, who had strong purpose, belief and determination and were willing to fight the internal and external problems, did far better.

Simonton said he believed that we all have a part of us that wants to live, socially sanctioned and in conscious awareness, and we all have a part of us that wants to die. The latter is largely out of consciousness and socially unacceptable.

He emphasised the significant part played in the development and progress of disease by the emotions, dietary factors and exercise. He also drew attention to the fact that stress is very complicated and difficult to research: what is stressful to one person is not stressful to another, and what is stressful at one time of life may not be stressful at another. He mentioned animal experiments, one in which by varying the stress factors and keeping other things constant the experimenter could vary the development of malignant breast cancers in mice from seven per cent to ninety-two per cent, and another in which mice which were exercised to an optimum level had decreased cancer development, a decrease in the incidence of malignancy and a decrease in the cancer growth rate. However, the mice which were overexercised increased the development of cancer and the cancer grew more quickly.

Simonton also described an exciting study being done at Boston University Medical School on "killer cells" (the white blood cells known as T-lymphocytes, which destroy alien malignant cells). They took three groups of undergraduates at Harvard and correlated their life change events with their "killer cell" activity. Compared to the other groups, and compared to what is considered usual, one group had little stress and little "killer cell" activity, another group underwent a great deal of stress and displayed symptoms such as irritability, nausea, not sleeping well, being depressed and anxious. This group had decreased "killer cell" activity. The third group experienced a lot of major changes in their lives but had none of those symptoms, their feeling of wellbeing being at about the same level as the first group. They had dramatically increased "killer cell" activity.

It has since been found that while one type of lymphocyte, the T-lymphocyte, identifies and destroys cancer cells, antigens are somehow formed to block this destruction, and these blocking agents are sometimes harboured and protected by the other type of lymphocyte, the B-lymphocyte.

Simonton said it has become clear that depression, anxiety and resentments play a significant part in the development and course of a malignancy by altering the hormones, changing the amount of cancer cells produced from a given amount of carcinogen and by influencing the body's basic defence mechanisms.

Simonton continued:

The most important thing is that the person is willing to participate . . . we try to get patients who strongly believe that they can alter the course of their malignancy by addressing significant emotional issues in their lives. We ask them to list five stressors that they had six–eighteen months prior to their diagnosis. These tend to be financial problems, marriage problems, family problems, problems with work and problems with their purpose in life. The most nebulous are probably the most important. Then we look at secondary gains: what is the person getting out of being sick? We all get something out of being sick. I strongly believe if we didn't we wouldn't be sick. Again, I see sickness as a tool we use when our other coping strategies break down, it is serving an important function. We work with [the patients] about early life decisions which were made and continue to cloud the way that they see their lives; if they change their views and change some of these decisions then they can change their perspective. We also deal with death and the possibility of recurrence. We help them make contact with the internal healing sources inside themselves and help them to develop realistic goals.

The importance of exercise, which is incorporated into the programme, and diet, were also emphasised. His basic stance on diet was, in general, to eat less, to move away from meats, fats and oils and stay with more fresh fruit and vegetables: "It is coming through loud and clear in all the literature that overeating and being overweight is detrimental in the course of malignancy."

More recently in the programme Simonton and his fellow researchers have focused on spiritual awareness as another way of dramatically changing people's perspective. They also looked at the family systems, types of communication within families, the healthy and unhealthy aspects of the family dynamics. Simonton maintains that emotional and spiritual factors must be addressed in the cancer victim. Among the tools available to do this are classical hypnosis, self-hypnosis and various meditation techniques and psychotherapies.

Similarly to Dr Walt, Simonton said that he believes there is

symbolic significance in the part of the body where we develop
our disease:

> It appears that women who develop breast cancer tend to have
> a special personality configuration. Sexual identity is a big
> factor — role conflict, sex role, whether to have children,
> whether to be a mother or a working woman. These women
> tend to have had relatively poor relationships with their
> mothers and they tend to have very poor relationships with
> their children, particularly their female children.

He suggested that if a person is in psychological conflict about a
part of his or her body, abnormal hormones may be produced
which affect that particular area. Hence certain personality types
are associated with certain types of cancer, as Dr James Walt also
points out. The lung cancer personality tends to be one of the
most emotionally repressed and inhibited, with poor self-esteem,
poor communication and feelings of helplessness. Simonton
concluded: "So I think there are both physiological and
psychological reasons why we attack the specific part of our body
that we do. I don't understand it very well, and it's a tenuous
area, but a rich area that will give a lot of valuable information
the more we understand it."

Another speaker at the conference, Dr Fadiman, said that it was
increasingly likely that disease processes would be changed by
mental intervention; that if you get your head straight the disease
will find it harder to coexist with you. He cited an example of a
woman who was thirty-three and very beautiful, and was told by
a surgeon that she had cancer of the cervix. She said, "When I
refused to let him cut it out he told me I had an unnatural
attachment to my uterus." She quit her job, and devoted herself
full time to meditation, in which she pictured a normal, healthy
uterus. Her cancer disappeared, and when she went back and told
the doctor he said she was crazy.

In a talk by Bob Gilley, from North Carolina, called "Learning
to Live Without Cancer", he described how in 1973 a lump was
discovered in his groin. Two years prior to this he had dropped a
weight on his leg and suffered traumatic muscle pull, and he was
despondent because he was getting very little exercise when,
before this, he had been extremely active. At the same time he
was a bit depressed because he had reached his business goals and
had nothing left to strive for. A biopsy gave him a thirty to
eighty per cent chance of recovering, but he was later told he had
less than a one per cent chance of recovery. He took inspiration
from his favourite childhood story, "The Little Train Who
Thought He Could", and went to a cancer clinic for

chemotherapy, which he said was a ghastly experience. At one stage he was so sick from the chemotherapy that he gave up the fight, but his wife rallied him. Nine months later when he was close to rock bottom, a mere skeleton, and had tried everything, he read about Dr Simonton's idea that a person had within them the power to combat disease through meditation and mental imagery. When he dragged himself along to see the Simontons at Fort Worth, he had been ten months on chemotherapy and could have taken no more without irrevocable tissue damage.

After practising meditation and visualisation three times every day for six weeks, he was checked out by his oncologist. The cancer had shrunk seventy-five per cent in mass, and he was on no other treatment except daily walks and the vitamins he had been taking all along. Two weeks later after another test he was totally clear of disease. His doctor was so amazed that he started using Simonton's techniques with his patients. He also got good results with some people, noting that results tended to be positive with those people who *believed* in what they were doing.

Simonton had also found that people's beliefs and expectations correlated with the results — those who were enthusiastic about the visual exercises had the best results, those who were half-hearted had average results, and those who were not interested or not convinced had poor results.

Professor Frank, Professor Emeritus in the School of Psychiatry at Johns Hopkins School of Medicine, gave some examples of how the body and the mind interact, and told of his objection to the placebo effect not being recognised as a legitimate source of healing. He estimated that forty to fifty per cent of the effectiveness of a treatment is placebo. He told of experiments with mental patients in which some were given a small to moderate dose of Stellazine, a powerful anti-psychotic drug, and some were given a placebo. There was a thirty-two per cent improvement with Stellazine and a thirty-five per cent improvement with the placebo. They then doubled the dose and doubled the contact time with the doctor, after which they reported a sixty-seven per cent improvement with Stellazine and a seventy-two per cent improvement with the placebo!

The Australian psychiatrist Ainslie Meares has for many years been treating terminal cancer patients using relaxation and meditation techniques (meditation can be looked upon as hypnosis without specific suggestions). He found that meditation reduced the level of cortisone in the body, freeing the immune system to fight against the cancer. Sadly, there does not appear to be any psychiatrist or psychologist following in his footsteps. However, one of his patients, Ian Gawler, a veterinary surgeon from Victoria, received considerable publicity due to his remarkable recovery from cancer of the bone, chest, lungs and pelvis. He mounted a three-pronged attack on the cancer: a complete overhaul of his diet, intensive meditation and keeping a positive attitude. He said that a positive attitude is crucial. When he was told he had a few months to live, he arranged to be married. "I never at any stage thought I would die. I was absolutely confident of finding a way to beat it," he said. He and his wife conduct the Melbourne Cancer Support programme, hold regular group sessions and distribute cassette tapes.

A recent edition of *Australian Wellbeing* carried a story by Maurice Burke, a Canadian, entitled "My Successful Fight Against Cancer". Burke used to work as an industrial designer with clients in several countries. In 1976 while he was shaving he discovered a small lump in his neck. By 1978 this had grown to the size of an apple and had spread to adjoining areas, the carotid vein and the nerve which controls speech. It was only then that it was diagnosed as a carcinoma. He tells the story of how he went through the whole arsenal of orthodox treatments and finally combined a fighting spirit and the intense determination to live with massive doses of vitamins. He commenced with twenty grams of vitamin C administered intravenously and worked this down to twelve grams orally, vitamin A, selenium, vitamin E and so on, and in about fourteen weeks his cancer had disappeared.

He went to see the professor who had been treating him in Switzerland, who when he had recovered from his shock said it was the most remarkable thing he had ever seen.[34]

CANCER SCRIPT

From this time forward the immune system in your body is going to fight the biggest battle it has ever fought . . . picture your white blood cells, the T-lymphocytes, getting together in large numbers, massing in powerful and strong ranks . . . picture them attacking the cancerous growths, the foreign invaders in your body . . . picture them attacking the cancerous growths and eating away at them until they gradually shrink away and finally disappear . . . dwindling away to nothing . . . attacking and attacking until there is nothing left to attack . . . all there is left is healthy tissue.

At the same time, those B-cells of a particular size that have been protecting the tumorous cells will no longer do so . . . they will simply cease to do so.

As the T-cells attack they are flanked by your medication . . . the radiotherapy or chemotherapy is there as another strong and powerful force to attack the unhealthy growth

... it attacks only the cancer and leaves the surrounding tissue untouched ... unharmed.

Antibodies will develop to fight the tumorous masses and will continue to develop until the cancer is killed ... these antibodies will go precisely and directly to the tumours and will not harm surrounding tissue.

Other body systems spring into action to help with the attack and destruction of the unhealthy tissue ... the blood supply is cut off from the tumour to assist with the shrinking and dying of the tumorous growth ... all the blood will be diverted so the tumour will be destroyed.

Your unconscious mind knows exactly where the growths and tumours are, and it will stop any blood being supplied to them in future and will keep the blood flowing as usual to the healthy tissues ... your unconscious mind will also assist the medication in finding its way to the tumours and concentrating solely on them, leaving all surrounding healthy tissue unharmed.

At the same time, while you are having radiation treatment, an increasing supply of oxygen will flow to the tumour to assist the treatment, but as soon as the treatment is over the tumour will be starved of any further supplies of oxygen so that the cells still alive cannot repair themselves ... they will be killed by lack of oxygen.

Together, your unconscious mind, your immune system, your blood and oxygen flow will work together with your medication in a mighty effort to fight and destroy the cancerous cells in your body ... at the same time they will leave your healthy tissues quite unharmed.

From now on you will be more and more confident of your ability to fight, of your conscious ability to fight, and of the ability of your body to fight ... you will believe, and it is true, that your unconscious mind as well as your conscious mind can contribute to this fight ... your unconscious mind can locate lesions and tumours and can find a way of halting their growth and reversing their progress ... it can and it will find a way ... perhaps by cutting off the supply of blood to these tumours ... whichever way it finds of stopping them, it will do this in such a way that it doesn't cause any other problems ... you can trust your unconscious mind ... it has the power and ability to put a stop to these cancerous growths ... you will find that from now on your conscious mind and your unconscious mind will fight well together ... will fight better and better ... you will feel stronger and fitter, more alert and energetic ...

you won't dwell on yourself and your difficulties.

Picture it now, your unconscious mind gearing up the healthy cells to fight the cancerous cells ... martialling your immune system to destroy the cancerous cells by cutting off the blood supply to these cells, or whatever method is most effective.

Your immune system will in future remain sensitive to changes in cells so that cancerous cells will be recognised and completely destroyed, immediately ... you will be calm and serene, completely sure of your body's ability to fight and win.

I have incorporated in that script a suggestion about the blood supply being cut off to the cancerous growth. This idea comes from an article by an American physician and a psychologist who suggested that as hypnosis could control massive bleeding and pain and remove warts by stopping the blood flow to them, perhaps the blood flow to cancerous tumours could likewise be controlled.[35] This could destroy them outright, or could at least be a useful adjunct to chemo- or radiotherapy.

They point out that, as in wart removal, the suggestion is to stop the blood flow to the cancers wherever they are and not to stop the blood flow to specific anatomical areas: ''We suspect that the subconscious mind may 'know' where the warts or tumours are, and the suggestion to stop flow to all tumours may be as successful as our stopping blood flow to all warts.''

They suggested the ways in which blood-flow control through hypnosis could be useful in cancer treatment:

• Completely stopping blood flow to tumours, thus destroying them outright

• Concentration or retention of drugs used in chemotherapy in the relevant areas

• Controlling oxygen distribution from the blood into tumours as an aid to radiation therapy; that is, to increase the oxygen supply to the tumour cells during radiation treatment and then immediately afterwards to reduce the available oxygen in order to minimise the repair of the cells still alive, if not to kill them outright.

It is important to include in the suggestion that normal tissue is not to be interfered with.

There are numerous ideas which can be included in a cancer script — it is just a question of finding something suitable.

Milton Erickson used displacement of the intractable pain of cancer of the prostate into an equal pain in the patient's left hand. In the new location it was endurable, since it did not have the same threatening significance. In another case of Erickson's the patient went into a trance state in response to post-hypnotic suggestions. In this trance state she took herself mentally away from her sick body. In her mind she climbed into her wheelchair and went into the living room to watch television — free of pain — while her suffering body remained in the bedroom.

Ernest Hilgard suggested returning to a time before the present illness began, to an activity in which there was great pleasure and absorption. Patients can relive happy experiences such as camping, bushwalking, playing sports, swimming or watching favourite TV shows. While the patient is in the midst of these experiences pain goes unnoticed. It is then possible to suggest that, although the experience itself will end, there will be a tendency to ignore any discomfort and that the feelings of wellbeing and pleasantness will persist for a long time. [36]

Paul Sacerdote successfully induced what he called "mystical introvertive and extrovertive experiences" for cancer patients suffering intractable chronic pain and no longer responding to other techniques. Introvertive mystical experiences culminate in the subjective experiences of "nothingness", the absolute void, in which people abandon identification of the senses, relinquish ego-identification and dispense with the usual logical categories of distinction. Extrovertive mystical experiences expand the person's awareness to unlimited universal experiences, across barriers of time and space. [37]

Suggestions of pleasant dreams, particularly dreams of flying, is another way in which hypnosis can help the cancer patient. Amnesia for the pain experienced previously can also be induced. As remembrance is dulled or erased, anticipatory dread can be eliminated.

22

SOCIAL INTERACTION, PUBLIC PERFORMANCE AND SELF-IMPROVEMENT

SOCIAL SKILLS AND COMMUNICATION PROBLEMS

Following closely upon loss of concentration and interest, and examination anxiety, the most common problem with which students approach me is difficulty relating to other people and forming friendships. At its worst this can result in agoraphobia, paranoia, depression or even suicide. In its more severe form sufferers feel isolated, having been unable to form friendships while at school, work or social events. They overreact strongly when others tease them and in doing so attract more teasing. They usually appear a little aloof as a defence, saying they find other people have little in common with them, that others are too superficial. They look for deep, meaningful relationships and scare people off with their intensity. They often become involved in odd religions or philosophies.

These people feel they are boring, unattractive — all kinds of negative things. They find it hard to locate good qualities in themselves, and withdraw more and more, especially following rejection. They may have experienced real or perceived rejection in the home, where nothing they do ever seems to be right. They are often overshadowed by their parents' or brothers' and sisters' performances. Frequently they are children of academics, medicos and (ahem!) psychologists, with overly high demands and expectations placed upon them, either subtly or openly.

Students with this problem have trouble starting or maintaining conversations, remain silent in a group, and are sometimes incapable of speaking in public. Some students have abandoned a course rather than give a seminar in front of their class, and where courses require students to band together to work on assignments, they may decide to give up a course because of their inability to do so.

There are less severe forms of social anxiety. Scratch most of us and you will find a somewhat shy person underneath. We are uncomfortable at parties with strangers, nervous about giving a

194

speech, shy with the opposite sex and sometimes with the same sex, wonder what to talk about, how to act, what other people think of us. We are afraid we are boring and worried about making *faux pas*.

Quite often I see students who have been confident for most of their school or tertiary years, but have suffered a sudden, seemingly unaccountable loss of confidence. This often follows some change or shock. They may have started at a new school, or close classmates may have left school, their parents may have gone on holiday and left them in charge of younger brothers and sisters, or they may have suffered a broken relationship.

SOCIAL SKILLS AND COMMUNICATION SCRIPT

From this time forward you will find it easier to appear more confident . . . you will work at presenting yourself as self-assured and confident . . . and gradually you will become the way you appear to be.

You will be less conscious of yourself, less preoccupied with yourself, you will concentrate on other people and show genuine interest in them . . . what they are doing and how they are feeling . . . you will *really* listen and ask questions.

You will look the other person in the eyes, smile readily, look approachable . . . from now on you will try to make yourself worth knowing . . . read as widely as possible . . . expand your activities and your circle of acquaintances . . . make a mental note of interesting things you have done or read, short funny jokes, anything you can use as a conversational item . . . But be prepared to be silent . . . you don't have to try to fill up gaps in the conversation all the time.

Be prepared to go more than half way when making friendly overtures to other people . . . be prepared for rejection . . . it will hurt less and less as time goes by.

In all social situations you will be much less self-conscious, much less aware or concerned about other people's opinions of you . . . teasing remarks will have less and less effect on you . . . you will realise they are said more in fun than with the intention of upsetting or hurting you . . . and they will soon cease to bother you.

You will be more adventurous where making friends is concerned, much more outgoing . . . your confidence will increase, day by day, steadily . . . your mind will be clearer and you'll be able to speak up and express your opinions easily.

RATIONAL THINKING

Albert Ellis, as I have already mentioned, believes that most emotional misery can be traced to the existence and continued application of one or more irrational beliefs, and these are arrived at by the person arranging irrational sentences in his head. So for the person to feel better he had better change his thinking.[1] Ellis teaches people to rewrite these irrational sentences into rational statements, such as, "It is not the end of the world if I fail this exam".

RATIONAL THINKING SCRIPT

I have converted some rational-emotive ideas into scripts so that you will get some idea of how to go about writing something that is relevant for you. It is a good idea to include a list of your good qualities so that at an unconscious level you can change any unflattering labels you have been applying to yourself.

For example:

> You know you have many excellent qualities, you are intelligent, loyal, trustworthy and honest . . . you have a very pleasant face and you are kind and considerate and thoughtful . . . from now on you will be far more aware and proud of your many good qualities . . . your confidence and self-acceptance will rapidly increase.

And here are some irrational ideas revised and rationally reformulated:

> Day by day you will do more and more of what you enjoy doing, rather than what other people think you ought to do in life. You will realise that it is not necessary to be approved of by almost everyone for almost everything you do.
>
> As each day passes you will become more competent and successful as you try to improve your performance, but you will give up the notion of being too much of a perfectionist . . . you will accept failures and setbacks as a nuisance . . . not a disaster . . . more and more you will realise you are a worthwhile person yourself and not just because of your achievements . . . you will be able to think more clearly, sort out your priorities, and decide what you would like to do with your life.

If that seems to be falling on deaf ears, try this approach:

> Now look inside your mind and find what you have been

saying to yourself to make you feel this way ... go back through the past and see if you can recall the experiences that caused your thoughts to be so negative ... back through the years ... try to relive an experience that upset you, and the thoughts and feelings you had at the time ... now you are going through the experiences that were important all over again.

Now you are coming back to the present time ... back up through the years ... when you wake up you will recall the experience ... the understanding you have will help you to rewrite the negative thoughts you have had ... things will no longer seem as black or depressing ... you will not worry nearly so much if things go wrong, if someone rejects you, or if you feel you have made a fool of yourself ... you will be far more placid and less easily upset.

ASSERTIVENESS

As I have explained, assertiveness involves standing up for your rights without pushing others around. You should say, "Excuse me, I was here first," in a shop when others are about to be served out of turn before you; you should return unsatisfactory goods; and you should learn to say "No" politely and firmly.

Lack of assertion is not considered to be a serious psychological disorder, but it can disable many people. In a recent survey, forty per cent of Americans, that is, eighty-four million people, considered themselves shy.

Nonassertion has been defined as: "Violating one's own rights by failing to express honest feelings, thoughts, beliefs and consequently permitting others to violate oneself."[2]

As a lot of nonassertive people have been found to have more negative mental self-statements than assertive people, assertiveness training is often combined with rational-emotive therapy.

ASSERTIVENESS SCRIPT

From this time forward you will become more and more assertive, more able to stand up for yourself without undue anxiety, to express your honest feelings comfortably and obtain your rights without interfering with the rights of others ... you will act firmly by speaking up if someone is served out of turn in front of you in a shop or if the food is unsatisfactory in a restaurant ... if someone asks you a favour you do not wish to grant you will simply say, "I'm sorry, but no" ... you will be more outgoing and friendly with people ... you will be able to talk quite confidently with strangers at a party ... you will accept compliments gracefully and pay other people compliments in return ... you will look directly at the other person when you are speaking, directly into their eyes as much as seems necessary ... you will choose your words more and more skilfully ... stand and sit confidently and straight, and smile whenever it seems appropriate.

The more assertive and spontaneous you become, the more confident you will feel, the better you will feel about yourself and the more other people will respect and admire you.

Remember, when you choose to do so you will be able to assert yourself more and more in situations you would once have found difficult to handle ... remember also that by being assertive you are not pushing others around ... as you become more assertive, you will also become more sensitive to the feelings of others, so your relationships will be *mutually* satisfying.

MEMORY FOR NAMES

Everyone has experienced times when they have suddenly forgotten names they should remember. Some people even forget the names of their best friends or their children. One of *my* best friends remembers with mortification his brother's wedding where his mother was about to introduce him to a guest saying, "This is my son, er, er ... " — and she only had two children!

I remember running into two people I knew in a restaurant and forgetting both their names *and* the name of the man I was with, when I had known them all for some time. I think I concealed this by saying to the other two, "Will you excuse us a minute," drawing him aside and whispering, "I've forgotten the names of those people." Co-operatively, he approached them, hand extended ready to shake, saying, "I'm so and so." Phew!

A friend of mine told me of a graceful way to proceed when you are stuck with this problem, and this is to say, "I know this is ridiculous, but I've forgotten your name", and when they reply, "George," you say, "Oh, not your first name, George, I'd never forget that (perish the thought), I meant your surname," and alter this suitably if they proffer their surname.

I must admit I generally bluff it out, hoping the name will come to me or that I can get away without using it.

I helped an ex-student construct the following script. He had gained a responsible position in marketing and wanted to be able to remember several names at once, upon first meeting the people. He found the tape helped considerably; he had a better memory for names and felt much more relaxed in high-pressure situations.

MEMORY FOR NAMES SCRIPT

You will find to your pleasure and surprise that your ability to remember names and faces will greatly improve . . . you will pay much closer attention when the names are spoken . . . and commit them rapidly to memory . . . distracting thoughts will be kept to a minimum . . . you will find a steadily increasing motivation and ability to concentrate on these names and faces, and on the effort of committing them to memory . . . it will become more and more easy for you to do this and much more difficult to distract you when you are doing this . . . you will concentrate well on this task even in the presence of what are usually distracting influences . . . you will be completely absorbed and comfortable and confident.

From now on you will find that your memory rapidly improves . . . you will remember what you have learned and you will retain it in your memory for longer and longer.

You will no longer get flustered when the pressure is on you to remember names of people you should remember in a social situation — you will remain cool and the names will come to you easily and effortlessly.

Remember, you will have far, far greater retention than ever before for names and faces of people you have met.

JOB INTERVIEW PREPARATION

It is not just the shy student who is nervous about an impending job interview. Even for those who have plenty of self-confidence it is a daunting prospect, especially in these days of high unemployment. There is no disguising the fact that one is being evaluated, quite critically, during the process of an interview for a job, and a poor interviewee may miss an important opportunity.

JOB INTERVIEW SCRIPT

As your confidence improves, as you become generally calmer and more composed, you will find you can think much more quickly and clearly in situations you once found difficult . . . when you are being interviewed for a new job you will feel in command of the situation, cool and confident of your ability to handle the job and your ability to handle the situation you are in . . . you will be able to reason clearly while looking the interviewer in the eye . . . perfectly relaxed and at ease.

You will have made inquiries about the employer and have a list of questions to ask . . . you will ask about the prospects of promotion, the training either on the job or formally that they are prepared to support, what kind of staff evaluation or appraisal you can expect . . . you will have anticipated the kind of questions they will ask: what your strengths and weaknesses are, why you have chosen them, what your future plans are . . . you will have prepared a résumé covering all your experience, qualifications, interests and activities, and you will have obtained references from academic, previous employment and private sources . . . you will be honest and tactful, and show you are eager and enthusiastic to work and, most important, you will dress appropriately for the interview.

Remember, you will be relaxed and confident in your job interview . . . you will be well prepared and able to think clearly and feel at ease.

PUBLIC SPEAKING

When speaking in front of people dress simply, don't wear jangling jewellery, and make sure your face is clearly visible — no sunglasses or hats over the eyes.

Look either at the middle distance (not over people's heads or at the floor) with a general encompassing gaze, or else pick a couple of responsive faces to focus on from time to time.

If people are obviously becoming bored and restive, cut down your talk and finish as quickly as you can, with grace. Naturally, try to make sure in the first place that the talk you prepare is not too long.

Speak clearly and loudly enough for everyone to hear and don't speak too quickly. Ask at the beginning if everyone can hear you. If there is a microphone, allow a little distance between yourself and it, to avoid producing peculiar sounds.

Try to make your talk interesting, and speak with conviction. If you make a joke, try to make it a deadpan one in case your audience does not laugh. And don't allow questioning throughout your talk; leave it until the end.

Rehearse your talk beforehand, and time yourself. If possible, gain access to a videotape machine, and try to enlist one or more people as an audience for a trial run-through.

A friend of mine, Bill Peters, has conducted a very useful study of public speaking anxiety, or seminar anxiety as it is known in the academic world.[3] Bill lectures at the New South Wales Institute of Technology, and has degrees in civil engineering. For his own interest and curiosity he completed an honours degree in psychology at the University of New South Wales and for his honours research thesis he treated people for public speaking anxiety. Along with his wife and some others, I assisted with rating the speakers before and after treatment, and there was surprising improvement in most cases. I heard some most interesting talks — one on what it is like to work at the Pizza Hut (it doesn't *sound* interesting, but it was), and another on travelling through the countryside in Japan.

Bill combined and contrasted treatments comprising skill training (practice in public speaking with tasks graded from least to most anxiety-provoking) and rational-emotive therapy (see section on Behaviourism in Chapter 10).

The twelve skill training tasks ranged from:

1. Reading a few paragraphs while *seated*, the therapist being the only other person present.

2. Reading for two minutes while *seated* to a group of three or four people.

. . . up to:

11. Making an impromptu speech in front of a group of three or four people on a topic of your own choice.

12. Making an impromptu speech in front of a group of three or four people on a topic selected by the therapist.

Examples of subjects' *irrational* self-sentences include:

• I am afraid that what I want to say in a seminar will be thought to be stupid by the other people.

• I feel inadequate and unable to ask sensible questions or make sensible comments.

• The image I try to project is that of calmness, and if I say something without thinking about it whatever I say is likely to detract from this image.

• These people are not really interested in anything I have to say.

• When I find people staring in my direction, I immediately think they are critically assessing me.

• I worry that they might disapprove.

- This is unpleasant — I will try to get it over with as soon as possible.
- I do not commit myself to speak in front of a group unless I am a hundred per cent sure of the correctness of what I want to say.
- It is often easier to *avoid* difficult situations such as speaking in front of a group of people.
- My speech must be perfect. I must not make a slip when I speak — if I do people will think I'm stupid.
- I haven't been able to speak in front of a group of strangers before, therefore I won't be able to do it now.
- I always forget what it is I want to say and get into a real muddle if I try to speak in public.

Examples of subjects' *rational* counter-statements include:

- Because I couldn't speak out before doesn't mean that I can't now.
- I understand that I have been upsetting myself in the past by telling myself nonsense, trying to please everybody and not wanting to make a mistake in public. It is irrational to think this way and in future I will concentrate on what it is I want to say rather than what I think the audience are thinking.
- I will write short notes or headings on a card or piece of paper so that I won't forget what I wanted to talk about.
- I will *not* get in a muddle because I will concentrate on what I want to say and will avoid attending to the audience's reactions.
- I don't need to know everything about a subject before speaking about it in front of a group. Nobody knows everything about any topic; therefore, if I have something I would like to say I should get up and say it.
- My concern with being negatively evaluated is irrational. No one is perfect and very few people expect perfection. I can't expect everybody to like me all the time and I can't expect to please everybody all the time.
- People's reactions to me aren't necessarily good measures of me as a person. *Their* reactions depend more on *their personality* than mine.
- I should concentrate on what it is I want to say rather than on the reactions of the audience when speaking in public.
- An isolated failure when speaking in public means nothing much really. Even numerous failures do not mean I'll never be a success in life. I'll still be happy and a worthwhile person.
- I must forget my failures and try to do better next time.
- I accept that it is self-defeating to avoid life's difficulties.
- I must *force* myself to do those things I once avoided. I must be prepared to take risks and accept setbacks if they occur.

Speakers were assessed by the presence or absence of such indicators of anxiety as avoiding eye contact, grimacing, quivering voice, shuffling, heavy breathing and so on.

Bill's analysis of the results showed that both the training in public speaking skills and the rational-emotive therapy approach are effective treatments used separately and in combination, but he felt that the practice of combining the two should be adopted, as it presented a broader base to treatment.

PUBLIC SPEAKING SCRIPT

As your nerves become stronger and steadier, and your confidence continues to grow, you'll become less conscious of yourself, less preoccupied with yourself ... you will find yourself more and more at ease and confident and able to speak naturally in front of a group — any group — at a seminar in your course, or later when you are at work ... whether you are making a response at an informal gathering, or addressing a large group of people ... you will be able to look at the faces in front of you and feel completely at ease.

You will speak clearly and loudly enough to be heard by everyone, and deliver your lines with complete confidence ... you will be sensitive to the feelings of your audience and will adapt what you have prepared if it becomes necessary, easily and naturally.

Remember, in future you will be completely comfortable speaking in front of a group, confident and at ease, just as if you were speaking to a few close friends.

Picture yourself now, speaking fluently and effortlessly ... completely in control of the situation.

PUBLIC PERFORMANCE

The following scripts were written with the help of an actor and a radio announcer, who both have at times found themselves self-conscious and lacking in confidence during their performances.

RADIO INTERVIEWER'S SCRIPT

As you become more relaxed, more calm, and your confidence continues to grow, you'll become less conscious of yourself, less preoccupied with yourself and your performance ... you'll be more and more at ease and able to speak naturally in front of the listeners ... you'll be completely at ease.

You'll be much less self-conscious, far less aware or

concerned about other people's opinions of you, you won't hesitate to ask pointed, perhaps even provocative questions, where these are justified . . . you know how important it is to yourself and your listeners that the person you interview should back up or justify points of view or actions . . . you will concentrate solely on the interview and pay no attention to distractions . . . your confidence will increase day by day, steadily . . . your mind will be clear, you'll speak up and express your questions and comments fluently and easily.

ACTING SCRIPT

As your calmness and confidence increases, and as you become able to bring tension under conscious control whenever you wish, by relaxing, breathing deeply and filling your mind with pleasant memories, you will find that you will be able to produce exactly the right amount of tension needed for a particular task or event . . . when you are performing on the stage you will have just the right amount of tension to allow you to perform at your very best; neither too little nor too much . . . before the performance you will be perfectly calm . . . your powers of concentration will increase, steadily, day by day, until very soon you will be able to exclude distracting thoughts from your mind when you are acting . . . you will notice only things that are vital to your performance . . . you will be responsive and sensitive to the audience's reactions or to any mistakes other actors may make, such as skipping lines, so you can make the appropriate adjustments to your lines and actions . . . everything else will be excluded from your attention . . . other things that are happening around you and distracting thoughts will recede into the distance . . . you will pay no attention to them and concentrate solely on your acting.

Because your confidence and concentration will grow steadily, day by day, your mind will be clear, you will find learning your lines much easier, you will speak them clearly and fluently, with dramatic impact, and your movements on stage will be relaxed, fluid and suitable for the character . . . you will feel perfectly comfortable.

Remember, from now on when you are on stage you will concentrate intensely on your acting to the exclusion of everything except those things that are important to your performance . . . you will become deeply involved in your performance, and will completely take over the role of the person you are portraying.

SELF-IMPROVEMENT

Here are a few simple scripts for improving your outlook and attitudes, making it easier to live with yourself and for others to live with you.

CAUTION AND PRIORITIES SCRIPT

From now on you will be able to assimilate and process far more ideas, problems and information than before . . . you will be able to sort out priorities and deal with the most important things first, leaving the least important things till last . . . wherever possible you will resist taking on duties and obligations that will overload your coping capacity.

You will find that you will be able to abstain from making hasty and rash decisions . . . from now on you will not make important decisions in the absence of thorough deliberation . . . you will hold off any such action until such time as you are calm, rational and able to make sound decisions based on objective, clear, valid reasoning.

You will find that those things which usually irritate or upset you will flow over you and become quite remote . . . you just won't be upset . . . you will be calm and remote and detached.

Remember, conflicting ideas and problems will be assimilated and processed far more easily, priorities will be set and wherever possible excessive pressure will be avoided.

From now on you will worry less and less about things you have no control over, or things that are not important . . . you will set aside a relatively small amount of time each day for constructive planning instead of useless worrying.

EXPECTATIONS OF SELF SCRIPT

You will find that in future you will not expect so much of yourself, you will not make such strong demands upon yourself . . . you will find it easier to relax, to set your priorities and stick to them, and not worry about anything else that needs doing.

People will have very little power to upset and bother you from now on, you will be calm and remote and detached, not worried about things you have no control over, or anything that is not really important . . . as you do this you will find the time you set aside for work will pass more quickly and enjoyably, and your efficiency and creativity will increase rapidly.

From now on you will think much more quickly ''on your

feet'' and make appropriate responses to people . . . you will relate more and be more sensitive to the cues that they give . . . also you will be silent when the occasion demands.

(Or this:)

You will find that in future you will not expect so much of yourself . . . you will not make such strong demands upon yourself . . . you will find it easier to relax, go fishing or play golf, go to agreeable social events, spend time with friends and family . . . you will enjoy the time you set aside for leisure more and more . . . as you do this you will find the time you set aside for work will pass more quickly and enjoyably, and your efficiency and creativity will increase rapidly.

23

ACADEMIC AND
STUDY PROBLEMS

While there are numerous suggestions for improving techniques in studying, note-taking, examinations and reading skills, the major problem with studying is actually sitting down to do it. There are too many distractions — sport, social life, television and noisy environments, to name a few, as well as difficulties in concentrating and lack of interest in the subject matter.

In a set of audio tapes called "From Schoolyard to Campus" I talk at length about the problems students have with studying and settling into tertiary institutions. In these tapes Sydney journalist Ros Bowden, who specialises in audio productions, asked me and several students vital questions about problems of adjustment, socialising, dealing with stress and so on when entering a tertiary institution for the first time.[1]

GENERAL STUDY HINTS

BASIC LEARNING PRINCIPLES

Rates of learning differ between individuals as well as between tasks or subjects — do not be too despondent if you are behind others.

Spaced learning is more effective than massed learning — if you are studying five subjects it is best to divide the time between them each day rather than spend the whole day on one subject, the next on another, and so on.

Allow a few minutes for relaxation at the end of about one hour of study. Get up, relax your muscles and if possible have a breath of fresh air.

The learning of one skill may interfere with the learning of another — so do not follow an hour of study on one topic with an hour of study on a similar topic.

Memory is better tested by recall than by recognition. Check your memory by recalling the main points made, then check with your notes and fill in the gaps.

Learning is improved and increased by repetition. Learn and re-learn, as you forget most of what you learn almost immediately unless it is reinforced.

TIME SCHEDULING

Get three blank timetables. On the first fill in how you spent the first week of the semester, the hours you spent at formal lectures, tutorials, practical classes, travel, meals, sport, recreation and study. Examine this carefully and then work out a trial timetable for the next few weeks. Give more time to subjects in which you are poorest, making sure you include time for recreation (and make sure you eat nutritious food). Have a study period before and after a lecture dealing with the subject matter of the lecture. Don't waste time between lectures; make use of it. After a couple of weeks, revise this timetable where necessary.

BAD READING HABITS

The commonest problems are:
  • Vocalisation: Saying the word to yourself aloud slows down the process of eye to brain presentation for processing, recording and fitting the material into thoughts. So does sub-vocalisation (saying the word in your mind, but not out loud), but to a lesser extent.
  • Fixations: Too many eye stops of too long a duration; the average adult has eight to ten fixations in a ten-word line, a superior reader about five.
  • Regressions: Reverse movements to re-read what has just been read; the fewer of these the better.
  • Rereading: Returning to a previously read sentence, passage, paragraph or page, usually due to inattention.

EXAMINATION PREPARATION

Revise your work constantly. Obtain past exam papers and complete them in the time allotted for practice. Predict from previous exams and from lecturers' hints the areas you think will be examined. Try to plan your preparation so that your intensive revision prior to the exam is timed correctly. If necessary, rest, then gear yourself for the big effort. If there are several exams in a row, you have to be careful not to run out of steam halfway through them. Timing is very important.

Make sure you are rested before you enter the examination room, otherwise you will have a jumble of confused facts in your head. A good system is to relax for half an hour before the exam, putting all thoughts of the exam out of your head. When you have any leisure time in the pre-exam period, relax completely and forget about study; when you do study, work as hard as you possibly can.

Keep away from other students just before the exam. You can

get into a panic if they talk about an unfamiliar topic or a topic you have not covered properly. There may be some one-upmanship; even your friends can turn into gremlins at this time!

EXAMINATION TECHNIQUES

A certain amount of anxiety is fine, but too much will prevent you from performing well during exams. Prepare a tape from the script on page 213 to help ease anxiety.

On examination day, read the directions on the exam paper carefully, underline key words, note the number of questions, the value of questions, the time given, compulsory questions, limitations on answering. Don't get beaten on a technicality. Know the difference between "discuss", "evaluate", "compare", "contrast", "describe", "differentiate between", "enumerate", and so on.

Once you have decided which questions you should attempt, select the one you can answer best. Write a plan — paragraph headings and main points. Keep to your time schedule. If the question allows only thirty minutes give it no longer.

Answer the question according to directions given. Don't just bring forth the prepared answer, alter it to suit the question. State your line of argument in the opening paragraph, elaborate on it, then tie up loose ends in the final paragraph. For each paragraph you should have a topic sentence and a core thought. Attempt the question about which you know least last of all.

Use short uncomplicated sentences. If you quote be sure it is accurate. If not, paraphrase. If you are forced into answering a difficult question don't sit and stew; your thoughts will often become clear as you write. If you run out of time jot down the plan for the rest of your answer.

MEMORY IMPROVEMENT

Since there is general agreement that hypnosis can improve memory skills and enhance learning, I often suggest that students include in the shortened induction some data that they wish to learn by rote, as well as have it recorded in a conventional manner on a tape to be played when they are doing things like washing up, or ironing, or cleaning the car.

MEMORY IMPROVEMENT SCRIPT

You will find to your pleasure and surprise that your memory will improve rapidly from now on . . . you will

remember what you have learned and you will retain it in
your memory for longer and longer . . . it will be easier and
easier for you to commit things to memory, and much more
difficult to distract you when you are doing this . . . you will
learn your work far more quickly than ever before . . . in
five minutes of studying and learning you will learn and
have available for recall as much as if you had been working
for ten minutes effectively and efficiently.

You will be able to solve problems with greater speed and
remember the problems and their solutions quite vividly.

From this time forward you will read faster and
comprehend better, you will recall what you have read and
understood much more effectively than you have in the past,
and you will process the information you receive much more
quickly.

Remember, you will have an increasing ability to
concentrate on what you are studying and learning and to
commit it to memory even in the presence of usually
distracting influences . . . you will remember what you have
learned and you will retain it in your memory for immediate
recall for longer and longer.

LOSS OF CONCENTRATION
AND INTEREST

I would estimate that ninety per cent of my work consists of
seeing students who have lost interest or concentration, or who
suffer from severe examination nerves. Exam nerves is relatively
simple to deal with, as it is not generally part of other more
complex psychological problems.

Loss of, or lack of, interest or concentration can be very
complex and stem from a number of possible causes. For a couple
of sessions I usually ask the student to talk while I listen, and try
to build up a good general picture of what seems to be happening.
Sometimes students know what is bothering them, but when the
problems are obscure and deep-seated they often do not. Because
of the pressures of simply being a student very little extra
pressure is needed to make them start to fray at the seams.

It may be that the problems are simple, but it needs an
objective person to point out that travelling long distances,
working in a full-time job, taking on too many subjects and trying
to study in a noisy family environment with the TV blaring are
not likely to contribute to a good academic performance.

Students may choose the wrong course and career and be reluctant to face the fact, they may have upsets in their personal relationships, they may just need a rest for a while, or they may not be capable of handling the course they have chosen. I often see students at the end of their courses who have only a few months to go and have decided they can no longer cope. Perhaps when students have been studying for a long time they feel safe in the institution and loathe to face the outside world. In these days of high unemployment the outside world can seem very threatening.

Here is a script that has been helpful, particularly with students who have ground to a halt for no apparent reason:

CONCENTRATION AND INTEREST SCRIPT

You will find to your pleasure and surprise that a feeling of interest in your studies will increase ... during lectures and tutorials you will pay closer attention to what is happening ... distracting thoughts will be kept to a minimum and time will seem to pass more quickly and enjoyably ... you will also find a steadily increasing motivation and ability to concentrate while you are studying, or doing assignments, or learning for quizzes or exams.

Again, it will seem that these times pass more quickly than usual and are used more efficiently and economically. It will become easier for you to settle down and begin to study and do assignments, and much more difficult to distract you when you are studying ... you will no longer put things off, but will firmly and easily tackle the necessary tasks at the right time ... you will find it much easier from now on to commence writing your assignments and exams and stick to tasks until they are completed ... you will learn your work more rapidly, and the things that you learn will be easier to recall, especially during examinations ... you will concentrate well even in the presence of noise or other usually distracting influences ... you will be completely absorbed in your studies.

From now on you will find that your memory rapidly improves ... you will remember assignments you have completed and what you have learned from them ... you will retain them in your memory for longer and longer ... remember, you will have far, far greater retention than ever before of the things you have learned.

You will be able to undertake longer hours of study without undue fatigue ... you will feel surprisingly fresh and energetic the next day.

Sometimes it is difficult to tell whether the tapes have been successful especially with these kinds of nebulous problems. It seems to me that the student is not always a good judge of what is happening. One student told me the tape had not had any effect, and then wènt on to describe a fascinating book he had read about public administration, how he and his wife were getting along a lot better and how he was no longer bothered by the friction between himself and a fellow employee. These were all suggestions included in the cassette that was made after he had come to see me in a bad state a few weeks before! Conversely, some students report that everything is fine when quite clearly it is not.

EXAMINATION NERVES

My first experience with this problem was just after I had started counselling when a student came to me in tears. Exams reduced her to such a state that she was failing them and was close to a breakdown. It disturbed me a lot that I did not know what to do (behavioural techniques had not been included in my course) so I went back to the University of New South Wales to attend a course in which I learned how to use systematic desensitisation for examination anxiety as well as other problems.

Part of my training was to treat a student whose great fear was that he would get honours class IIA instead of first class honours in his course. This taught me two lessons: that if you think you have a problem you have one, regardless of how trivial an objective observer would regard it, and secondly, that almost without exception sufferers of severe exam nerves are superior students.

It later became clear that there are two ways in which exam nerves can manifest themselves. One is by making students so disturbed before the exam — unable to sleep or eat, irritable, and so on — that by the time the exam arrives they are too debilitated and exhausted to perform well. The other form, which is very common at the Institute of Technology, almost invariably effects science and engineering students. The student does not feel tense or anxious prior to the exam, but cannot think well during it — the brain just does not function. Usually, the minute this student walks out the door the information comes flooding back, but too late. This form of examination nerves does not respond at all to systematic desensitisation, but hypnosis is enormously success-ful. And as hypnosis is much quicker than systematic desensitisa-tion I tend to use it for either type of exam nerves.

EXAMINATION NERVES SCRIPT

From now on you will find that you will feel far less anxious, far less tense, about your examinations ... when the exams are approaching you will be relaxed, calm and even-tempered, you will work and study steadily and efficiently ... you will gear your greatest efforts to when they are most needed ... your timing and organising ability will be greatly improved ... the more preparation you do, and the more absorbed you become, the more your calmness and confidence will increase ... from now on when you are studying you will try to enjoy your studies instead of thinking about the exams to follow.

During the examination you will have just the right amount of tension to allow you to perform at your very best ... you will feel more confident, more relaxed and will perform as well as you possibly can ... your mind will be clear, you will work quickly and efficiently.

Remember, you will do as well as possible in your exams because you will feel more relaxed, more confident, much calmer than you usually do at this time.

24

HYPNOSIS AND SPORT

THE INNER GAME

In a book called *The Inner Game of Tennis*, W. T. Gallwey puts forward the idea that the opponent in our head is our main problem and not the opponent on the tennis court or the golf course. By playing the inner game we observe our mental states, watch our reactions and stay uninvolved so we can see that the problem is more in the mind than the external event, and can prevent these mental obstacles from stopping us giving our best.

There are two selves: one is the teller and one is the doer. "Poor tennis" is when your teller takes over and you talk to yourself thus: "Stupid idiot, smarten yourself up ... throw the ball higher." "Good tennis" is giving instructions to yourself on how you want something done and letting it happen freely, as if it were happening by itself, effortlessly. We have to learn to concentrate on the *present* and not keep remembering the shot or two we have missed or keep fearing that they will be repeated in the future, because both dwelling on past mistakes and future fears hampers our ability to perform in the present.[1]

Gallwey's ideas are applicable to life in general, not only to tennis and golf.

SPORTS PSYCHOLOGISTS

Many football teams have their own sports psychologists. At the Annual Conference of the Australian Psychological Society in 1982, I attended a sports psychology symposium, one of the most popular areas covered at the conference. Addresses were given by psychologists and coaches of football teams, skiing and other sports on the methods they use for motivating sportsmen.

One of the speakers was Carlton Football Club sports psychologist, and it seems the team had done very well since he took over the psychological preparation for training and competitive events. He used relaxation training, mental rehearsal of the game to come, and trained the team in methods of intensifying concentration, and techniques of pre-match arousal.

He also worked with players on an individual basis, dealing with problems that could not be dealt with adequately with the team approach.

There was an address by Jeffery Bond, a psychologist from the Institute of Sport in Canberra, where a scientific team was studying and advising 180 elite athletes and their coaches. He spoke about the ethical and moral problems encountered with psychological assessment, client confidentiality and the invasion of individual freedom that can be associated with the practice of sports psychology.

Desmond Drinkwater from the University of New South Wales talked about whether becoming a champion, with its accompanying adulation, was likely to foster psychological health of either the champion or the "also rans". He felt that organised sport which de-emphasises competition in favour of participation, and emphasises the doing rather than the deed, can provide athletes with the skills, drive and perseverance to cope with becoming champions.

Harry Stanton, the Tasmanian psychologist previously mentioned, talked about his hypnotic method of treating a football player who had lost confidence. First he demonstrated to the player that he had control over his own body. Then he explained that everything is recorded in the unconscious mind and that the player's unconscious mind was going to re-experience the three best matches he had ever played. After this the footballer was to imagine a television screen, on which he could generate new behaviour. At first he was to see himself playing as he did not wish to, then he was to create images of himself playing in various effective ways. He was to practise these latter visualisations at home before drifting off to sleep and before each match. Stanton also made use of the "secret room" technique of Diana Elton and Graham Burrows, with some changes, and the player imagined himself dumping all his fears, self-doubts, anxieties and physical discomforts down a chute in his secret room.

In an article written in 1983[2], Stanton described how he helped a cricketer who had suffered a drop in performance. He used a technique of Erickson and Bandler and Grinder: talking to the unconscious mind and asking it to do whatever is necessary to achieve the desired outcome. He likened the cricketer's unconscious mind to a computer containing in its memory everything that had ever happened to him, and from all these memories the unconscious would locate a very important experience, study it thoroughly and from it gain fresh understanding of what was necessary for him to change. After this it was to use this new learning to achieve the necessary change. As Stanton points out, the cricketer never looked back; he had helped him convert failure into success in the space of one fifty-minute session.

That reminds me of the point Bandler and Grinder made in reply to a question on the difference between systematic desensitisation and one of their techniques: "About six months." Their techniques are also a lot speedier than psychoanalysis, which sometimes goes on for years.

In the same article, Stanton describes the case of a weightlifter who had reached a plateau he could not go beyond. Stanton had the weightlifter re-live the experience of performing in a weightlifting championship, seeing himself, hearing the crowd and even smelling the sawdust, and then told him that neither he, Stanton, nor the weightlifter's conscious mind, could tell him what weight he was capable of lifting. However, the weightlifter's unconscious mind knew what weight he was capable of lifting, and as he concentrated he would "see" the weight he was preparing to lift, would lift it successfully, and furthermore would be able to do so from that time on. An hour later the man telephoned to say he had lifted twelve kilos more than he had ever lifted before, and since then lifted about twenty-five kilos more than his previous limit.

At the International Congress of Clinical and Experimental Hypnosis in Melbourne in 1979 a Swedish visitor, Dr Lars-Eric Unestahl, spoke about his thirty-week programme with the Swedish Olympic Team.[3] The first six weeks were spent in training the team in physical and mental relaxation techniques and then training them to be detached, as if they existed in a shell where nothing could bother them, released from anxiety and pain and fatigue, and dissociated, as if they were outside themselves looking at their performance, "spectatoring". Then there was goal programming, turning goals from negative into positive terms, sorting out the realistic from the unrealistic, problem-solving and assertiveness training, and finally training them to concentrate intensely both prior to and during the competition. They mentally rehearsed the performance they aimed for, reactivated the "winning feeling" from past experiences, and decided on goal scores, times or other results they wished to achieve.

So for your forthcoming sporting events you should have a regular mental rehearsal. Lying in a quiet room, play the round of golf or the tennis match, and run the marathon in your mind; imagine playing the shots, rehearse the golf swing, or the tennis stroke, in your mind. Train yourself to concentrate. Keep thinking about the best performances you have given; re-live them.

Make yourself tapes incorporating any of these ideas, but specifically those suggestions that *you* personally need. Recreate your best performances in your tapes, so that you recall them again and again, and give yourself amnesia for poor performance or mistakes. If you are a runner, put yourself in a new dimension, floating on a cloud, or experiencing a feeling of timelessness or effortlessness. Include suggestions of detachment and dissociation, become a detached spectator of your automatic muscular activity. Use time distortion and visual distortion: the ball is larger and easier to hit; it appears to be coming in slow motion so you have plenty of time to plan tactics. You have an automatic pilot of such inner security and certainty that you cannot help but succeed, unconsciously.

I have often found that sportspeople need only a pointer in the right direction and they can easily see the potential of self-hypnosis, because nobody knows what is needed for a particular athlete to improve performance as well as that very athlete knows.

BIKE RIDING

Here is a bike riding script I compiled for a competition bike rider, immediately followed by the script he constructed for himself. After using this he qualified for the State team:

BIKE RIDING SCRIPT I

As your calmness and confidence increases, and as you become able to bring tension under conscious control whenever you wish to by relaxing, breathing deeply and filling your mind with pleasant memories, you will find that you are able to produce exactly the right amount of tension needed for a particular task or event; while you are riding your bike in competition, for example, you will have just the right amount of tension to allow you to perform at your very best — neither too little nor too much.

Your powers of concentration will increase, steadily, day by day, until very soon you will be able to exclude everything from your attention — everything except things that are vital for you to attend to — everything else will be excluded from your attention ... things that are around you and things passing through your mind will recede right into the distance, you will pay no attention to them and concentrate solely on your bike riding — remember, from now on you will concentrate intensely on your riding to the exclusion of everything except that which is vitally important.

Picture yourself now, picture yourself riding the way you would like to, having just the right amount of tension to allow you to perform at your best, and total, intense concentration on your task . . . see yourself riding at your best, feeling confident, sure of your power, far, far less aware of pain or discomfort from effort or fatigue . . . and this is how it will be when you compete.

The only thing that will run through your mind as you compete, when your mind is not occupied in planning tactics against your fellow competitors, will be the word ''concentrate'', repeated over and over again.

Remember, you will have just the right amount of tension, you will have vastly increased powers of concentration, you will be extremely confident and will be much less aware of pain or discomfort from now on when you compete.

BIKE RIDING SCRIPT II

Every time you race as well as you are able your confidence will grow, you'll become less conscious of yourself, less preoccupied with yourself, you will find yourself more and more at ease talking to others, you will stop worrying about trying to impress them . . . you will realise that it is not necessary to be loved and approved of by almost everyone for almost everything you do . . . more and more you will realise you are a worthwhile person in yourself and not just because of your performances . . . you will find you will be able to think more clearly and sort out your priorities, figure out what you want to do with your life.

You will no longer ride to impress others . . . now you will simply wish to do as well as you can, as well as your body will allow you . . . you will never stop trying until your body tells you it simply can't go any further — and you will be perfectly happy, perfectly content when you know that you have done as well as you can.

You won't blame officials for your failures, you won't feel it necessary to criticise other riders or even show them you are better than they are . . . you will ride because you know you're good at it . . . your heart, your lungs, your legs all enable you to ride better than most. You enjoy riding because it is something you can do well.

You will never care why other people race, you will only
know that you race because you are happy doing as well as
you possibly can ... Your goal in racing will always be to
train and race as hard as your body will allow and only you
will know when you are achieving that goal ... you know it
will often hurt and make you feel uncomfortable, but you
will be happy when you feel you could not have ridden
better, regardless of whether or not you win.

PISTOL SHOOTING

For two pentathletes who had just the tiniest tremor when it
came to the pistol shooting event, I constructed the following
script:

PISTOL SHOOTING SCRIPT

As your confidence and calmness increase and as you
become able to bring tension under conscious control when
you wish to by relaxing, breathing deeply and filling your
mind with pleasant and calm thoughts, you will find that
you will be able to produce just the right amount of tension
needed for a particular task or event ... for example, you
will find that where almost no tension at all is needed with
pistol shooting, you will easily be able to control the
steadiness of your hand and arm.

Right now, project yourself into a competition situation
with your pistol, one where your performance suffered from
too much tension ... now, relax and imagine that same
situation with you performing at your very best ... just as
you do when you are practising ... at that time you must
keep constantly in mind the word "steadiness" ... you will
associate the word "steadiness" with a relaxed, confident
feeling, a steady hand and arm, and intense concentration
... by saying the word "steadiness" or, if you prefer,
"steady", to yourself you will perform exactly as you do
during practice sessions when you perform at your best ...
it will be just as if you were practising, trying your hardest
to better your performance for your own satisfaction ...
your aim and timing will be excellent.

You will feel a little remote when you compete, as if you
were standing outside yourself and watching, as if someone
else, completely cool and confident, in total control of the
situation, were pulling the trigger.

You know you are capable of performing well and from
now on you will have complete confidence in yourself . . .
Remember, from now on when you compete you will be
relaxed, confident, and you will concentrate completely . . .
you will associate the word "steady" or "steadiness" with
all these good feelings and will perform at your best, just as
you do in your practice sessions.

Both of the pentathletes had considerably improved scores in
their next event, and it struck me how important it can be that
you feel exactly the right amount of tension for each purpose or
activity. For instance, for pistol shooting you probably do not
need any, or hardly any, and for examinations you probably need
quite a lot, but not too much.

When one of the pentathletes was interviewed by a reporter
from the *Sydney Morning Herald* he explained that he had tapes
designed specifically for each event, which he played at training
and before competing. His pistol-shooting tape begins: "You are
in the shoot. You have been in this situation many times before.
It is a big event, you are nervous, but you know how to shoot
well. There is no reason why you can't shoot well every time.
You have to think: sights and squeeze." He repeats these words
over and over again until they have become locked into his
subconscious and there is no time to become nervous or to fear
failure during the event.

"If you can tap that area of the brain (the subconscious) you are
in a position to perform at your best," he is quoted as saying.
"The subconscious is far more powerful than the conscious.
When you do things subconsciously, you do them without
thinking about them. You don't get put off by nervousness. You
only deal with the facts and concentrate only on the tasks
necessary to winning." His pistol-shooting script deals with a
pistol malfunction, teaching him not to panic but to reload
calmly, think "sights and squeeze", and shoot ten out of ten.[4]

TABLE TENNIS

Here is a script for a student who played championship table
tennis:

TABLE TENNIS SCRIPT

Whenever table tennis matches are taking place, especially
the important ones, you will be relaxed and alert — you will

have exactly the right amount of tension to allow you to
perform at your very best . . . your head will be clear, you
will anticipate your opponents' moves, you will react as
quickly as possible, the ball will seem larger and appear to
move more slowly, giving you plenty of time to plan your
shot . . . you will concentrate on playing the shot fluidly and
to completion . . . you will play just as if you were playing
for yourself alone, to achieve your personal best . . . your
powers of concentration will increase day by day, until very
soon you will be able to exclude everything but the game
from your attention while you are competing . . . you will
be completely absorbed in the game.

Remember, you will have just the right amount of tension,
and vastly increased powers of concentration, to assist you
to perform at your very best during all table-tennis
tournaments.

GOLF

Here is a golf script I helped prepare for a golfer. You may use it as
a basis for your own script, incorporating more technical details if
you wish:

GOLF SCRIPT

From now on when you are playing golf you will find you
have far greater powers of concentration and far more
confidence than before . . . you will play as you played at
your very best in the past . . . your very best golfing
performance . . . the ball will seem larger, much larger than
before . . . you will have excellent judgment of the most
appropriate club to use for the distance . . . your swing will
be at the right angle and speed . . . you will address the ball
correctly and keep your eyes on the tee till after you have
hit the ball.

You will spend time before your game rehearsing in your
mind, planning just how you wish to play . . . mentally
rehearsing your drive, your iron shots, your chips and your
putts.

Remember, from now on you will play golf accurately and
coolly, with greater powers of concentration than ever before
. . . confident that you will play as you played at your very
best in the past.

MARATHON AND TRIATHLON

A marathon runner I treated found it a little difficult to put in the necessary number of hours of training, and he constructed a script to impress upon himself the need for several years of well-planned hard work. His suggestion was that he would look forward to this hard work, get out and run every day, and be patient enough to make slow progress but tough enough to keep persevering.

The director of the unit in which I work, Neill Robinson, is a triathlon competitor. This involves running, swimming and bike riding, and he was at one stage having trouble with a stitch when he ran. He constructed his own tape, and after playing it he made the following comments:

For the past three years I have had stitches, only in competition and from about the two-and-a-half-hour mark on, and they go all over my body. Even though there is still drive in my legs, my body is cramped up; it is very debilitating. I've been told my stomach muscles aren't strong enough, but I've done heaps of work on my stomach muscles, so I know that's not the problem. The other thing I experimented with is drinking. It is only when I am in competition that I drink when I'm running; I can run for three hours normally, but not in competition. Thinking that maybe it was the drinking, I eliminated that, which is a pretty dangerous thing to do, especially if you sweat as much as I do, and particularly in a summer event which goes over three hours. Anyway, I conditioned myself to running over three hours without water, and that was not only risky, but very tiring.

That had no effect, I still had a cramp in mid-summer, so I thought maybe what I was doing was breathing irregularly, because in competition you rush everything and as you lose form you also lose breathing form. I decided that if I told myself to breathe regularly, that might make all the difference.

I made a tape, and played it twice. The tape consisted of a normal, very brief relaxation induction and I went through the three events and told myself to hold form, and how to hold form. For example, in swimming to stroke deeply, put my shoulders in, be conscious of the shoulders sitting square, stay on the plane all the time, and continually drive. The difference between competing and not competing is that you can rest when you aren't competing, but when you are competing you have to drive all the time, so you have to concentrate and keep your mind on the job all the time.

In a long event, and this event was four hours plus, it is difficult to concentrate all the time and your mind might wander a little, and you may have slowed down for up to ten minutes.

So, the basis of the tape was to tell myself how to keep form in the three events, and then I said that my breathing would be regular and controlled and that I wouldn't get a stitch. Well, in the same event last year as soon as I got into the swim I had a stitch. But this year I went through the swim and the bike ride beautifully, and in the run it was not until the last thirty minutes that I experienced any discomfort at all. That was because I swung around when I was descending to see who was catching me, which caused a slight muscle strain, and I got a bit of a cramp, but nothing, nothing really, and no real discomfort at all, which I would say was a miracle as I've tried everything else.

Part Four

MISCELLANEOUS IDEAS AND SCRIPTS

25

IDEAS FROM ERICKSON

TIME FALSIFICATION

Erickson played many games with time. He made it appear to speed up or slow down, or he moved people forward or backward in it to suit a particular purpose.

He would ask, "Do you want to get over that habit this week or next? That may seem too soon. Perhaps you'd like a longer period of time, like three or four weeks." And, "Time can be of varying intensity. Will it be condensed? Expanded?"

He would say:

Before today's interview is over your unconscious mind will find a safe and constructive way of communicating something important to your conscious mind. And you really don't know how or when you will tell it. Now or later . . .

Your unconscious mind will set the time at which your symptom will disappear [or insight will occur, or whatever] . . .

In this difficult situation in which we find ourselves we will have to sit back and wait and wait for the unconscious answers. [1]

Erickson would give a hypnotised patient suggestions deliberately falsifying his past or future so that the patient could divert energy from underlying conflicts to more constructive use. He employed amnesia for these suggestions so that the person never became consciously aware of them.

One example of this was in the case of a young woman whose problem was too complex and deep-seated to deal with. Erickson therefore gave her a whole new set of past experiences, including a meaningful, pleasant and close relationship with "The February Man" who was actually himself. He introduced her at various stages of her life to this person and when he brought her back to the present she was able to relate to him and subsequently developed normal relationships with other people. [2]

One of my students used a similar device to help her put up with an unpleasant change her father had undergone when she was quite young. She chose to believe that the person who pretended to be her father was an impostor and her real father had been spirited away in a foreign submarine.

Another patient of Erickson's, Harvey, was "his mumma's dish rag if ever there was one, colourless, coatless, discouraged ... he had a pain here, and then he had a pain here, and then he had another pain here ... he was wonderful — as a pathological specimen."

A group of psychiatrists sceptical about hypnosis had challenged Erickson to demonstrate its usefulness on Harvey, whom they had chosen specially. As well as his aches and pains Harvey had very low self-esteem and was unable to assert himself at work.

Erickson began with Harvey's problem of illegible handwriting. He used crystal balls conjured up by hallucination, which were, he said, cheaper and more plentiful than the other kind, in which the patient saw himself at ages six, twelve and twenty, always very, very unhappy. At six the teacher was walking away from him with a ruler in her hand after punishing him for writing left-handed, and at the same time his pet puppy was shot because it had rabies. When he was twelve he went shooting with his brother and another pet dog was accidentally killed. At twenty he also saw the same boy, still very unhappy. "They're the same boy at different ages, but they all have the same feeling. They're very unhappy," he said.

While Harvey was in a waking state Erickson had one of the psychiatrists who was present write nicely and clearly, "This is a beautiful day in June." Harvey said he would give anything to write like that. When Harvey was back into a trance Erickson told him to write the same words in the way the six-year-old would have liked to, which he did in perfectly good script, and upon awakening he was shown what he had just written. He didn't believe it at first, accusing the group of teasing him and lying to him. When he was convinced that the handwriting was indeed his own the session was concluded. The next day, they found out later, Harvey began to stand up for himself in his work situation. He asked his boss for a promotion and an increase in salary. After that he went to his psychiatrist and said, "I don't know what you've done to me. You know, I'm thirty-two years old and I think it's about time I got a girl. Don't you think so?" The psychiatrist said, "Well, you know, I've got nothing to say about that. You'll have to consult Dr Erickson." And Harvey said, "To hell with Dr Erickson! I'm going to get a girl." Soon Harvey was happily married, and writing legibly.[3]

Erickson was impressed by the research investigating time perception in hypnosis, which found that an event which took ten seconds to hallucinate was estimated by the subject to take half an hour. He decided to make use of the way that hypnosis distorts time. He got one patient to speed up memory and remember everything that had happened to her in her first eight years by the time he had dropped his pencil.

He asked another client to see:

> ... *everything in slow motion so that she could memorize and recall and understand everything ... and although she would be seeing things in slow motion it wouldn't take very much time for her to describe what she saw. Twenty seconds later she had covered 16 months of the most traumatic period imaginable.*

It took him ten seconds to obtain from that same client a completely repressed memory concerning the accidental death of her baby.[4]

TIME FALSIFICATION SCRIPT

Imagine you are gazing into a crystal ball ... you have all the time you need to look into this crystal ball, and in it you will see something that happened during a certain period of life that was of considerable importance ... you will see everything in slow motion in the crystal ball so that you can memorise and understand and recall everything and can remember and understand it later ... if your unconscious mind wishes you to do so.

It will put past experiences and learning together in a way that is illuminating and satisfying, and you will have new learning and better understanding ... this experience will be safe, always protecting you and not disturbing that which it is important not to disturb.

Now go forward in time, as if flipping forward through the pages of a book ... keep going forward in time, to when you are free, or almost free, of your problem ... you have made excellent progress and your life is most satisfactory.

Review in your mind what has been done ... what has transpired, what insights you have developed ... what you have achieved ... what tasks have been completed ... and how you have managed to complete them.

The energy that has been consumed and created and invested in your symptom or problem has been diverted to something else ... something far more constructive and useful ... there is no energy left to vitalise your symptom or problem.

AGE REGRESSION SCRIPT

Something very interesting is about to happen . . . in a little
while you are going to go back to the time when your
problem did not exist, back before it began . . . picture
yourself again on the escalator, about to go down . . . as you
move slowly down you will go back through the years,
moving slowly back, younger and smaller, further back in
time . . . younger and smaller . . . now you are at the
bottom.

Where are you? What is happening to you? What is
happening around you? What are your feelings? What are you
experiencing? Are there any smells, sights, sounds that you
notice?

Now you no longer have the problem that bothered you so
much when you grew older . . . it is so good to be without
it . . . you will find when you grow up again that the
problem will have disappeared, or almost; you will be just as
you are now as far as the problem is concerned.

You can grow up again now . . . coming forward now,
slowly . . . slowly getting older and older, back to the
present time . . . Everything is as it was, except that your
problem has gone, or nearly gone . . . just continue to be
relaxed.

If you prefer you can use the image of flipping back through the
pages of a book, or of standing in a room in a cottage with a
window through which you can look back on the past and bring
to consciousness forgotten memories.

You can, if you like, create a television screen:

. . . and the important events in your life will be replayed on
the screen . . . you can watch them being replayed but you
are not personally involved . . . one step removed, protected
and safe and detached . . . now you can see the screen . . .
watching carefully . . . what effect is it having on you?

DREAMS

Erickson made substantial use of hypnotic dreams. One of his
clients suffered from an irregular menstrual cycle resulting in
severe headaches, vomiting, and actual invalidism for five days.
She was told, while in a deep trance, that on any Saturday night
she chose she would have a dream in which she would telescope
time. In the dream she would experience a whole week's

menstrual invalidism but she would then sleep soundly and wake up refreshed. She would wake up with amnesia for the dream and would subsequently experience a satisfactory menstrual period. Two weeks later, after experiencing painful menstruation for years, she found to her surprise she was menstruating without any difficulty. She returned to Erickson to ask him what had happened as she had no awareness whatsoever of the process.[5]

Hypnotic dreams can take place within the hypnosis session or as a consequence of a post-hypnotic suggestion. Here is an example of the former:

DREAM SCRIPT

I am going to allow you to rest for a while, about a minute, and you are going to have a dream during that rest . . . a real dream, just like the kind you have when you are asleep at night . . . when I stop talking to you shortly, you will begin to dream . . . the dream will be relevant to your problem and will partially work through this problem in some way so that it becomes far less of a problem.

It will be a very comforting dream, and the good feelings attached to it will pervade your everyday life for several days or even longer after your dream is over and you have woken up.

Now you are falling asleep, soundly asleep . . . you will begin your dream . . . when I speak to you in about a minute's time, you will listen to me just as you have been doing . . . now, sleep and dream, deeply asleep . . .

(*After sixty seconds*) The dream is over . . . you will remember every detail of it clearly.

DREAM REVIVIFYING MEMORY

The following script was constructed when a student came to me and said he needed to recall details of a car accident that had occurred a couple of days before. Everything had happened so quickly and in such a blur that he could remember very little of the car that had crashed into his and driven off. He was uninsured, and his car had been damaged beyond repair, so he was hoping that hypnosis would help him remember the colour and make of the car, something of the driver and (he thought) passenger, and perhaps the licence number.

He did not let me know the outcome, so I do not know whether hypnosis helped at all, but it was certainly worth a try. It is a reasonable assumption that if he had recorded this information at an unconscious level he may have been able to salvage it.

I also recall a lady telling me that before she went away on an overseas trip she had hidden all her valuable jewellery so carefully that on her return she could not remember where it was. Two years had passed and still there was no clue as to where she had hidden it. It is quite conceivable that hypnosis could unearth such information, tucked away as it is from conscious recall.

DREAM REVIVIFYING MEMORY SCRIPT

I am going to allow you to rest for a while, about a minute, and you are going to have a dream during that rest . . . a real dream, just like the kind you have when you are asleep at night.

When I stop talking to you shortly, you will begin to dream . . . the dream will shed a considerable amount of light on the incident you have forgotten.

Sooner or later, all the information that your unconscious mind recorded at that time will gradually filter through to your conscious awareness . . . each time you dream, more and more information will return. Whatever you registered at an unconscious level at the time will become available to your conscious mind in a way that is safe . . . you will remember as much of what happened as you wish to or need to or feel comfortable with . . . people, faces, colours, smells and impressions, all will become available, as necessary, to your conscious mind . . . sooner or later, all these will filter through to your conscious mind, as much as is necessary . . . bit by bit as you continue to dream . . .

Now, sleep and dream, deeply asleep . . .

(After sixty seconds) The dream is over . . . you will remember every detail of it clearly.

26

IDEAS FROM BANDLER
AND GRINDER

REFRAMING

Bandler and Grinder use a technique called "reframing" — contacting the part of the person that is causing a certain behaviour to occur, or that is preventing certain other behaviour from occurring, and trying to find new and more acceptable behaviours that achieve the same purpose.

The script below is an example of this technique altered and abbreviated sufficiently to be added to a self-hypnosis script. I used it with a student whose problem I never did find out because he was too embarrassed to talk about it. It was something to do with sex, that much he admitted, and I had an idea it was something to do with unwelcome fantasies.

Feeling at an impasse, I used the reframing script, as you do not actually need to know what the problem is to employ it. He came back later looking slightly mystified and said he couldn't quite understand how, but it had worked!

REFRAMING SCRIPT

I want you to go deep inside yourself and ask a question . . . go deep inside yourself and ask that part of yourself that is creative or inventive or responsible for planning if it would be willing to undertake the following task: Ask it to go, at the unconscious level, to the part that is organising the problem you have, and ask it to begin to create alternative ways by which this part can accomplish whatever happens to be its intention . . . as many other ways as it can generate to accomplish this intention.

Now, ask it to select three ways that will work at least *as* effectively, and hopefully *more* effectively, than what you have been doing before, three new ways of accomplishing what is intended . . . *(very long pause)*

Now you have three new ways of behaving more effectively, achieving the same purpose, than the old way you had before, whether you know it consciously or not . . . now go inside and ask the part responsible for your problem if it will take responsibility for making those alternatives

233

happen in your behaviour at the appropriate time from now on ... make those three new ways, or one or more of them, happen in your behaviour from now on ... now ask that part if it will let you have these new alternative ways of behaving and try them out for a period of six weeks ... try them instead of the old way you were behaving ... so for the next six weeks you will behave in three possible new ways instead of the way you did before ... and this will achieve the same purpose ... so from now on for the next six weeks you will have three new choices ... instead of what you have been doing up till now.

ANCHORING

To deal with a problem or habit that interferes with a person's proper functioning, Bandler and Grinder use a technique called anchoring, which changes the way the person actually experiences unpleasant or upsetting past events in his or her life by a kind of emotional reconditioning procedure. I have adapted an anchoring procedure to be added to a self-hypnosis script:

ANCHORING SCRIPT

Dwell for a while on what it is you want to change ... close your eyes and try to experience the unpleasant feelings associated with the unwanted situation or memory or habit ... as you do this you will become aware of body feelings of anxiety ... your heart will beat faster or your pulse will race.

As you experience these unpleasant feelings place your hand heavily on your left knee, so that whenever you do this you will recreate the unpleasant feelings.

Examine the qualities and resources you possess now, that you did not have in the past ... such things as more confidence, greater self-esteem and maturity, which would have changed the experience you had back then if they had been present at that time ... as you dwell on these qualities you now possess, and the good feelings they bring ... press your hand firmly on your right knee ... (long pause)

Now, go back to the unpleasant situation in your mind, touch your left knee and bring in all your current resources so that you respond in a new way.

From now on you can deal with any similar, unpleasant experience by grasping your left knee to evoke your more recently acquired resources and strengths.

STRUCTURED REGRESSION

Bandler and Grinder programmed a person to rewrite her personal history as she slept. While she was in a deep trance they suggested that while she slept at night her dreams would generate the requisite personal history, which she would recall in the waking state the next day. She was instilled with memories of things that had not happened but were preferable to her real life history.

STRUCTURED REGRESSION SCRIPT

Go back through the years as if you are leafing back through the pages of a book . . . as you turn back the pages you get younger and smaller . . . younger and smaller.

Now, imagine you are floating up and out of your body . . . look past yourself and experience the feeling of strength and adult resourcefulness . . . evaluate the situation again with new strengths and new choices.

Allow the younger part of you to go through the old experience for the last time with the new resources.

Now, go through it again, in your mind . . . experiencing again the understanding and learning that is embedded in that experience in your past.

When you see that the younger version is reassured . . . pull it close and feel it enter your body.

In *Frogs Into Princes*, Bandler and Grinder point out something that had not occurred to me with such force before: "We have noticed this peculiar trait about human beings: when they find something that doesn't work, they do it again." They use as an example an experiment comparing the behaviour of a rat and a human in a T-maze. The rat quickly learned to adapt his behaviour to achieve his goal, and the human kept perpetuating his error.

Here are some other ideas taken from *Frogs Into Princes* and turned into scripts for achieving change and perhaps insight:

You will change and your conscious mind won't have anything to do with it . . . I know that you have a vast array of resources available to you that your conscious mind doesn't even suspect . . . you have the ability to surprise yourself . . . somewhere in your personal history you have resources available or something that will serve as a resource . . . or you have admired someone whose resources you can borrow . . . and you will acquire new choices, new behaviour patterns, new understanding and learning.

Your unconscious mind will make use of the natural processes of sleep and dreaming, to review any experiences that have occurred recently and sort out those things that are useful, making a useful representation at the unconscious level, meanwhile allowing you to sleep soundly and deeply so that in the days and weeks and months to come you can discover things that you didn't know . . . so you can constantly increase the choices you can make.

Get comfortable, relax . . . sometime in the past you have had a very strong experience in which you learned something of great value for yourself as a human being . . . allow that experience to come up into your consciousness . . . see and hear again what it was that happened to you back there.

Now, go through it again, in your mind . . . experiencing understanding and learning that are embedded in that experience in your past.

I strongly suggest you include a script to protect yourself from too many unpleasant revelations:

If anything begins to occur to your conscious mind which is too painful in any way, your unconscious mind has the right and the duty to keep from your conscious mind anything that is too unpleasant . . . your unconscious resources can and should protect you from thinking about things which are unnecessary in that way, and thus are able to make your conscious experience more pleasant.

CONCLUSION

I would like to make a couple of observations, and then have a grizzle. I have had many insights in the course of my work, but what comes across most strikingly both in my smoking research and in my job is the aspect of control — the need to be in *control* of one's life and destiny. People cannot cope if they feel they are not in control, although the feeling that their lives are under the control of benign and predictable outside forces, giving them a strong sense of order and security, of being in safe hands, may be acceptable.

But the out-of-control feeling, of either being under the influence of someone or something, of being helpless and powerless, seems to feature in most of the problems listed in my specific scripts.

While you may not get any closer to having much control over natural disasters or political decisions which affect your life, you can aim to take more control over those things that *are* within your sphere of influence.

Secondly, I have noticed that quite frequently symptoms seem to take on a life of their own, completely independent from what had initially caused them. This explains why, in many instances, therapy aimed at insight and understanding of the symptom in lieu of change and improvement is not very effective.

And thirdly, I have been struck by the fact that for so many problems a major component of the treatment is relaxation, deep breathing and calming mental imagery — so it would seem to be a good idea for everyone to practice these things regularly whether currently undergoing difficulties or not.

And now, a grizzle.

It is appalling considering the power that hypnosis can generate that there is no restriction on people calling themselves hypnotists – a drover's dog is free to do so. Anyone can do a short course or even no course at all and call themselves a hypnotherapist with the attendant potential for unethical and unsafe practices. So make sure you consult someone subscribing to a code of ethics, a doctor, dentist or psychologist who is a member of the relevant professional hypnosis body. In Australia that body is the Australian Society of Hypnosis.

Another grizzle: It would seem that the community is fairly poorly provided for when it comes to dealing with the minor psychological problems of life. School and tertiary student counsellors cater for the student population, and psychiatrists cater for the more severely disturbed, and some of the more disabling conditions, such as anxiety and depression, are covered by the Medicare system.

However, there are no medical benefits for treatment of ordinary people with ordinary problems.

I recall reading a statement by the famous clinical psychologist and researcher, Hans Eysenck, in his book *Uses and Abuses in Psychology*, that the way things are going, with increasing numbers of stress-induced psychological disorders, one-half of the world will soon be on the couches of the other half of the world.

There are many problems that it would be foolish to attempt to treat without help from qualified experts, but for some of the problems I have covered people can go a long way toward helping themselves.

When you make a recording please keep in mind the warnings and suggestions I have given throughout this book. The unconscious mind is very literal, and it can also take its time, so one must be both careful and patient.

Avoid suggestions that are potentially harmful or unrealistic or that could overreach normal physical capacity. A simple example of a physically harmful suggestion would be to remove all pain, or awareness of pain. Also, to remove all tension would rebound in most cases as there is an optimal amount of tension required for different activities — sometimes a lot, sometimes very little.

Harm can also be done in the sporting scripts. If you try to achieve anything supranormal, you just might do so. Your mind's influence over your body will continue long after the body has given up, so always try to optimize your potential, not overreach it.

It may take quite some time before the hoped-for changes occur. If you eventually become convinced the recording has not had the desired effect, go back to the drawing board as you may need more ingenious suggestions. Always emphasize that whatever ways are found to achieve the desired change, they will be *safe* ways, especially if you have an uneasy feeling that your unconscious may not always be trying to do what is best for you.

Wherever possible, turn negative statements into positive ones.. To say "do not do such and such" is a subtle encouragement to actually do it.

Alter the scripts carefully to suit your personal situation, or they may fall on deaf ears. I am not at all clear just how many different suggestions can be made at once, but I would be inclined to think that it is better to concentrate on one major problem, or perhaps a couple of minor ones, at a time.

If you have any doubts at all, consult your medical practitioner, psychologist, or other suitable professional person or contact me: www.selfhypnosis.net.au, pamelayoung@selfhypnosis.net.au

Finally, I hope that the suggestions in this book will help you to alleviate your own distressing problems or conditions, and enable you to take greater control of your own life.

NOTES

CHAPTER 1

1. Sigmund Freud, "Hypnosis" (1981) *The Complete Psychological Works of Sigmund Freud*, James Strachey (ed.) in collaboration with Anna Freud; Standard Edition, Vol. 10, Hogarth, London, 1966, pp. 105–114.
2. Frederick H. Frankel, *Hypnosis: Trance as a Coping Mechanism*, Phenum Medical Book Co., New York, 1976.

CHAPTER 2

1. William C. Wester II (ed. D.), "The Phreno-Magnetic Society of Cincinnati — 1842", *Am. J. Clin. Hyp.*, Vol. 18, No. 4, April 1976, p. 277.
2. J. Christopher Clarke and J. Arthur Jackson, *Hypnosis and Behaviour Therapy: The Treatment of Anxiety and Phobias*, Springer Publishing Co., New York, 1983, citing E. G. Boring, *A History of Experimental Psychology*, Appleton-Century-Crofts, New York, 1950.
3. James Esdaile, *Natural and Mesmeric Clairvoyance*, H. Bailliere, London, 1852, repr. Arno Press, New York, 1975, p. 272.
4. Milton V. Kline, "Freud and Hypnosis: A Re-evaluation", *Int. J. Clin. and Exp. Hyp.*, Vol. XX, 4, 1972, pp. 205–223.
5. Sigmund Freud, "Turnings in the Ways of Psychoanalytic Therapy", in E. Jones (ed.), *Sigmund Freud, Collected Papers*, Vol. 2, Hogarth Press, London, 1924, pp. 392–402.
6. Clark L. Hull, *Hypnosis and Suggestibility — An Experimental Approach*, Appleton-Century-Crofts, 1933, pp. 271–275.

CHAPTER 3

1. Theodore Xenophon Barber, "Suggested Hypnotic Behaviour: The Trance Paradigm Versus an Alternative Paradigm", in E. Fromm and R. E. Shor (eds) *Hypnosis Research Developments and Perspectives*, Aldine-Atherton, Chicago, 1972.
2. C. L. Tuckey, "Psychotherapeutics; or treatment by hypnotism", Woods Medical and Surgical Monographs, 1889, 3, pp. 721–795, in John Chaves and Theodore X. Barber, "Hypnotic Procedures and Surgery; A Critical Analysis with Applications to Acupuncture Analgesia", *Am. J. Clin. Hyp.*, Vol. 18, No. 4, April 1976.
3. Theodore R. Sarbin, "Contributions to Role-Taking Theory: 1. Hypnotic Behaviour", *Psychological Review*, 57, 1950, pp. 255–270.
4. Ernest R. Hilgard, *Divided Consciousness: Multiple Control in Human Thought and Action*, Wiley, New York, 1977.
5. Martin T. Orne, Peter W. Sheehan and Frederick J. Evans, "Concurrence of Post-hypnotic Behaviour Outside the Experimental Setting", *J. Pers. and Soc. Psych.*, 14, 1968, pp. 61–78.
6. Martin T. Orne, "The Nature of Hypnosis: Artifact and Essence", *J. of Abn. and Soc. Psych.*, 58, 1959, pp. 277–299.
7. James Jupp, Senior Lecturer in Psychology, Macquarie University, personal communication.

8. Marita McCabe, John K. Collins and Ailsa M. Burns, "Hypnosis as an Altered State of Consciousness. II. A Review of Contemporary Theories and Empirical Evidence", *Aust. J. Clin. and Exp. Hyp.*, Vol. 7, No. 1, 1979, pp. 7–25.

CHAPTER 4

1. Josephine R. Hilgard, *Personality and Hypnosis: A Study of Imaginative Involvement*, University of Chicago Press, Chicago and London, 1970, 1979.
2. Barbara M. Ashford, "The Use of Intermittent Photic Stimulation During Hypnotic Induction", Doctoral dissertation, Macquarie University, 1983.
3. Ernest R. Hilgard, A. M. Weitzenhoffer, J. Landes and R. K. Moore, "The Distribution of Susceptibility to Hypnosis in a Student Population: A Study Using the Stanford Hypnotic Susceptibility Scale", *Psychol. Monographs*, 75, (8, Whole No. 512), 1961.

CHAPTER 5

1. Frederick J. Evans and Wendy A. Thorn, "Two Types of Posthypnotic Amnesia: Recall Amnesia and Source Amnesia", *Int. J. Clin. and Exp. Hyp.*, 14, 1966, pp. 162–179.
2. William Penfield, "Functional Localization in Temporal and Deep Sylvian Areas", in H. Solomon, S. Cobb and W. Penfield (eds), *The Brain and Human Behaviour*, Assn. Nerv. Ment. Dis. Vol. 36, Williams and Wilkins, pp. 210–226.
3. Ivan P. Pavlov, *Conditioned Reflexes*, Oxford University Press, 1934.

CHAPTER 6

1. Richard Bandler and John Grinder, *Frogs Into Princes, Neuro Linguistic Programming*, Real People Press, Moab, Utah, 1979.
2. Louis L. Dubin and Sandor S. Shapiro, "Use of Hypnosis to Facilitate Dental Extraction and Haemostasis in a Classic Haemophiliac with a High Antibody Titer to Factor VIII", *Am. J. Clin Hyp.*, Vol. 17, No. 2, October 1974, pp. 79–83.
3. Fred Frankel and R. C. Misch, "Hypnosis in a Case of Long Standing Psoriasis in a Person with Character Problems", *Int. J. Clin. and Exp. Hyp.*, Vol. XXI, No. 3, 1973, pp. 121–130.
4. A. A. Mason, "A Case of Congenital Ichthyosiform Erythroderma of Brocq Treated by Hypnosis", *British Medical Journal*, 23 August, 1953, pp. 422–423.
5. M. A. Wenger and B. K. Bagchi, "Studies of Autonomic Functions in Practitioners of Yoga in India", *Behavioural Science*, 6, 1961, pp. 312–323; Theodore X. Barber, "Hypnosis, Suggestions and Psychosomatic Phenomena: A New Look From the Standpoint of Recent Experimental Studies", *Am. J. Clin. Hyp.*, Vol. 21, No. I, July 1978.
6. Neal E. Miller, "Learning of Visceral and Glandular Responses", *Science*, 163, 1969, pp. 434–445.
7. David Cheek, "Maladjustment Patterns Apparently Related to Imprinting at Birth", *Am. J. Clin. Hyp.*, Vol. 18, No. 2, October 1975.
8. Elena Fiore, "Hypnotic Regression Into Past Lives: A Case of Resistance to Hypnosis", in G. D. Burrows, D. R. Collison and L. Dennerstein (eds), *Hypnosis 1979*, Proceedings of the 8th International Congress of Hypnosis and Psychosomatic Medicine, Melbourne, Australia, 19–24 August 1979, Elsevier, North Holland Biomedical Press, Amsterdam, 1979.
9. Vladimir Raikov, "Theoretical Substantiation of Deep Hypnosis", *Am. J. Clin. Hyp.*, Vol. 18, No. 1, July 1975.

CHAPTER 7

1. Sigmund Freud, "Hypnosis" (1891), *The Complete Psychological Works of Sigmund Freud*, James Strachey (ed.) in collaboration with Anna Freud; Standard Edition; Vol. I, Hogarth, London, 1966.
2. Milton V. Kline, "Freud and Hypnosis: A Re-evaluation", *Int. J. Clin. and Exp. Hyp.*, Vol. XX, No. 4, 1972, pp. 252–263.
3. Jacob H. Conn, "Is Hypnosis Really Dangerous", *Int. J. Clin. and Exp. Hyp.*, Vol. XX, No. 2, 1972, pp. 61–79.
4. "Rapport des Commissaires Charges Par Le Roi de L'Examen du Magnetisme Animal", Paris, 1784, in C. Burdin and F. Dubois, *Histoire Academique du Magnetisme Animal*, Bailliere, Paris, 1841, pp. 26–88.
5. Conn, op. cit.
6. Lann Dawes, incomplete doctoral thesis, personal communication.
7. Martin T. Orne, "The Use and Abuse of Hypnosis in Criminal Investigation", in G. D. Burrows, D. R. Collison and L. Dennerstein (eds), *Hypnosis 1979*, Proceedings of the 8th International Congress of Hypnosis and Psychosomatic Medicine, Melbourne, Australia, 19–24 August 1979, Elsevier, North Holland Biomedical Press, Amsterdam, 1979.
8. Bruce Duncan and Campbell Perry, "Uncancelled Hypnotic Suggestions: Initial Studies", *Am. J. Clin. Hyp.*, Vol. 19, No. 3, January 1977.

CHAPTER 8

1. Hans Selye, *The Stress of Life*, McGraw-Hill, New York, 1956, revised edn., 1975.
2. Thomas H. Holmes and Richard H. Rahe, "The Social Readjustment Rating Scale", *Journal of Psychosomatic Research*, II, 1967, p. 213.
3. Selye, op. cit.

CHAPTER 10

1. Ivan P. Pavlov, *Conditioned Reflexes*, Oxford University Press, 1934.
2. Joseph R. Cautela, "The Use of Covert Conditioning in Hypnotherapy", *Int. J. Clin. and Exp. Hyp.*, Vol. XXIII, No. I, 1975, pp. 15–27.
3. N. H. Azrin and W. C. Holz, "Punishment", in W. K. Honig (ed.), *Operant Behaviour*, Appleton-Century-Crofts, New York, 1966, pp. 380–447.
4. Joseph Wolpe, *Psychotherapy by Reciprocal Inhibition*, Stanford University Press, Stanford, 1958.
5. Robert E. Alberti and Michael L. Emmons, *Your Perfect Right: A Guide to Assertive Living*, 4th Edn, © 1982, reproduced by permission of Impact Publishers, San Luis Obispo, Ca, USA.
6. Albert Ellis and Robert A. Harper, *A New Guide to Rational Living*, Wilshire Book Company, North Hollywood, California, 1972, repr. 1980.
7. Arnold A. Lazarus, *Behaviour Therapy and Beyond*, McGraw-Hill, New York, 1971.
8. Milton H. Erickson, "Hypnotic Approaches to Therapy", *Am. J. Clin. Hyp.*, Vol. 20, No. 1, July 1977.
9. Richard Bandler and John Grinder, *Frogs Into Princes, Neuro Linguistic Programming*, Real People Press, Moab, Utah, 1979.
10. John O. Beahrs, "The Hypnotic Psychotherapy of Milton H. Erickson", *Am. J. Clin. Hyp.*, Vol. 14, No. 2, October 1971, pp. 73–96.
11. J. Haley, *Uncommon Therapy: The Psychiatric Techniques of Milton H. Erickson, M. D.*, Norton, New York, 1973.
12. Bandler and Grinder, op. cit., p. 80.

13. John Grinder and Richard Bandler, *Trance-Formations*, Real People Press, Moab, Utah, 1981.

CHAPTER 11

1. Morton Prince, "Experiments to Determine Co-conscious (Subconscious) Ideation", *J. Abnorm. Soc. Psychol.*, 1909, 3, 37.
2. Daniel Dunnett, speaking in TV documentary "The Human Brain".
3. Richard Bandler and John Grinder, *Frogs Into Princes, Neuro Linguistic Programming*, Real People Press, Moab, Utah, 1979.
4. Ernest R. Hilgard, "Consciousness and Control: Lessons from Hypnosis", *Aust. J. Clin. and Exp. Hyp.*, Vol. 7, No. 2, August 1979, p. 105.
5. Morton Korenberg and Catherine Jones, *The Eye of Childhood*, Don Mills, Longman, Ontario, Canada, 1970, p. 109.
6. Albert A. Ellis, "A Rational Approach to Interpretation", in E. F. Hammer (ed.), *Use of Interpretation in Treatment: Technique and Art*, Grune and Stratton, New York, 1968, p. 233.
7. Milton H. Erickson, Ernest Rossi and Sheila Rossi, *The Induction of Clinical Hypnosis and the Indirect Form of Suggestion*, Irvington Publishers, New York, 1976.
8. John O. Beahrs, "Integrating Erickson's Approach", *Am. J. Clin. Hyp.*, Vol. 20, No. 1, July 1977, pp. 55–75.

CHAPTER 12

1. Herbert Spiegel, "An Eye-Roll Test for Hypnotizability", *Am. J. Clin. Hyp.*, 15, 1972, pp. 25–28.

CHAPTER 13

1. Wendy-Louise Walker, "Going Further With Floating Leaves — An Imagery Based Deepening Technique", *Aust. J. Clin. and Exp. Hyp.*, Vol. 10, No. 1, May 1982, p. 1.
2. Wendy-Louise Walker and A. D. Diment, "Music as a Deepening Technique", *Aust. J. Clin. and Exp. Hyp.*, Vol. 7, No. 1, 1979, pp. 35–36.

CHAPTER 14

1. Jean Holroyd, "Hypnosis and Smoking, A Review", *Int. J. Clin. and Exp. Hyp.*, Vol. XXVIII, No. 4, 1980, pp. 341–355.
2. Milton V. Kline, "The Use of Extended Group Hypnotherapy Sessions in Controlling Cigarette Habituation", *Int. J. Clin. and Exp. Hyp.*, No. 4, Vol. XVIII, 1970.
3. H. B. Crasilneck and J. A. Hall, "The Use of Hypnosis in Controlling Cigarette Smoking", *Sth. Med. J.*, 61, 1968, pp. 999–1002.
4. Philip Marcovitch, Robert Gelfand and Campbell Perry, "Hypnotizeability and Client Motivation as Variables Influencing Therapeutic Outcome in the Treatment of Cigarette Smoking", *Aust. J. Clin. and Exp. Hyp.*, Vol. 8, No. 2, 1980, pp. 71–81.
5. W. A. Hunt and D. A. Bespalec, "An Evaluation of Current Methods of Modifying Smoking Behaviour", *Journal of Clinical Psychology*, 30, 1974, pp. 431–438.
6. Milton V. Kline, Lester L. Coleman, and Erika E. Wick, *Obesity: Etiology, Treatment and Management*, Charles C. Thomas, Springfield, Ill., 1976.
7. J. K. Collins, J. J. Jupp and J. Krass, "Hypnosis and Weight Control: A Preliminary Report on the Macquarie University Programme", *Aust. J. Clin.*

and Exp. Hyp., Vol. 9, No. 2, 1981, pp. 93–99.
8. William S. Kroger, *Clinical and Experimental Hypnosis*, 2nd edn, J. P. Lippincott and Son, Philadelphia, 1979, p. 406.
9. M. M. Miller, "Hypnoaversion Treatment in Alcoholism, Nicotinism and Weight Control", *Journal of the Nat. Med. Assn*, 68, 1976, pp. 129–130.
10. J. Christopher Clarke, "Hypnotherapy in the Treatment of Alcoholism", *Aust. J. Clin. and Exp. Hyp.*, Vol. 7, No. 1, 1979, pp. 1–5.
11. Thomas Wadden and James Penrod, "Hypnosis in the Treatment of Alcoholism: A Review and Appraisal", *Am. J. Clin. Hyp.*, Vol. 24, No. 1, July 1981.

CHAPTER 15

1. Milton H. Erickson, "Hypnotic Approaches to Therapy", *Am. J. Clin. Hyp.*, Vol. 20, No. 1, July 1977.
2. Milton H. Erickson, "A Clinical Note on Indirect Hypnotic Therapy", *J. Clin. and Exp. Hyp.*, 2, 1954, pp. 171–174.
3. Harry E. Stanton, "Short-term Treatment of Enuresis", *Am. J. Clin. Hyp.*, Vol. 22, No. 2, October 1979.
4. id., "Enuresis, Homeopathy and Enhancement of the Placebo Effect", *Am. J. Clin. Hyp.*, Vol. 24, No. 1, January 1981.
5. Keith E. Bauer and Thomas R. McCanne, "An Hypnotic Technique for Treating Insomnia", *Int. J. Clin. and Exp. Hyp.*, Vol. XXVIII, No. L, 1980, pp. 1–5.
6. A. Jacobson, J. D. Kales and A. Kales, "Chemical and Electrophysiological Correlates of Sleep Disorder in Children", in A. Kales (ed.), *Sleep: Physiology and Pathology*, Lippincott and Co., Philadelphia, 1969.
7. Thomas S. Eliseo, "The Hypnotic Treatment of Sleepwalking in an Adult", *Am. J. Clin. Hyp.*, Vol. 17, No. 4, April 1975.
8. Crisetta MacLeod-Morgan, John Court and Russell Roberts, "Cognitive Restructuring: A Technique for the Relief of Chronic Tinnitus", *Aust. J. Clin. and Exp. Hyp.*, Vol. 10, No. 1, 1982, pp. 27–33.
9. J. L. Baker Jr, I. S. Kolin and E. S. Bartlett, "Psychosexual Dynamics of Patients Undergoing Mammary Augmentation", *Plastic and Reconstructive Surgery*, June 1974, pp. 652–659.
10. L. M. Le Cron, "Breast Development Through Hypnotic Suggestion", *Journal of the American Society of Psychosomatic Dentistry and Medicine*, 16, 1969, pp. 58–61.
11. J. E. Williams, "Stimulation of Breast Growth by Hypnosis", *Journal of Sex Research*, 10, (4), 1974, pp. 316–326.
12. Allan R. Staib and D. R. Logan, "Hypnotic Stimulation of Breast Growth", *Am. J. Clin. Hyp.*, Vol. 19, No. 4, April 1977, pp. 201–208.
13. R. D. Willard, "Breast Enlargement Through Visual Imagery and Hypnosis", *Am. J. Clin. Hyp.*, Vol. 19, No. 4, April 1977, pp. 195–200.
14. Jack A. Gerschman, Graham D. Burrows and Patrick J. Fitzgerald, "Hypnosis in the Control of Gagging", *Aust. J. Clin. and Exp. Hyp.*, Vol. 9, No. 2, November 1981.
15. Kevin A. Bartlett, "Gagging. A Case Report", *Am. J. Clin. Hyp.*, Vol. 14, No. 1, July 1971.

CHAPTER 16

1. Thomas J. Galski, "The Adjunctive Use of Hypnosis in the Treatment of Trichotillomania: A Case Report", *Am. J. Clin. Hyp.*, Vol. 23, No. 3, January 1981.

2. Robert Rowen, "Hypnotic Age Regression in the Treatment of a Self-destructive Habit: Trichotillomania", *Am. J. Clin. Hyp.*, Vol. 23, No. 3, January 1981.
3. David J. Horne, "Behaviour Therapy for Trichotillomania", *Behaviour Research and Therapy*, 15, 1977, pp. 192–196.
4. Alma C. Spithill, "Treatment of a Monosymptomatic Tic by Hypnosis: A Case Study", *Am. J. Clin. Hyp.*, Vol. 17, No. 2, October 1974.
5. John L. LeHew III, "Use of Hypnosis in the Treatment of Long Standing Spastic Torticollis", *Am. J. Clin. Hyp.*, Vol. 14, No. 2, October 1971.
6. Milton H. Erickson and Ernest L. Rossi, "Varieties of Double Bind", *Am. J. Clin. Hyp.*, Vol. 17, No. 3, January 1975.
7. L. Leshan, "The Breaking of a Habit By Suggestion During Sleep", *J. Abn. Soc. Psychol.*, 37, 1942, pp. 406–408.
8. Philip H. Bornstein et al, "Hypnobehavioural Treatment of Chronic Nailbiting: A Multiple Baseline Analysis", *Int. J. Clin. and Exp. Hyp.*, Vol. XXVIII, No. 3, 1980, pp. 208–217.

CHAPTER 17

1. S. Agras, N. Chaplin and D. Oliveau, "The Natural History of Phobias: Course and Prognosis", *Archives of General Psychiatry*, 26, 1972, pp. 315–317.
2. J. B. Watson and R. Rayner, "Conditioned Emotional Reactions", *Journal of Experimental Psychology*, 3, 1920, pp. 1–14.
3. Sigmund Freud, "Analysis of a Phobia of a Five-Year Old Boy", (1909a), in *The Complete Psychological Works of Sigmund Freud*, James Strachey (ed.) in collaboration with Anna Freud, Standard Edition, Vol. 10, London, Hogarth Press, 1955, pp. 3–149.
4. A. A. Lazarus and A. Abromovitz, "The Use of Emotive Imagery in the Treatment of Children's Phobias", *J. Medical Science*, 108, 1962, pp. 191–195.
5. Evelyn D. Lawlor, "Hypnotic Intervention with School Phobic Children", *Int. J. Clin. and Exp. Hyp.*, 1976, Vol. XXIV, No. 2, 74–86.
6. M. A. Basker, "A Hypnobehavioural Method of Treating Agoraphobia by the Clenched Fist Method of Calvert Stein", *Aust. J. Clin. and Exp. Hyp.*, Vol. 7, No. 1, 1979, pp. 27–34.
7. Doctor Claire Weekes, *Simple, Effective Treatment of Agoraphobia*, Angus & Robertson Publishers, 1977. Reprinted 1983.
8. Richard M. O'Brien, Lewis E. Cooley, Joseph Cicotti and Kathleen M. Henninger, "*Augmentation of Systematic Desensitisation of Snake Phobia Through Hypnotic Dream Suggestion*", *Am. J. Clin. Hyp.*, Vol. 23, No. 3, January 1981.
9. *ibid.*
10. W. L. Marshall, J. Boutilier and P. Minnes, "The Modification of Phobic Behaviour by Covert Reinforcement", *Behaviour Therapy*, 5, 1974, pp. 469–480.
11. Paul L. Deyoub and Seymour J. Epstein, "Short-term Hypnotherapy for the Treatment of Flight Phobia; A Case Report", *Am. J. Clin. Hyp.*, Vol. 19, No. 4, April 1977.
12. David Spiegel, Brian Maruffi, Edward J. Frischolz and Herbert Spiegel, "Hypnotic Responsivity and the Treatment of Flying Phobia", *Am. J. Clin. Hyp.*, Vol. 23, No. 4, April 1981.
13. John O. Beahrs, "The Hypnotic Psychotherapy of Milton H. Erickson", *Am. J. Clin. Hyp.*, Vol. 14, No. 2, October 1971, pp. 73–96.

CHAPTER 18

1. I. Stevenson and R. Matthews, "Facts and Fantasy in Psychosomatic Medicine", *Journal of Nervous and Mental Disease*, 118, 1953, pp. 289–306.

2. H. A. Lyons, C. R. McFadden, T. Lupanello and E. R. Bleecher, "Emotions in Asthma", meeting of American College of Physicians, in C. W. Moorefield, "The Use of Hypnosis and Behaviour Therapy in Asthma", *Am. J. Clin. Hyp.*, Vol. 13, No. 3, January 1971.

3. P. S. Clarke, "Experimental Exacerbation and Relief of Asthma Under Hypnosis", in G. D. Burrows, D. R. Collison and L. Dennerstein (eds), *Hypnosis 1979*, Proceedings of the 8th International Congress of Hypnosis and Psychosomatic Medicine, Melbourne, Australia, 19–24 August, 1979, Elsevier, North Holland Biomedical Press, Amsterdam, 1979.

4. David Collison, "Hypnotherapy in the Management of Asthma", *Am. J. Clin. Hyp.*, 1, 1959, p. 124.

5. C. W. Moorefield, "The Use of Hypnosis and Behaviour Therapy in Asthma", *Am. J. Clin. Hyp.*, Vol. 13, No. 3, January 1971, pp. 162–168.

6. Gordon Milne, "Hypnobehavioural Medicine in a University Counselling Centre", *Aust. J. Clin. and Exp. Hyp.*, Vol. 10, No. 1, 1982, pp. 13–26.

7. R. Asher, "Respectable Hypnosis", *British Medical Journal*, 11 February 1956, pp. 309–313.

8. A. H. C. Sinclair-Gieben and D. Chalmers, "Evaluation of Treatment of Warts by Hypnosis", *Lancet*, 3 October 1959, pp. 480–482.

9. David B. Sheehan, "Influence of Psychosocial Factors on Wart Remission", *Am. J. Clin. Hyp.*, Vol. 20, No. 3, January 1978.

10. Dabney M. Ewin, "Condyloma Acuminatum: Successful Treatment of Four Cases by Hypnosis", *Am. J. Clin. Hyp.*, Vol. 17, No. 2, October 1974.

11. T. A. Clawson and R. H. Swade, "The Hypnotic Control of Blood Flow and Pain: The Cure of Warts and the Potential for the Use of Hypnosis in the Treatment of Cancer", *Am. J. Clin. Hyp.*, Vol. 17, No. 3, January 1975.

12. D. Kent Welsh, "Hypnotic Control of Blushing: A Case Study", *Am. J. Clin. Hyp.*, Vol. 20, No. 3, January 1978.

13. Abraham J. Twerski and Ray Naar, "Hypnosis in a Case of Refractory Dermatitis", *Am. J. Clin. Hyp.*, Vol. 16, No. 3, January 1974, p. 202.

14. Fred H. Frankel and Robert C. Misch, "Hypnosis in a Case of Long-standing Psoriasis in a Person with Character Problems", *Int. J. Clin. and Exp. Hypnosis*, Vol. XXI, No. 3, 1973, pp. 121–130.

15. Robert E. Lehman, "Brief Hypnotherapy of Neurodermatitis: A Case with Four-Year Follow-up", *Am. J. Clin. Hyp.*, Vol. 21, No. 1, July 1978.

16. J. H. Schultz, *Das Autogene Training*, Georg Thieme Verlag, Stuttgart, 1932.

17. Neal E. Miller, "Learning of Visceral and Glandular Responses", *Science*, 163, 1969, pp. 434–445.

18. David R. Collison, "Cardiological Applications of the Control of the Autonomic Nervous System by Hypnosis", *Am. J. Clin. Hyp.*, 12: 150, 1970.

19. Herdis L. Deabler, Edward Fidel, Robert L. Dillenkoffer and S. Thomas Elder, "The Use of Relaxation and Hypnosis in Lowering High Blood Pressure", *Am. J. Clin. Hyp.*, Vol. 16, No. 2, October 1973.

20. David B. Case, David H. Fogel and Albert A. Pollack, "Intrahypnotic and Long-Term Effects of Self-Hypnosis on Blood Pressure in Mild Hypertension", *Int. J. Clin. and Exp. Hyp.*, Vol. XXVIII, No. 1, 1980, pp. 27–38.

21. J. Arthur Jackson, "Hypnosis in the Treatment of a Hypertensive patient: A Longitudinal Study", *Aust. J. Clin. and Exp. Hyp.*, Vol. 7, No. 3, 1979, pp. 199–206.

CHAPTER 19

1. "The Science Show", ABC Radio, 30 March 1985.
2. Robin Skynner and John Cleese, *Families and How to Survive Them*, Methuen, London, 1983.
3. George Matheson, "Modification of Depressive Symptoms through Posthypnotic Suggestions", *Am. J. Clin. Hyp.*, Vol. 22, No. 1, July 1979.
4. S. C. D. Gaunitz, Lars-Eric Unestahl and B. K. Berglund, "A Posthypnotically Released Emotion as a Modifier of Behaviour", *Int. J. Clin. and Exp. Hyp.*, 1975.
5. Details of Dr Antony Kidman's programme and other publications such as *Stress Management*, *Time Management*, etc., are available from Biochemical and General Consulting Service, P. O. Box 156, St Leonards, NSW 2065.
6. Diana Elton and Graham Burrows, "Specific Use of Imagery in Treatment by Hypnosis", *Aust. J. Clin. and Exp. Hyp.*, 6, 1978, pp. 17–25.
7. H. E. Stanton, "Elaborations on Elton's 'Secret Room' ", *Aust. J. Clin. and Exp. Hyp.*, Vol. 7, No. 3, November 1979.
8. Helen H. Watkins, "The Silent Abreaction", *Int. J. Clin. and Exp. Hyp.*, Vol. XXVIII, No. 2, 1980, pp. 101–113.
9. Harry E. Stanton, "Hypnotherapy and the Inner Game", *Aust. J. Clin. and Exp. Hyp.*, Vol. 10, No. 1, 1982, pp. 67–71.
10. Lin Yutang, *The Importance of Living*, William Heinemann Ltd, London, 1946.

CHAPTER 20

1. Robin Skynner and John Cleese, *Families and How to Survive Them*, Methuen, London, 1983.
2. William H. Masters and Virginia E. Johnson, *Human Sexual Inadequacy*, Little, Brown & Co., Boston, 1970.
3. Greta Goldberg, "Suggestion as a General Structure and a Specific Strategy in the Behavioural Treatment of Vaginismus", *Aust. J. Clin. and Exp. Hyp.*, Vol. 11, No. I, 1983, pp. 39–47.
4. M. Balint, *The Basic Fault*, Tavistock, London, 1968.
5. Mary L. Gottesfeld, "Treatment of Vaginismus by Psychotherapy with Adjunctive Hypnosis", *Am. J. Clin Hyp.*; Vol. 20, No. 4, April, 1978.
6. David B. Cheek, "Short-term Hypnotherapy for Frigidity Using Exploration of Early Life Attitudes", *Am. J. Clin. Hyp.*, Vol. 19, No. 1, July 1976.
7. Lorraine Dennerstein and Graham Burrows, "Psychosexual Dysfunction: Therapy Approaches", *Aust. J. Clin. Exp. Hyp.*, Vol. 7, No. 3, 1979, pp. 235–245.
8. Fred Belliveau and Lin Richter, *Understanding Human Sexual Inadequacy*, Coronet Books, London, 1970.
9. James H. Semans, "Premature Ejaculation: A New Approach", *Southern Medical Journal*, 49, 1956, pp. 353–357.
10. Masters and Johnson, op. cit.
11. Milton H. Erickson, "Psychotherapy Achieved by a Reversal of the Neurotic Processes in a Case of Ejaculatio Praecox", *Am. J. Clin. Hyp.*, Vol. 15, No. 4, April 1973.
12. Masters and Johnson, op. cit.
13. Herdis L. Deabler, "Hypnotherapy of Impotence", *Am. J. Clin. Hyp.*, Vol. 19, No. 1, July 1976.
14. Steve de Shazer, "Investigation of Indirect Symbolic Suggestions", *Am. J. Clin. Hyp.*, Vol. 23, No. 1, July 1980.
15. Harold B. Crasilneck, "The Use of Hypnosis in the Treatment of

Psychogenic Impotency", *Aust. J. Clin. and Exp. Hyp.*, Vol. 7, No. 2, August 1979.

CHAPTER 21

1. H. B. Crasilneck and J. A. Hall, "Clinical Hypnosis in Problems of Pain", *Am. J. Clin. Hyp.*, Vol. 15, No. 3, January 1973, pp. 153–161.
2. J. Liebeskind, J. Sherman and T. Cannon, *Neural and Neurochemical Mechanisms on Pain Inhibition*, I. A. S. P. Conference, Adelaide, January 1981.
3. D. Schafer and A. Hernandez, "Hypnosis, Pain and the Context of Therapy", *Int. J. Clin. Exp. Hyp.*, Vol. XXVI, No. 3, 1978, pp. 143–153.
4. James Esdaile, *Natural and Mesmeric Clairvoyance*, H. Bailliere, London, 1852, repr. Arno Press, New York, 1975.
5. A. A. Mason, "Surgery Under Hypnosis", *Anaesthesia*, 10, 1955, pp. 295–299.
6. Victor Rausch, "Cholecystectomy with Self Hypnosis", *Am. J. Clin. Hyp.*, Vol. 22, No. 3, January 1980, p. 126.
7. *ibid.*, p. 127.
8. Ernest and Josephine Hilgard, *Hypnosis in the Relief of Pain*, Kaufman, Los Altos, California, 1975. Updated paperback 1983.
9. Milton H. Erickson and Ernest L. Rossi, "Autohypnotic Experiences of Milton H. Erickson", *Am. J. Clin. Hyp.*, Vol. 20, No. 1, July 1977.
10. H. G. Wolff, *Headache and Other Pain*, (2nd ed.), Oxford University Press, New York, 1963.
11. J. D. Sargeant, E. E. Green and E. D. Walters, "Preliminary Report on the Use of Autogenic Feedback Training in the Treatment of Migraine and Tension Headaches", *J. Psychosomatic Medicine*, 35, 1973, pp. 129–135.
12. A. F. Baraboz and C. M. McGeorge, "Biofeedback, Mediated Biofeedback and Hypnosis in Peripheral Vasodilation Training", *Am. J. Clin. Hyp.*, Vol. 21, No. I, July 1978.
13. Edward E. Stambaugh and Alvin E. House, "Multimodeling Treatment of Migraine Headache: A Case Study Utilizing Biofeedback, Relaxation, Autogenic and Hypnotic Treatments", *Am. J. Clin. Hyp.*, Vol. 19, No. 4, April 1977.
14. H. Clagett Harding, *Workshop on Hypnotic Treatment of Migraine and Obesity*, Australian Society for Clinical and Experimental Hypnosis, Brisbane, March 1978.
15. William S. Kroger, *Clinical and Experimental Hypnosis in Medicine, Dentistry and Psychology*, Lippincott and Co., Philadelphia and Montreal, 1963.
16. N. Bruce Litchfield, "A Study of the Effectiveness of Hypnosis Prior to Intravenous Diazepam in Reducing Complications of Adverse Psychological Reactions and Prolonged Recovery", *Aust. J. Clin. and Exp. Hyp.*, Vol. 10, No. 1, 1982, pp. 57–65.
17. Ann M. Damsbo, "Trigeminal Neuralgia Treated by Hypnosis; A Case Report", *Am. J. Clin. Hyp.*, Vol. 17, No. 2, October 1974.
18. Ainslie Meares, *Relief Without Drugs, The Self-Management of Tension, Anxiety and Pain*, Fontana/Collins, 1970.
19. Kroger, op. cit.
20. Barbara Davenport-Slack, "A Comparative Evaluation of Obstetrical Hypnosis and Antenatal Childbirth Training", *Int. J. Clin. and Exp. Hyp.*, Vol. XXIII, No. 4., 1975, pp. 266–281.
21. Herbert B. Crasilneck, J. A. Stirman, B. J. Wilson et al, "Use of Hypnosis in the Management of Patients with Burns", *J. Am. Medical Assn*, 158, 1955, pp. 103–106.
22. Dabney M. Ewin, "Clinical Use of Hypnosis for Attenuation of Burn

Depth'', cited in R. John Wakeman and Jerome Z. Kaplan, ''An Experimental Study on Painful Burns'', *Am. J. of Clin. Hyp.*, Vol. 21, No. 1, July 1978.
23. N. Bernstein, ''Observations on the Use of Hypnosis with Burned Children on a Pediatric Ward'', *Int. J. Clin. and Exp. Hyp.*, 13, 1965, pp. 1–10.
24. J. Dahinterova, ''Some Experiences with the Use of Hypnosis in the Treatment of Burns'', *Int. J. Clin. Hyp.*, 15, 1967, pp. 49–53.
25. Donald W. Schafer, ''Hypnosis Use on a Burn Unit'', *Int. J. Clin. Exp. Hyp.*, Vol. XXIII, No. 1, 1975, pp. 1–14.
26. Wakeman and Kaplan, op. cit., pp. 3–13.
27. Dr Siegel borrowed this image from William S. Kroger and W. D. Fezler, *Hypnosis and Behaviour Modification: Imagery Conditioning*, Lippincott, Philadelphia, 1976.
28. Eleanor Fosco Siegel, ''Control of Phantom Limb Pain by Hypnosis'', *Am. J. Clin. Hyp.*, Vol. 21, No. 4, April 1979, pp. 285–286.
29. G. F. Solomon and K. M. Schmidt, ''A Burning Issue: Phantom Limb Pain and Psychological Preparation of the Patient for Amputation'', *Archives of Surgery*, 1978, pp. 185–186.
30. Milton H. Erickson, ''Hypnotic Approaches to Therapy'', *Am. J. Clin. Hyp.*, Vol. 20, No. 1, July 1877. Ernest and Josephine Hilgard, *Hypnosis in the Relief of Pain*, Kaufman, Los Altos, California, 1975, updated paperback, 1983.
31. Hilgard, op. cit.
32. Carolyn B. Thomas and K. Duszynski, ''Closeness to Parents and the Family Constellation in a Prospective Study of Five Disease States: Suicide, Mental Illness, Malignant Tumour, Hypertension and Coronary Heart Disease'', *Hopkins Medical Journal*, 134, 1974, pp. 251–270.
33. O. Carl Simonton, Stephanie Matthews-Simonton and James L. Creighton, *Getting Well Again*, Bantam Books, New York, 1978.
34. Maurice Burke, ''My Successful Fight Against Cancer'', *Australian Wellbeing*, March/April 1984.
35. T. A. Clawson and R. H. Swade, ''The Hypnotic Control of Blood Flow and Pain: The Cure of Warts and the Potential for the Use of Hypnosis in the Treatment of Cancer'', in *Am. J. Clin. Hyp.*, Vol. 17, No. 3, January 1975.
36. Hilgard, op. cit.
37. Paul Sacerdote, ''Theory and Practice of Pain Control'', *Int. J. Clin. and Exp. Hyp.*, Vol. XVIII, No. 3, 1970, pp. 160–180.

CHAPTER 22

1. Albert Ellis and Robert A. Harper, *A New Guide to Rational Living*, Wilshire Book Company, North Hollywood, California, 1972, repr. 1980.
2. P. Jakubowski and J. Lange, *Responsive Assertive Behaviour*, Research Press, Champaign, Illinois, 1976.
3. William G. Peters, ''Treatment Approaches to Public Speaking Anxiety'', Honours thesis, University of New South Wales, 1975.

CHAPTER 23

1. Pam Young, ''From Schoolyard to Campus, Transition from School to Tertiary Study'', Sound Information Pty Ltd, Sydney, 1983.

CHAPTER 24

1. W. T. Gallwey, *The Inner Game of Tennis*, Random House, New York, 1974.
2. Harry E. Stanton, ''Helping Sportsmen to Help Themselves'', *Aust. J. Clin.*

and Exp. Hyp., Vol. 11, No. 1, 1983, pp. 33–38.

3. Lars-Eric Unestahl, "Hypnotic Preparation of Athletes", in G. D. Burrows, D. R. Collison and L. Dennerstein, (eds), *Hypnosis 1979*, Proceedings of the 8th International Congress of Hypnosis and Psychosomatic Medicine, Melbourne, Australia, 19–24 August, 1979, Elsevier, North Holland Biomedical Press, Amsterdam, 1979.

4. *Sydney Morning Herald*, 7 March 1984, p. 50.

CHAPTER 25

1. Milton H. Erickson, "An Hypnotic Technique for Resistant Patients: The Patient, The Technique and Its Rationale, and Field Experiments", *Am. J. Clin. Hyp.*, 7, 1964, pp. 8–32.

2. John O. Beahrs, "The Hypnotic Psychotherapy of Milton H. Erickson", *Am. J. Clin. Hyp.*, Vol. 14, No. 2, October 1971.

3. Milton H. Erickson, "Hypnotic Approaches to Therapy", *Am. J. Clin. Hyp.*, Vol. 20, No. 1, July 1977.

4. *ibid.*

5. Milton H. Erickson, "Control of Physiological Functions by Hypnosis", *Am. J. Clin. Hyp.*, Vol. 20, No. 1, July 1977.

6. Hans J. Eysenck, *Uses and Abuses in Psychology*, Penguin, Harmondsworth, 1953, repr. 1970.

INDEX

www.ingramcontent.com/pod-product-compliance
Lightning Source LLC
Chambersburg PA
CBHW020606270326
41927CB00005B/204